SHE
DEVILS

SHE DEVILS

TRUE STORIES OF THE
WORLD'S MOST NOTORIOUS
FEMALE SERIAL KILLERS

ANNE McDUFF

JOHN BLAKE

Published by John Blake Publishing Ltd,
3 Bramber Court, 2 Bramber Road,
London W14 9PB, England

www.johnblakepublishing.co.uk

First published in paperback in 2009

ISBN: 978 1 84454 729 6

British Library Cataloguing-in-Publication Data:

A catalogue record for this book is available from the British Library.

Design by www.envydesign.co.uk

Printed in the UK by CPI William Clowes Beccles NR34 7TL

1 3 5 7 9 10 8 6 4 2

Papers used by John Blake Publishing are natural, recyclable products made from
wood grown in sustainable forests. The manufacturing processes conform to the
environmental regulations of the country of origin.

For KT and R Spence
'By perseverance and diligence'

ACKNOWLEDGEMENTS

With special thanks to DJ Howard, Edward Humes, Connie Nisinger, Will Johnson, Clive Hebard, Wensley Clarkson, John Wordsworth, the staff at Oystermouth Library and all those at Kew National Archive.

PROLOGUE

AN EVIL WITHIN

Very few women kill. When they do, it is by and large the tragic outcome of domestic abuse, drug addiction or mental illness. It is rare for women to kill for pleasure, yet a few of that breed emerge in each generation and they haunt our understanding of what it means to be human.

Not too long ago, we would try to explain terrible cruelty as a form of possession. It was easy to believe in demons and witches. Take the case of Erzsébet, or Elizabeth, Bathroy. A Hungarian Countess born in 1560, she could have led a life of quiet if remarkable privilege but instead, she embarked on a career of sadistic killings that earned her the name the Blood Countess.

She is said to have tortured young servant girls for her own pleasure, beating them with a heavy cudgel and barbed wire, dragging them naked into the snow and repeatedly dousing them with cold water until they froze to death. But Elizabeth made a fatal misjudgement. She began to trap and kill girls that belonged to minor nobility.

Some say this was because she believed that the blood of peasant girls, held in chains above her bath and slaughtered as she lay below, was no longer ensuring her youth. Blood of finer lineage would suit her aims better, but these girls had families that could speak out. Late in December 1610, Mattias the King of Hungary, ordered a Count named Thurzo to arrest Elizabeth.

The soldiers that led the night raid on Elizabeth's home, Castle Cachtice, found a girl lying dead in a hallway and many other victims locked in cells, either dead or dying. A huge public trial was held in January of 1611 and hundreds of witness statements were read out, some from survivors who had escaped, badly mutilated but still able to testify. They included accusations of mutilation of the face and genitals, burning with pokers, biting the flesh off faces and other bodily parts, starvation and satanic rituals.

How many girls and young women suffered cannot be known. Elizabeth's accomplices were tortured and confessed to 37 victims but other servants at the castle claimed numbers of between 100 and 200. One witness stated that Elizabeth kept a hand-written ledger which totalled over 650 names. But the ledger was not produced at the trial and it has never been discovered. Elizabeth was condemned as a witch and imprisoned in her own bedchamber where she died three years later.

Elizabeth Bathroy is only one example of a serial killer in history. Without doubt, as long as there have been human societies, there have been individuals who have inflicted terrible acts of sadism and torture on others. All that has changed is how we describe and choose to punish them.

Today, we would look for factors in Elizabeth's childhood to see if there is an explanation for her psychosis. As a child, she was said to suffer from fits and uncontrolled rage. She was married at 15 to Count Ferenc Nadasdy, a man who behaved savagely towards servants – although this was not uncommon for the time. He was said to have shown Elizabeth the art of pouring water on wrongdoers until they froze to death. Perhaps the most chilling account is that of a young Elizabeth watching the punishment of a gypsy who was accused of theft. The miscreant was sewn into the belly of a dying horse with only his head exposed and left to die.

Yet beyond trying to piece together a psychological explanation for her sadism, the most valuable lesson we can learn from Elizabeth Bathroy is that she operated in an environment that allowed her to kill. She grew up in a time when the casual and accepted misuse of servants was the norm. It allowed her to mask years of torture and she remained unchallenged until she crossed a line and murdered girls from noble families.

Society is key to understanding female serial killers. They do not emerge from a vacuum, they are shaped by their environment. They emerge from damaged childhoods and learn to exploit the hypocrisy and prejudice that surrounds them.

At the turn of the last century, Annie Walters could kill newborns as they were farmed out for being unwanted or born out of marriage with no adoption agency to protect them. Fast forward 90 years and Aileen Wuornos sold herself on the highways of Florida, a well-known hunting ground for men looking for prostitutes, until she saw fit to become the hunter. Rose West exploited lonely girls from nearby children's homes, Myra Hindley the blind trust of Britain in the 1960s, a time when it was thought that children were safe to walk the streets alone.

Then there are women like Beverly Allitt and Marybeth Tinning, who knew that as a nurse and a mother respectively, they would be seen as blameless and unfortunate as children in their care died one by one. Karla Homolka exploited a different prejudice. She was perfect, pretty, so caring as a veterinary nurse and married to good-looking Paul Bernardo. No one ever imagined she could be a sexual predator and killer.

Every one of the ten women that appear here reveal something extraordinary about our lives over the last century. These killers have acted in ways that outstrips anything you may have imagined, yet they are all products of their time. We see our weaknesses through their eyes.

Once we imagined that evil came from without, but it does not. Evil is incubated by extreme conditions, often in an abused childhood, and it takes root in a flawed mind that is stripped of humanity but hungers to inflict pain. Then all it needs is a stage – one we unwittingly provide.

This handful of women became monsters. Not demons from tales of ritual and black magic, but monsters all the same. It is an irony that some modern forensic psychologists suggest that our ancestors were right to fear that monsters could wear a human face and walk amongst us.

That may sound alarming but once you know the stories behind the most infamous of female killers, you question what it is that makes us human – and why this handful of women were allowed to act with such savagery, as if they never had been human at all.

CONTENTS

1

ANNIE WALTERS

THE BABY FARMER

'I never murdered the dear.'

ANNIE WALTERS, CAUGHT WITH A DEAD BABY IN HER ARMS.

The nurse stood between the legs of the mother, waiting for the moment that the baby would begin to emerge from the birth canal. She saw the crown and within a few seconds she was easing the head into her waiting hands. She placed a thick, wet linen cloth over the nose and mouth of the infant. Holding it in place while the baby's body followed, its new-born lungs distended and collapsed. Brain death followed in minutes. The child did not draw a single breath

The nurse examined the newborn, hoping there was no skin discolouration. In that way, once the doctor was called, the words 'stillborn' could appear on the death certificate with little fuss. If that didn't ease the doctor's conscience, the money that exchanged hands would be enough.

Childbirth is never easy. At the turn of the 20th century it was even more fraught. Even deliveries that proceeded without complication did so with a degree of pain and fear.

For a woman struggling to give birth in a low-rent room, with her identity hidden, away from loved ones, trusting her life to a backstreet nurse, the hours were hard to endure, both mentally and physically. It was the ideal killing ground for nurse Annie Walters.

The strict moral code of the time, meant to discourage premarital sex in the hope of making society better, ironically facilitated her grim work. Serial killers learn to manipulate expectations. They know that the best cloak for their evil is to fit in. They don't simply break into homes or attack people on the spur of the moment. They can be adept at both planning their kills and disguising their madness. They are predators. They often have jobs and families and go about their business quietly.

Female serial killers, not as physically strong as men, tend to focus on those weaker than themselves. That is why female predators usually target the very old or the very young. There are exceptions. Nannie Doss and Aileen Wournos killed men but they had to engineer a way to catch them with their defences down. In Nannie's case, it meant stirring poison into the meals she'd cook for her husbands, in Aileen's case, it meant luring men off a highway into a secluded setting and shooting them dead. But it is the very young who remain the most vulnerable members of society and are the easiest for serial killers to prey on.

To most of us, there is no greater crime than harming a child – it shatters every human instinct. But when the mother is an outcast and her child is not wanted, a hole opens up in the safety net of the community. Even in modern times, babies are abandoned, discarded by frightened and confused mothers. When such a story makes the headlines today, the state often swings into action. Nurses are pictured holding the newborn, who is given an identity by the maternity ward. Offers of help are broadcast in the hope is that the mother can be found and supported. Social services are on standby to find a home for the child. It is a scenario we've all watched unfold in newspapers and on television. What if there were no contraceptives, no legalised abortion, no financial help from the state for lone mothers and no adoption services? Welcome to Britain in 1900.

At that time the illegitimacy rate was as low as four per cent, compared to around 30 per cent now (the modern figure includes both those born to single mothers and those born to couples who are unmarried). The change in rate reflects the fact that the social penalties of having a child out of wedlock at the time were catastrophic. There are chilling accounts of fathers who would beat their pregnant daughters to death, of girls who drowned themselves, women committed to mental institutions for the 'morally insane' and even of women being stoned.

Some took desperate risks to avoid the stigma. They pushed needles inside themselves, used washing soda, slippery elm bark, quinine and hot baths to try and abort the unwanted foetus. Abortions were illegal and highly dangerous, often resulting in infection, haemorrhage or life-threatening injury to internal organs, such as puncturing or tearing of the uterus.

Institutions like the workhouse would not accept pregnant women. The church preached abstinence but this was hardly realistic. Charities were set up to guide fallen women back to a life of virtue. One, the Magdalene Laundries, or asylum, was originally established as a refuge for prostitutes. It was inspired by Jesus and his acceptance of reformed 'sinner' Mary Magdalene. The asylums soon evolved to become institutions where girls could be placed in the care of nuns if they were unwanted, if their mothers were found to be adulterers or if the girls themselves were fallen women, if they became pregnant. Unfortunately, they became well known not as a place of refuge, but of ill-treatment. Growing numbers of women committed to them came forward to give their accounts of neglect. Reports of psychological, physical and even sexual abuse emerged.

Set up in in the 19th century, the laundries were established in Ireland and on the British mainland. Young girls were often forced to work without pay all year round and in silence, symbolically 'washing away' their sins. Frequently, they were forced to bind their breasts once they reached puberty, some had their heads shaved and all wore shapeless smocks to remind them to be wary of the sin that lay within them.

The laundries were profitable, earning the refuge money through contracts with schools, hospitals and prisons. But the profits were raised from the labour of girls stripped of their rights. A number of the girls disappeared, thought to have taken their own lives, despite this being a terrible sin in the eyes of the Church. In 1993, an order of nuns in Dublin sold part of their convent to a commercial developer and the remains of 155 inmates, buried in unmarked graves, were exhumed. The belief is that these were girls who either committed suicide or were beaten to death.

Astonishingly, the last Magdalene asylum did not close in Ireland until 1996. In the UK, most had disappeared by the 1970s. One of the last was on East End Road, in East Finchley, London. It was an area that Annie Walters knew well. She would have walked past the laundry run by the Sisters of the Good Shepherd many times. She would have been aware of the fate that these young girls faced: a life of hard labour, shame and neglect. These were the harsh social and economic realities that she thrived in and she wasn't alone.

Annie worked in partnership with nursing home boss Amelia Sach and the two women knew that there was money to be made from adoption. The need was great, and not only from unmarried women. Without access to contraception, the average number of children each woman bore at the turn-of-the-century was four, but it was not uncommon to find households of up to ten children. It was unfortunate, but many older mothers wanted rid of the burden of an extra mouth to feed.

Advertisements for nursing homes for expectant mothers would appear in local newspapers. There was no illusion either from the women who used the service or those who provided it as to what the homes offered. This was not about skilled midwifery. This was an agreement whereby a woman at full-term could turn up anonymously and for an agreed sum of money, leave her baby, safe in the knowledge that her child would be farmed out to a new family and she could continue with her life.

Such nursing homes would have been widely spoken of, if in hushed terms. Amelia Sach, who presented herself as a midwife and qualified nurse, placed such an advertisement in *The Hendon and Finchley Times*. It read:

'Doctor recommends comfortable home; skilled nursing; every care; terms moderate.'

We can learn a good deal from those dozen words. First is the careful way in which the service had to be presented; Britain was riddled with hypocrisy and the advertisement was written in the accepted code of the day. It was offering a disposal point for unwanted babies.

The 32-year-old Amelia Sach had no qualms about posing as a nurse with the backing of medical practitioners. A doctor may well recommend a comfortable home but Sach had no formal training and no backup from the medical profession. The real incentive comes with the words 'terms moderate'. For impoverished women, scraping enough money together to pay for the placement of their child in a good home was a considerable worry.

Yet even though these types of services were frowned upon, they were accepted to the point where they appeared in popular literature. Oliver Twist, for example, spent his first year in a baby farm and it was known that the homes were not without scandal. In 1870, Margaret Waters was convicted of murdering a baby placed in her care by a desperate mother. She was hanged at Horsemonger Lane jail in London later that year. The stories scandalised polite society and with good reason.

When the case came to trial, a Dr Puckle told the court about what he found: 'The body was extremely emaciated, the bones almost protruding through the skin. It was miserable, wasted and nothing but skin and bone. It had been a fine child. It was in a thoroughly insensible state.'

And the boy was only one of several wasted babies found in Margaret Waters' care. The case helped promote new legislation, the Infant Life Protection Act of 1872. From that point on, the law called for all nurses to be registered if they were caring for more than one infant under the age of 12 months. Annie Walters and Amelia Sach would have known of the existence of the Act but they also knew that it was very poorly regulated. The new law had good intentions but desperate women still had a need for the baby farms.

East Finchley was once a rural community famous for its

pig markets, but overcrowding and industrialisation had changed the community hugely by the 1890s. The neighbourhood was dominated by a pottery works, a brick factory and a cricket bat manufacturers, but the main landmark was the 130ft spire of the Congregationalist church. The ale houses of East Finchley were as well attended as the churches. The tube extended overground by 1868 and it allowed inhabitants of East Finchley to access the rest of London quickly and easily.

It isn't known how Amelia and Annie met, but they would have made an incongruous sight as they walked down East End Road. Amelia was tall, stylishly-dressed and wore her dark hair fashionably pinned up. She was not unattractive and knew how to present a respectable front. She was married to a builder called Jeffrey Sach and according to the census of 1901, they had one child. Amelia was 32 but said she was still in her 20s. It was a touch of vanity, but faded by comparison with the number of lies Annie Walters regularly traded in.

Annie Walters was 54. She would say that she had been married for more than 20 years and lived with her husband in Drury Lane; or that she was a widow and that her husband had been a sailor and she lived on his pension; at other times she would say that she'd been a nurse at St Thomas' Hospital in London and that she had recently been a patient there, suffering with a 'disease of the throat'; on other occasions she claimed she had been recently widowed and was waiting for her possessions to be shipped to her from Yorkshire. None of it was true.

In essence, Annie span a web of lies to suit every individual she met, supplying just enough detail to make her unremarkable. It was a method that had served her, up to one cold November morning in 1902. She was short and heavily-built, once fair-haired, she now pinned back her grey hair in a tight bun and, with her snub nose and cold blue eyes, had a face that many would remember.

Annie Walters had settled into new lodgings at 11 Wanbury Street in Islington late in October 1902. She'd taken the back parlour for five shillings a week and made her first payment in advance. Taking in lodgers was how many families kept their heads above water and the family at No 11 already had another lodger in permanent residence, a Mrs Minnie Spencer. The house belonged to policeman Henry Seal, who lived with his wife Alice, daughter Isabel and son Albert, then aged 14. It was a fairly common setup. Annie would have known of Henry's profession as it was sure to have been something that Mrs Seal mentioned when she showed Annie the room. The older woman decided to move in all the same, despite planning to use her lodgings as a place to carry out the most evil of deeds. Annie must have been supremely confident that she could carry on without being caught. For the first time in her long career, she would be proved wrong.

Yet it wasn't constable Henry Seal who first became suspicious but the women in the house. Annie told her landlady and Mrs Spencer that she was a trained midwife and was skilled in setting up adoptions in the higher echelons of society. In fact, she told Alice and Minnie, she was waiting for a telegram from a lady willing to pay £100 to adopt a baby. This was a considerable sum at a time when the average weekly wage was less than £2. Annie created a beguiling picture of a waif transported to a life of privilege when she took the room. She didn't venture out for two weeks, only answering her door to young Albert, who asked if there were any errands he could run for her.

The telegram arrived on Wednesday 12 November: '5 o'clock tonight. Mrs Sach, East Finchley.' Annie duly left at 3.15pm and returned by 6.30pm with a small bundle in her arms. There was some excitement at the arrival and Annie gave Minnie Spencer money to buy a baby's feeding bottle, a comforter and a tin of Nestlé milk. The women welcomed being able to fuss over a newborn and he was a handsome boy too. Annie soon took him to her room and the door was closed. The next day Alice remarked that she had not heard a peep from the child but when she asked to see him, Annie brushed her aside, saying he was sleeping or that he was 'under the weather'.

There was no sight or sound of the child on Thursday either and the women began to talk. Too loudly. With Minnie out, Annie emerged from her room and said: 'I overheard a few words between you and Mrs Spencer this morning, she will have to answer for what she said if it costs me a few shillings. I hate liars and deception.' Alice felt her blood run cold.

It wasn't the first time Annie had made threats. She moved easily from affability to menace and had intimidated many in the past. Alice later spoke to her husband who, until that point, had given the new lodger little thought. Annie had always acted out the part of a respectable widow in his presence. The following day, Annie found both Alice and Minnie in the kitchen and Alice said as pleasantly as she could: 'I'd like to see the baby, Mrs Walters.'

'I will go and put my boots on and come down again,' Annie calmly replied.

To Alice's amazement, they soon saw Annie sauntering out of the back garden, a bundle in her arms. The baby was never seen again.

Annie did not get back until nightfall and it was clear that she'd been drinking, but she sat down and told the women how she travelled to Piccadilly where she was met by a beautiful lady in a horse-drawn brougham carriage. The lady loved the child from the moment she set eyes on him and Annie waited as it was dressed in fine lace, a full cloak and bonnet. The story was enough to allay the women's fears until the following day, when Albert handed Annie another telegram. 'Come tonight, 8pm, same place.'

When Annie left at 6.30pm, she did not realise that she was being followed by young Albert Seal on his father's instructions. Keen to impress, Albert tracked Annie carefully on her way to meet Amelia. He later gave the police a good description of her, watching as the women made their way into the Archway Tavern. By 10pm, Annie was back at her lodgings with a new bundle.

She placed the baby on the kitchen table and Alice and Minnie gathered around to ask questions. It seemed that this baby was to go to a coastguard and his wife on the Isle of Wight for the sum of £10. Annie took her things through to her room, leaving the baby. Alice wanted to warm the child and as she wrapped the clothing around it, was alarmed to note that the girl was in fact a baby boy. All was not as it seemed with this midwife lodger.

Again, Annie left the baby in her room and there was barely a sound from him, which she attempted to explain away as the effects of a bad cold. Alice persuaded her husband to consult his sergeant about her suspicions. A detective constable, George Wright, was posted to watch the house on 17 November, but noticed nothing out of the ordinary. It was on that day that the infant was last seen by Minnie Spencer. She knocked on Annie's door because the baby was 'making a funny noise'.

Irritated by Mrs Spencer's intrusion, Annie laughed it off saying: 'Hark, do you hear it? I think the mother had been frightened by a dog.' The subdued barking cough came from the bundle on the centre of the bed but Minnie Spencer was led out before she had a chance to see the child.

Wanbury Street, Noel Street, Clarence Street, Colebrooke Row, Duncan Terrace, St John Street, City Road. Detective Constable George Wright noted them all as he followed Annie Walters with the tiny bundle in her arms on the morning of 18 November. It was cold and grey as Detective Wright monitored the older woman cautiously on the way to the train station. Was she going to meet the coastguard? He paused as she disappeared into the toilets at South Kensington station. Quite some time passed. She must, he thought, be changing the child. He swung into action as she emerged. 'I am a police officer,' he said quietly, taking her firmly by the arm. 'I want to see the baby.'

Annie looked at him steadily and asked: 'Why?'

Unnerved by the woman's cold, direct stare, he said: 'Because I have reason to believe it is not as it should be.'

Annie was no fool. She knew she wouldn't be able to outrun the young detective and he was holding her close, by her elbow, so she could not slip into the crowds at the station. She held her ground and George Wright stood in silence, momentarily unsure of how to proceed. As the daily pedestrian traffic of London swirled around them, the woman was immobile, calm. He called a female attendant over to him and asked her to make sure that the ladies' toilet was free.

The attendant was wide-eyed for a moment, wondering if the plain-clothes officer had caught another pickpocket. The public toilet was empty and George Wright steered Annie towards it. The child still seemed to be asleep. Annie was unruffled as she placed herself in a chair inside the building. 'I suppose you will take me to the station,' she said.

'I want to see the child first,' replied Detective Wright.

She unwrapped the bundle. This is the statement George Wright later gave the court: 'She unwrapped the clothing and I saw she had a male child there. I noticed that part of the right side of its face was black. The body was cold, the lips a little black and the eyes tightly closed. The child's hands were clenched. The child was dead.'

Maintaining his composure, Detective Wright said simply: 'The child is dead isn't he?'

Annie, still sitting, said: 'I never murdered the dear.'

The detective read Annie her rights and formally arrested her. 'All right, I won't say anything,' Annie chimed, 'then I can't say wrong.' They travelled by cab to King's Cross Road police station and the other police constable noticed that Annie did not so much as glance at the dead child lying next to her.

By now, Inspector Kyd was searching Annie's lodgings. He found a baby's bottle, some 'dark liquid' he believed to be carbolic acid and a bottle of Chlorodyne. Chlorodyne was a well-known over-the-counter medicine, used to treat migraine, cholera and diarrhoea. It had a high laudanum content. It was an opiate that many became addicted to. He then made his way to Claymore House in East Finchley, home of Amelia Sach.

Amelia opened the door to two officers and Inspector Kyd asked to come inside. They quickly established that there were two women in the house, both having recently given birth. Amelia told him that this was a respectable nursing home but she would not allow him to go upstairs as one of the women was too ill to be disturbed. She denied knowing Annie Walters and denied that she had ever handed over any babies to her. She was asked to explain the telegrams Annie received at Wanbury Street and the five Annie had sent in return. Amelia backtracked, saying that she could now recall Annie Walters.

'She worked for me,' she told Inspector Kyd, 'but I never gave her any babies.' Amelia Sach was taken to the same police station that held Annie Walters.

The following day, both women were charged. Amelia's charge outlined the belief that her role was to 'abet, counsel and procure' for Annie Walters. Annie's charge was stark: 'That Annie Walters did feloniously, wilfully and of her malice aforethought kill and murder a male infant whose name is unknown.'

What concerned Inspector Kyd and his team was that the unknown child was not the only victim. To their alarm, a search of Claymore House uncovered nearly 300 items of baby clothing. Items sewn by expectant mothers as a last gift to the child they would not be able to care for.

The police knew that Annie had disposed of two infants in the short time that she lodged with the Seal family. They would pursue only one charge. As Annie was caught with the dead child, that was the safest way to secure a successful prosecution. But they were haunted by the idea that this squat and cold-eyed woman had run her business for years.

The coroner in Clerkenwell, George Danford Thomas, began to hear evidence of the death of the male infant found with Annie Walters on 21 November. Outside, there was much discussion of the fate met by these unwanted babies. They would be found in rubbish heaps, discarded at railway banks, or thrown into the Thames like so much refuse.

Police surgeon Dr Richard Counter gave his evidence. He believed the child had been dead for at least eight hours. His account was couched in medical terminology but it still made brutal hearing. The boy was less than four days old but he had suffered. His tongue was swollen, his lips purple black and he had been systematically starved. His stomach had no contents but mucus. His head was bruised on the right side from the temple to the jaw and there was evidence of a bleed into the tissue at the back of the child's head, under the scalp. Ultimately, he had been asphyxiated, probably with a Chlorodyne-soaked cloth held over his mouth and nostrils. Chlorodyne also contained chloroform. The saddest detail was the observation that the child's umbilical cord was 'about half dried'. Life had been cruelly stolen before it had really begun.

Inspector Kyd also found letters addressed to the nursing home from women looking for babies to adopt. There was a genuine need for couples to adopt babies. One note arrived from a Mrs Laura Bracey two days after the birth of the baby boy killed by Annie Walters. In it she carefully outlined her nice if modest home, how her husband was a good worker and how they would be 'pleased to take and give [a baby] a good home'. But Amelia knew that to give the babies up meant passing on the lion's share of the fee she charged the biological mothers. And why part with money at all, if Annie Walters was so content to dispose of the infants she handed over?

Other evidence revealed the extent Amelia would go to assure mothers whose children she delivered. Some insisted on a contract. This is a typical example: 'Received of Ada Charlotte Galley the sum of twenty-five pounds in consideration of which I undertake to have her child, born on the 15th day of November 1902, properly adopted and cared for, for the future, the said payment to relieve her of further liability in respect of the child. Amèlia Sach.'

Ada Galley left her baby with handmade clothes, including a shawl and a flannel gown. It is difficult to imagine what a heartbreaking task it must have been to sew clothes you knew you would never see your child wear. It is even harder to try and comprehend what mothers who had used Amelia Sach's nursing home must have felt on hearing the news of the arrests.

The Hendon and Finchley Times reported: 'Considerable sensation was caused in East Finchley on Tuesday night by the arrest of Mrs Sach,' and it must have sent to chill through many hearts.

As the case progressed, it was clear that other babies must have been at risk at Claymore House. Police continued their enquiries and talked to the doctors that were occasionally called out to assist some of the women in labour and a grim picture emerged. Some of the babies born there were recorded as stillborn. The police were not interested in pursuing the doctors involved as they were respectable figures and, once again, turning a blind eye to their activities was expedient.

The doctors maintained that their involvement with Claymore House was entirely professional. They came because they were called out to a medical emergency. An infant might be dead by the time of their arrival and attention would switch to the mother. It is very difficult, even today, to tell the difference between suffocation caused by complications during labour and deliberate asphyxiation. Both the medical profession and the police knew that nursing homes were little more than baby farms, they knew that money rather than benevolence drove the trade and they knew that money also bred criminal behaviour. The women and their unborn children were at risk from the moment they stepped through the door. But money was also the lifeblood of the professional class. There was no NHS and doctors had to be paid for. If that meant doing no more than shaking their heads as they walked away from nursing homes, then so be it.

The police were fully aware Annie Walters would have acted as midwife at other deaths. But they also knew the safest course was to plough on with the case in hand, the dead child found in Annie Walters' arms, a child without a name. It was evidence from an unexpected source which would prove to be Annie's undoing.

When Theresa Edwards had read about the arrests and the horror unfolding at Claymore House, she was paralysed with fear and guilt. She knew the police would come for her. Two years earlier, Theresa had been just another desperate customer in Amelia's house of horrors. She was a pretty young barmaid who had been working at the White Bear in Berwick Street, Soho. It was the summer of 1901 and Theresa had found Amelia Sach through an advertisement placed in *The People*. She was six months pregnant and no longer able to hide the fact. She was also unmarried but had no intention of telling Mrs Sach who the father was. Theresa protected him and it is likely that he was already married.

Amelia was then operating from 4 Stanley Road, another street in East Finchley. Amelia led Theresa into the parlour and explained her terms of business. To stay, Theresa would need a guinea a week – simply beyond her means as she was no longer able to work. Other women in Theresa's situation were either supported by the father of the child or by her family. Theresa had no one to support her but she was a woman blessed with a rare determination, as Amelia was to discover.

Theresa opened negotiations. She would stay in the house, would cook and clean and run the household, allowing Mrs Sach to a free hand to operate her business, and would take no wage. Theresa was bright and articulate and Amelia decided that a hard worker was what the house needed. She moved in at the start of June 1901 and stuck to her side of the bargain.

Having spent years serving behind a bar, Theresa had developed a keen eye for character and detail and watched the comings and goings at Stanley Road with interest. Amelia was not a well-bred woman but she was literate, ambitious and prickly when it came to how others thought of her. She had airs and graces and it amused Theresa to see her acting like the wife of a barrister rather than that of a bricklayer. Theresa knew that socially she was an outcast but she would not be cowed by Amelia Sach. The women came to clash as time went on. Amelia liked her household to feel indebted to her, but Theresa had no intention of bowing and scraping to a woman she knew was making money from others' misfortune.

On 18 September, Theresa went into labour. It was difficult and the baby was not born until late the following day when a Dr Owen had to be called out. No doubt the extra expenditure would have grated on Amelia. Dr Owen asked Theresa if she intended to keep the child. She had to reply that she did not and the doctor advised her not to suckle the child but to bottle-feed it. But as Theresa cared for her little girl over the next few days, a determination grew that she would raise her herself. It was an extraordinary decision to make as she would have been fully aware that they both faced a hard life. But once decided, she would not turn back and she renegotiated with Amelia, asking to be kept on. Again, she would not ask for money, just a roof over her and her daughter's head. Amelia agreed. It is doubtful that she did so out of the kindness of her heart. The women did not get along and it can only have been Theresa's skills as a housekeeper that meant she could stay. With her keen powers of observation, Theresa might have guessed that children were at risk.

She later told the police about her first year with Mrs Sach: 'Five parted with their children and these were all sent away before the mothers had recovered.' There were also stillborns. A Dr Wylie wrote out a death certificate for one and a Mrs Raymond's infant was also signed off as a natural death. She knew where the other children were sent. A 'Mrs Laming' would appear at the appointed time, either to assist with the births or to remove the babies. Theresa knew that Laming was an alias for Annie Walters.

Theresa later told police: 'I have sent telegrams to Mrs Laming. The wording was always the same: "Come to Finchley."'

She also explained that she helped Amelia Sach with the move to Claymore House in June 1902, while tension was growing in the household. Theresa took her daughter out more and more. She still completed all her household chores but she invented reasons to spend time away from the property. Amelia's temper snapped and one evening in September 1902 she locked Theresa out. They had a fierce quarrel and Theresa and her daughter, now a year old, left for good that same evening.

The court adjourned until 11 December. It was only a matter of days but it was long enough for a growing sense of guilt to prompt Theresa to change her testimony. One conversation with 'Mrs Laming' had haunted her for months. Theresa had been sitting in the kitchen, playing with her daughter, who was then six months old. She could sit up and grin and was able to eat the fingers of bread Theresa had cut for her. Her mother marvelled at her little girl every day. Annie Walters walked in. 'Mrs Laming' always referred to Theresa as 'Auntie'. Watching the young woman carefully she said: 'Auntie, wouldn't you like to part with your baby?'

'No,' was Theresa's simple reply.

'You're a fool,' Annie said. 'It stands in your light for getting work.'

Theresa ignored the older woman but carried on playing with her little girl. Not used to silence, Annie chimed in again: 'I will take it for £5.'

'I would not let the King take my baby,' said Theresa firmly and she met the older woman's cold stare directly. After a moment, Annie laughed and walked out.

When the court came back to session, Theresa broke down. She had denied any involvement with Annie and Amelia other than keeping house and said she knew nothing about money changing hands. Now she stood in tears and said: 'I took one from Stanley Road to Mrs Laming in 20 Glasgow Road, Plaistow. It was Mrs Baker's baby. I handed over £3 to Mrs Laming.

'Mrs Laming asked me, "Did you meet any inspectors on the way as there were enquiries being made?"

'I said, "I don't know any Inspectors."

'Then Mrs Laming said, "They know you. They have asked me who is that young girl there with Mrs Sach? And I have told them it was Auntie and that she had a baby there."'

Annie had not been under investigation at that point. It seemed clear that she was attempting to menace Theresa, hinting that she was now involved in an illegal adoption trade and that both she and her baby were vulnerable. Her intimidation worked and Theresa kept her mouth shut for a while. When she confessed, it was to say that her conscience would not allow her to remain silent about all she knew about the nursing homes. She gave a list which provided an insight into the bleak nature of Annie's trade.

Mrs White	26 years old	£12
Mrs Dredge	38 years old	£12
Mrs Smith	33 years old	£10
Mrs Young	27 years old	£12
Mrs Harris	19 years old	£30
Mrs Owen	40 years old	£15
Mrs Baker	age unknown	£15

Theresa knew in detail the terms of business of the illegal baby-farming Amelia profited from. She knew too of the doubts she had about 'Mrs Laming' and she also had to live with the guilt of knowing that she had delivered one baby directly into her arms.

It was probable that Annie Walters had murdered dozens of babies, either asphyxiating them at the moment of birth or disposing of them in the days or weeks that followed. Of the one murder for which she was tried, she denied everything. Her statement showed that she was canny enough to arrive at a plausible explanation for the infant's death and through her spelling and errors, it is eerie to hear how her accent rings through:

I cant tell you any moor as I don't know any think else.
I gave the baby 2 drops of Chlordine not in ten thin to

*arm it only to mak it sleep. I have taken a bottle full
and it don't hurt me. I gave it nothink but that. I was
grealty surpirse.*

For her part, Amelia Sach claimed to have no involvement, but
her defence was pulled apart when the authorities traced
payments. They followed money found in her home and paid
into her bank account. One of the men whose child had been
given up for adoption had recorded for his own accounts the
serial number of a £10 note given to Amelia. It emerged she
also lied about knowing Annie Walters and her story had
changed so often her credibility was destroyed. Both women
were found guilty and sent to Holloway to await execution.
The newspaper reports that followed believed they deserved
little mercy as they had shown none to the infants in their care.

Even Holloway did not dampen Amelia Sach's sense of
self-importance. She had requested that a number of items be
sent to her, including clothes and money raised from the last
two women who stayed at Claymore House, a Mrs Pardoe
and a Mrs Galley. When the clothes parcel arrived, Amelia
put pen to paper and, in doing so, revealed something of her
haughty disposition:

'I am surprised Mrs Bell at you sending me in that dreadful
old chemise and you have sent me in one of my husband's
under vests. I cannot wear them so I will send them back
tomorrow.' She added a further list of demands.

Female executions had previously taken place at
Newgate prison and the pair had the dubious honour of
being the first women to be hanged at Holloway jail on 3
February 1903. It was the last female double-hanging in
Britain. The women were by then well-known and shared a
grave alongside two other women executed at Holloway,

now located in Brookwood Cemetery in Surrey. Their bodies were removed in 1971 when the grounds and buildings of Holloway were extended.

At the time of their death, the two young baby boys Annie brought to the Seal household should have been learning to walk. It will never be known how many children died at the hands of Annie Walters and Amelia Sach – perhaps 30 or more. We can, however, for the first time, piece together the identity of the baby found with Annie Walters by Detective Wright.

Two baby boys were born at Claymore House in mid-November 1902. The police listed the details of the two women confined there when they searched the house as a Mrs Rosina Pardoe and a Mrs Ada Galley. In truth, neither woman was married. Rosina Pardoe was a domestic servant working at 1 Sandford Villa in Lincoln Road, East Finchley. She had the misfortune to become pregnant and it is probable that the man responsible was an employer. The sum turned over for the adoption was a not inconsiderable £30. She left and returned to domestic work, but not at Sandford Villas.

Ada Galley had travelled from Fryerning, a village in Essex, to stay at Claymore House. Her labour was long and traumatic and after 36 hours, Amelia Sach called for Dr Wylie. In the two years that Dr Wylie had done business with Mrs Sach, he estimated that he had been called about a dozen times. This was a difficult birth and he was forced to use forceps. When he returned the following day to check on Mrs Galley, the child was gone. Dr Wylie asked about its whereabouts and Mrs Sach said that Mrs Galley's mother had it. The next day, the story changed to a 'sister in Holloway' and later still to having 'to get someone to adopt the child'. Dr Wylie reported these inconsistencies to the police only after the arrests and because he was required to make a signed deposition for the coroner.

There was one further detail about Ada Galley that made her stand out from the other women that came through the doors of Claymore House. The father of the unborn child knocked on the door. A clerk from Fryerning, Mr Reginald Golding, arrived on 15 November with the sum of £25. He was concerned to know how Ada was. She had just delivered a baby boy and, as usual, Annie Walters was sent for.

The vital piece of evidence leading to the identity of the child found dead with Annie Walters at South Kensington Station emerged at the coroner's court but was overlooked. During his evidence, police surgeon Dr Richard Counter noted the bruising on the right-hand side of the newborn's face and at the back of his scalp. It measured approximately four-by-three inches. He did not believe that the pressure applied to produce such bruising and the corresponding bleed into the tissue, resulted in the cause of death. He was right. Had he spoken to Dr Wylie, he would have learnt that the mark was a result of the forceps used at the time of the baby's birth. The child died because it was starved and asphyxiated by Annie Walters. The child found in Annie Walters' arms at South Kensington station belonged to Ada and Reginald.

Reginald Golding had been questioned by the police about why he visited Claymore House. He admitted paying the sum of £25 but believed it was to secure the baby's future. Had he any idea of the true nature of the nursing home, he said, 'I should have refused to pay the money.' He was a broken man.

In the harsh social realities of life in turn-of-the-century

Britain, something prevented Ada and Reginald marrying and starting a family. Perhaps Reginald already had a wife, perhaps Ada was forbidden by her family from having anything to do with the clerk. It is unlikely that we will ever know. All we do know is that the couple travelled a good distance from their village to conceal the pregnancy and that they made plans for the child's adoption. Reginald still cared for Ada. He arrived at Claymore House in person. Perhaps if he had seen the boy, if Ada had been allowed time with the baby as Theresa had, the outcome would have been very different. But the technological wonders of the telegram and the railway meant that the child's fate was sealed the very same day.

Annie killed and killed without mercy and it is very probable that she did so with a degree of enjoyment at the sensation of power it gave her. Even newborns struggle and fight for life. It would have taken no more than a few minutes to hold a cloth over a baby's airways but the awareness of watching life ebb away would have been acute. We cannot know what drove Annie Walters to want to take the lives of innocent babies but research with female serial killers today gives some chilling insights.

Criminal profiler and author Dr Deborah Schurman-Kauflin noted how many female serial killers find their way into traditional roles as carers, as nurses for example. They are attracted to these positions as it gives them access to the vulnerable and the infirm and few ever expect the carer to become a killer. But for the deeply damaged psyche of the serial killer, it is precisely this cloak that edges them to what they want – to determine the moment the victim will die, to have control.

One convicted serial killer gave Dr Schurman-Kauflin a

glimpse inside her mind, the mindset of a predator. She agreed to keep the murderess' identity secret and, in doing so, gathered a greater degree of cooperation. This killer told her something remarkable, something that shed light into the mind of a killer acting a century earlier. She said: 'I knew at some point, the power would come to me. All I had to do was wait it out. There was going to be somebody who was dependent on me for help and all I had to do was wait. Waiting is kind of like a death. You know it's coming and it hurts bad. But it's something you have to go through. And after all the waiting, it's finished. I was finished by the time I was through waiting, but I got my chance. I finally had control.'

Annie Walters closed the door of the room she was renting at 11 Wanbury Street on 29 October 1902. Alice Seal noted with some surprise that she did not emerge until 12 November. Two weeks of solitude. Alice would have no inkling why. She would not have known that her lodger was enjoying her wait.

2

NANNIE HAZLE DOSS
THE GIGGLING GRANNY

'Samuel? He got on my nerves.'

<small>NANNIE DOSS, IN A STATEMENT ABOUT HER FOURTH HUSBAND</small>

After four days of severe stomach cramps, diarrhoea, vomiting, delirium and a dramatic weight loss of 16 pounds, Sam Doss, a 59-year-old highway inspector, was admitted to Hillcrest Medical Centre, in Tulsa, Oklahoma. With his polite and cheerful wife at his side, the medical team hoped that Mr Doss would soon be on the road to recovery. Yet it took another agonising three weeks for his condition to stabilise. Sam Doss' greenish vomit was streaked with blood, he suffered from prolonged convulsions and cramps and, although his symptoms seemed centred in the bowels, he also had to endure both unending thirst and burning pains when urinating. But by early October 1954, Sam Doss' system had stabilised and hospital staff decided to discharge him, back into the care of his wife. Within 36 hours, he was dead.

Sam had returned home on 5 October. His wife had been at his side as they travelled back to their modest but well-kept house in the quiet town. Sam was proud of the home he had established with his wife, Nancy. They had only met the previous June and it had been something of a whirlwind romance. A lonely hearts column had brought them together and Sam was delighted after many years alone, to find a smiling homemaker willing to be his bride.

Nancy was the name his wife was given at birth but she had always been known as Nannie. Although no longer the attractive woman of her youth, at 49, Nannie still charmed with her infectious laugh and bright black eyes. She was a widow, she told Sam how she'd always struggled to make a home for her and her children and said that her one hope now was to enjoy her remaining years as a grandmother and wife of Sam Doss.

It came as little surprise to neighbours in Tulsa to see that Nannie had spring-cleaned the house in anticipation of bringing Sam home. Freshly-washed laundry had been hung on the line and the smells of baking wafted through the windows. So the sense of shock in the close-knit community was great when news leaked out that Sam had passed away shortly before midnight on 6 October.

While the neighbourhood rallied around, the news also reached the hospital and a young intern, Dr W Dean Hidy, was more than shocked. He was adamant that Sam Doss could not have suffered such a fatal relapse – a relapse that led to total organ failure – only a matter of hours after being released from the medical centre's care. He requested an autopsy. It was the first autopsy to be ordered for any of the men who had married sweet Nannie Hazle and it was the trigger point for a startling story of love, murder and retribution. It showed that Sam's roast dinner had been accompanied by enough arsenic to slay a man three times his size. The home cooking that Sam had thought of as such a comfort had been the weapon used to kill him.

The sense of humour shared by police officers is often bleak but it is far from heartless, acting as a safety valve to keep the horror of what they see at bay. But when detectives sat down to talk to a serene Nannie, they were to find the laughter rolling from only her side of the interrogation room. Nannie was having the time of her life. She flirted, chuckled and flicked through magazines. The investigative team, led by Special Agent Ray Page, had to admit that they had never questioned a suspect quite like Nannie.

Since her arrest, Nannie had tried to beguile and cajole the officers into believing that they were mistaken. Questioned about Sam's demise, she coyly remarked, 'Oh, boys, come on now, I killed nobody. I don't know why you think I did.' Many of those present might have been inclined to believe her. For when Nannie wanted to turn on the charm, there were few that could resist her, but the evidence against her was overwhelming.

This was to prove no simple tale of unfortunate domestic homicide. The officers gathered in Tulsa that day were unaware but they had taken the first step into uncovering a story of a serial killer who had been systematically murdering family members for almost 30 years.

Arsenic has been in use for centuries. It was thought of as a cure for conditions such as syphilis but has been favoured as a poison because it has neither taste nor odour. It has frequently featured in books and films and is perhaps best known as the substance used by two sweet old ladies in Frank Capra's comedy classic *Arsenic and Old Lace*. The 1944 film stars Cary Grant as a man who realises to his horror that his aunts are doing away with their tenants. As a plot device, it works like a charm but its use as a murder weapon can be all too real.

In small doses, someone can live for years but the effects will accumulate and have been linked to diabetes, cancer, liver disease, problems with the digestive system and a coarse thickening of the skin. It can take as little at 60 grams to kill an adult male outright and it is never a painless death.

The officers interviewing Nannie did not have an in-depth understanding of arsenic but they did have toxicology reports that Nannie could not explain away. They had also found out that Sam was Nannie's fifth husband and that only one of those husbands, the first, was still alive. The chance that four men should die suddenly and inexplicably struck the investigators as suspicious. Nannie had had a lot of explaining to do but the team were making no headway. She was still impassive and friendly, smoking Camel cigarettes and flicking through her favourite magazine, *Romantic Hearts*.

When Special Agent Ray Page pressed her into discussing the circumstances surrounding the deaths of her other husbands, Nannie responded with yet another giggle. She said: 'Are you saying, young man, that I killed all my husbands? You're a nice-looking young man, but so foolish.'

Ray Page's patience had reached breaking point. Snatching the magazine from Nannie he raised his voice and told her to end her charade and face up to the many ghosts that stood with her in the room that day. To his surprise, the light that gave Nannie's eyes their shine was snuffed out. She stared coldly and directly at him and Page admits that he felt an unearthly chill. This woman has the devil in her, he thought, and pulling himself back into his usual professionalism, he sat whilst Nannie began to talk.

After many hours of questioning, although Nannie's energy had shown no sign of flagging, she was bored of the game. Calmly, she admitted to poisoning Sam's coffee. Page wanted to know why. Her answer was: 'He wouldn't let me watch my favourite programmes on the television, and he made me sleep without the fan on the hottest nights. He was a miser and... well, what's a woman to do under those conditions?'

At first glance a confession as glib and as trivial as that might seem an attempt by a killer to evade the seriousness of their actions. And yet psychologists who have spent many hours interviewing convicted serial killers will recognise the tone of Nannie's remarks. Dr Helen Morrison has talked extensively to infamous killers such as John Wayne Gacy and Ed Gein. In one of her conclusions, Dr Morrison states: 'Serial murderers have no emotional connection to their victims. Not only do they not care but they also have no ability to care.'

Unlike a killer who may work themselves into a rage and snap, causing fatal damage to another human being, Dr Morrison argues that there is no such emotional outburst from serial killers. She states: 'For them, killing is nothing, nothing at all.'

After admitting that she poisoned Sam, Nannie's mood brightened again: 'Okay, there, you have it,' she grinned. 'Can I have my magazine back now?'

Looking at Nannie Hazle, the officers thought that the only explanation for her behaviour was insanity, for they'd never encountered a serial killer. Page composed himself and said that she could have her magazine back if she told them about her other husbands.

'It's a deal,' she smiled and she chatted about the other men in her life.

Richard Morton, Arlie Lanning and Frank Harrelson. Nannie sighed as she talked about the romantic hopes that she had harboured for all of them, she had always sought her knight in shining armour but had been let down by these men time and time again. Remembering Page's taunt about the ghosts that surrounded her, Nannie quipped: 'If their ghosts are in this room, they're either drunk or sleeping.'

Yet there was far more to come. Not from Nannie, she had tired of her talk with Tulsa's law enforcement officer and decided to sit and wait for her trial the following year. What developments were to follow came from exhumations of not only the men that Nannie had been married to but others who had suddenly died when in her care. The press had got hold of the story too and dubbing Nannie the 'Giggling Granny', they had begun investigations of their own. The facts as they emerged were almost impossible to believe.

Nannie's start in life was unremarkable. She was born in November 1905 in the small rural outpost of Blue Mountain, Alabama. Nannie's parents were James and Loulisa Hazle. Loulisa was known as Lou and on the census of 1910 it was noted that the couple had been married for nine years. Nannie was thought to be close to her mother but it was James Hazle that was to dominate Nannie's early life.

James Hazle was a farmer but the farm Nannie, her three sisters and a brother were raised on was no idyll. The work was intensive and that meant backbreaking tasks for the whole family. The children were soon used to being sent out to weed the land, clear it of stones, help bring in the harvest and cut wood either side of the school day. School was often missed if James decided that the farm demanded it but even when he agreed to let the children go, the walk was a tiring four-mile round trip. Nannie may have resented her chores but plenty of children her age living in the area would have been in exactly the same predicament.

Nannie spoke little about her childhood but she made it clear that she loathed James. He had a quick and violent temper and thought little about beating Nannie, her siblings and even his wife if he felt that he was not receiving the respect he deserved. Again, this would not have been unusual for the time. Men were the head of the household and if they were not obeyed and obeyed quickly, the switch could be used to impose discipline. Although it wasn't simply harsh punishment that fuelled Nannie's hatred, it never became clear what else took place on the farm.

The people of Blue Mountain were hard-working but knew how to enjoy what little leisure time they had. The church would organise social events and there were dances held at halls or barns. To Nannie's immense frustration, James would not allow his daughters to attend. Though this may have seemed severe, James was under no illusion that young men were only interested in dancing. His solution was to keep his girls away from potential suitors and he announced that when the time was right, he'd be the one to pick out suitable young men. But matters did not quite proceed as James had planned.

In 1921, Nannie found work at a textile mill. It was probably a great relief for Nannie to be beyond the bullying control of James. Far from the bleak atmosphere of home, Nannie revelled in the mixed-sex environment. She soon noticed that her dark hair and eyes and trim figure brought her plenty of male attention and her girlish giggle made her a hit. Nannie wanted more than flirtation, however, she was looking for a way out of her family home and reasoned that marriage was her surest way to leave quickly.

One of her co-workers was a tall and handsome boy called Charley Braggs. He was only 16 years old but Nannie liked what she saw. She soon learned that he had no one in his life except his widowed mother, and that meant no siblings to have to accommodate. Within a few months, Charley and Nannie were married, apparently with James Hazle's approval. Nannie moved into the home of her mother-in-law.

Any hopes that she may have had for an easier life were soon dispelled. Charley's mother was highly demanding and quick to throw a fit if she felt she was not getting her way. What was more, Charley always backed his mother over his wife. It was probably not what Nannie was expecting but, before long, there was more on her mind than difficulty with her mother-in-law. Between 1923 to 1927, Nannie gave birth to four girls and exhaustion was unavoidable. Nannie found it harder and harder to cope and began to turn to drink and chain-smoked constantly. No alarm bells would ring with her husband, however, as his dependence on alcohol outstripped Nannie's.

Charley began to spend more and more time away from the family home, at bars and chasing women. Nannie's response was simple. She was soon spotted drinking in bars too, leaving her babies with her mother-in-law and openly accompanying other men around the small town. Both parents could go missing for days, but the worst offender was Charley, who was engineering more time away from Nannie to spend in the arms of another woman.

By then in her early 20s, Nannie knew her marriage was effectively over but that seemed not to be her main concern. The grim setup in the Bragg household had taken a tragic turn for the worse. By the end of 1927, two of Nannie's daughters were dead. They were both claimed by sudden stomach complications. It was said that the girls were fine at breakfast but dead by lunchtime. Another report had the toddlers writhing on the ground in agony before they died, but much of this detail emerged after Nannie's arrest. The deaths were recorded as accidental and Nannie buried two of her daughters in one year with little comment. Postnatal depression can cause a psychosis so severe that a woman will harm her child, which is perhaps something that could be considered in Nannie's case. However, her conduct undermines this theory.

Nannie would go on to kill many more with a dispassionate and methodical precision. Her utter lack of compassion for those around her more clearly fits the profile of a serial killer than that of a woman with postnatal depression.

This was a woman who decided that she had too many dependants and that ridding herself of some suited her. This wasn't a cataclysmic moment of horror, where a mentally unbalanced mother takes the lives of all her children and herself. Nannie had selected two. Having made a cold assessment of her needs, she decided who would live and who would die.

If Charley had any suspicions, he kept them to himself. After Nannie's arrest, he became something of a minor celebrity, always ready with a quip such as: 'If she was in a bad mood, I made sure I didn't eat.' This was probably no more than playing the part of 'the one that got away' for newspapers but what is known is that by 1929, Charley and Nannie were divorced and Nannie was looking for work once more. Divorce at that time was not rare and claimed one in every seven marriages and so Nannie moved back in with her parents and found a job at a cotton mill in Anniston. This was the start of another clear pattern in her life as she developed the urge to keep moving and keep dating.

She was said to be an incurable romantic and Nannie encouraged that image, spending hours reading trashy magazines. They were filled with corny love stories and she talked about the hope that one day she would find true love. It is unlikely that Nannie had any true sense of how to create a lasting relationship. This was probably little more than role play. Role play suited Nannie very well. Serial killers are not the lone and wild-eyed creatures of fiction. On the contrary, the majority of serial killers are articulate, have above average intelligence and hold down steady jobs. Some even excel at appearing as upstanding citizens, such as John Wayne Gacy, a married man who ran a successful building company. He hosted charity fundraising events in his back yard – on the very property where he had buried the remains of 27 of the 33 young men he had raped and killed. Nannie's appearance as a good homemaker did not falter or crack until the very end.

Nannie began placing ads in lonely hearts pages and corresponded with many men this way. The more dripping with sentiment a letter was, the more likely Nannie was to continue writing. One of the lonely hearts was Robert Harrelson, sometimes known as Frank, who replied to Nannie with gushing verse. Nannie sent him a cake and he replied with an offer of marriage and the suggestion that they set up home in Jacksonville. Somewhat confusingly, when Nannie later talked about Frank, she said they married in 1937, yet Frank's brother told reporters that they did not marry until 1945 – the year of Frank's eventual death. And a 1930 census reports Robert Harrelson as married to Nancy, aged 24, living with her four-and-a-half-year-old daughter, Melvina.

If 1929 is when they married, then this at 16 years would be by far the longest of Nannie's marriages. The earlier marriage date does not fit with the rest of Nannie's matrimonial career as she would later move quickly from one marriage to the next, often in a matter of months rather than waiting for years for her next husband to come on the scene. If they did not marry until 1937, however, this would not discount Nannie meeting someone else and setting up home in the years in between. Nannie's movements are difficult to trace year by year, as she frequently travelled, even staying away for months at a time when she was married. She would tell curious neighbours that she had been caring for a sick relative. Nannie also relied on the fact that the US is a country so large and diverse that anyone determined enough can put time and space between them and their past.

Whatever the true date of the Harrelson wedding, the honeymoon period was soon over. Frank was not the clean-living, hard-working man he presented himself as in his courtship of Nannie. The new bride soon learned that as far as drinking was concerned, she had flipped out of the frying pan and into the fire. Frank was a devoted drinker and hell-raiser and had even served a prison sentence for assault. Frank was happy to spend a night in the cells, drying out after causing a disturbance. The marriage, such as it was, dragged on until the end of World War II. In 1945, there must have been a trigger point.

Nannie continued to live her life as Mrs Harrelson until her daughter Melvina was around 19 years old and planning her own wedding. Perhaps seeing Melvina's excitement at the amount of male attention she was receiving gave Nannie pause for thought. It was probably then something relatively minor that prompted her to take matters into her own hands and rid herself of Frank.

As she later told it, Frank had been out on a huge drinking binge with some friends back home from active service. He'd eventually arrived back at the family home and demanded that they have sex. Nannie wasn't happy to consent and he raged that she should or there was a good chance that he wouldn't be around next week. These were the words that sealed Frank's fate. Nannie had been manipulated and threatened before and knew that she had the power to end it. Nannie knew Frank's weaknesses. She knew that as a seasoned alcoholic, he hid liquor in the house and even in the garden. She knew where to find the bottle he had hidden in a flowerbed and carefully poured some away. She topped the rest up with rat poison. Within a few hours, Frank was dead. He was 38.

His passing would have been far from easy. Thallium sulphate is the active substance found in commercial rat poison and ingesting it leads to excruciating skin and joint pain, paralysis and respiratory failure as it overwhelms the nervous system. All of which Nannie sat and watched.

Melvina married a man called Mosie Haynes in 1947 and their names appear again in the public record in 1952, this time to record their divorce. There are conflicting accounts about the arrival of Melvina's children: some claim that her son, Robert, was born in 1943 but this seems unlikely as Mosie was enlisted in the US army and was posted abroad for the duration of the war.

Melvina was said to have had a difficult labour with her daughter, though when she eventually arrived, the baby was in good health. Nannie was present throughout and Melvina drifted into sleep as she watched Nannie rock the newborn. But when Melvina awoke, her daughter was dead. The nursing team could offer no explanation for the sudden death of the infant. Melvina, on the other hand, struggled with a reoccurring nightmare.

Ether had been administered to Melvina during labour and its effects would have had an impact during the hours that came after delivery and yet she swore that she had groggily awoken to see her mother inserting a large hatpin into the head of her new-born daughter. Asking questions of other family members in the hospital afterwards, most confirmed that Nannie had indeed spent some time toying with a hatpin. It can be argued that Melvina was suffering from a drug-induced hallucination but with the inexplicable death of her daughter, doubt would remain.

Melvina must have dismissed her doubts sufficiently to leave her toddler son with her mother when she was called away from Jacksonville. Nannie gladly took the little boy in and insured his life for $500. Then Melvina was told that Robert had suddenly died of a fever. It wasn't until there was an exhumation following Nannie's arrest many years later that it was discovered that Robert had been asphyxiated. Yet remarkably, Melvina never lost faith in her mother. Children of serial killers are often blind to their parent's true character and it is a sign of how credible Nannie could be that she was able to keep her daughter in check.

Despite the hasty arrangements for Robert's life insurance, money was never a motivation for Nannie. She always maintained that a search for enduring love drove her, yet this would not explain the deaths of children at her hands. It is probable that Nannie saw those in her life as little more than objects to experiment on and her desire to watch as she inflicted pain would not leave her. And with Frank gone, she was back on the marriage market.

By placing ads in lonely hearts columns, Nannie once

again embarked on a whirlwind romance, this time with a man called Arlie Lanning which resulted in another move, to Lexington, North Carolina. This was a marriage destined to last five years and it began well. Arlie was not as prone to hell-raising as Frank and he would avoid fights if he could, yet he was undeniably a womaniser who drank heavily. How much this bothered Nannie will never be known but neighbours did note that she could be absent for weeks and even months at a time. The absences were easily explained and there was some basis of truth around certain visits as one of Nannie's sisters, Dovie, was ill with cancer. There were fresh responsibilities too as Arlie's elderly mother, Sarah, expected a degree of care from her new daughter-in-law but in 1949, Sarah passed away in her sleep. It was only an exhumation after Nannie's arrest that established that 84-year-old Sarah had been smothered. The helpless old woman must have proved an inconvenience.

Nannie played the part of a doting wife and regularly attended the Methodist church, without Arlie if he was suffering with a hangover. Appearing as a martyr to marriage suited Nannie. It was only after her arrest that her daughters came forward and talked about the darker side of Nannie's personality and her sudden and violent black moods. Her neighbours in Lexington would have had a hard time believing this as they saw her being devout in church, even becoming a stalwart of their ladies auxiliary, there to support and assist other Christian ladies. Nannie was an inspiration. She'd bake for Arlie, kept a neat and ordered home and suffered her husband's alcohol dependency with grace.

It is a common characteristic that serial killers are able to maintain a plausible persona to the outside world. Nannie had done so for many years and was clearly able to entice men into marriage, even though her looks were no longer what they once were. What Nannie also shared with other serial killers was an ability to talk fluently and keep her composure even under questioning – at least up to a point. Forensic psychologists have found that hours into interviews with killers, their carefully compiled personas crack and kaleidoscopic fractures appear. Initially they respond well to questioning, appearing helpful and cooperative. But then there is a sudden and violent rupture, an overwhelming change in personality that suggests that when they kill, it comes out of nowhere.

Special Agent Ray Page saw that flicker in the deadening of Nannie's eyes during his time with her, that shift into anger when the real world intruded and became irksome. Nannie traded a confession of serial murders for the return of a magazine. The switch from smiling and amiable talker was instantaneous. It would have been a chilling moment that grandson Robert would have seen and a split second that 84-year-old Sarah would have witnessed, as carer Nannie turned on them. It would have been a moment of sheer terror. It was far from Nannie's last.

The year 1952 proved to be a momentous one for Nannie. As a man, even a drunk, could physically overpower Nannie, asphyxiation was not an option. Coldly assessing the methods that would suit her best, she turned once again to poison – specifically, to arsenic – as she prepared Arlie's food. What Arlie's transgression had been we will never know. Nannie reached a decision about her husband's fate and watched as he suffered with sweating, vomiting, dizziness and respiratory failure. It took Arlie an agonising two days to die and a tearful Nannie confided to neighbours: 'Poor, poor Arlie. You know what he said to me before he breathed his last? "Nannie," he said, "Nannie, it must have been the coffee."'

The local doctor did not order an autopsy. Arlie Lanning's death was recorded as heart failure and once again it wasn't until years later that answers were provided through an exhumation.

After the funeral Nannie stayed in the home she shared with Arlie and passed the time indulging in her new passion: watching television. It would have come as some annoyance to her to have learnt however that Arlie had not left the house to his wife. Rather, the beneficiary was to be his sister. Out of the blue, two months after Arlie's death, the house burnt to the ground. Nannie was not hurt and miraculously, neither was the TV, as it sat next to Nannie in the car. The TV was on its way to be repaired, Nannie explained and within a few more weeks and with a little more quick thinking, she had cashed the insurance cheque and left North Carolina.

Her next stop was to visit her ailing sister in Gadston. Dovie had asked for Nannie's help to recuperate. Again, it is fascinating that family members continued to trust Nannie, either not able to believe that she was capable of murder or not witnessing her sudden shift into a fatal state of mind until it was too late. Whatever took place between Dovie and her elder sister cannot be known but once more, the exhumation would uncover another brutal asphyxiation.

It is not typical for serial killers to kill members of their families. It is widely recorded that many present themselves as doting parents and spouses. Very often, the families of serial killers simply do not believe the reports of their loved one's horrific acts. It is chilling to read spousal accounts about the many acts of kindness their husbands showed them during years when they were preying on the vulnerable and savagely attacking them. But there are also sickening accounts of parents like Rose and Fred West who systematically abused their children. Nannie fell into their group, those who looked for love in order to abuse it horrifically.

When Richard L Morton, a retired businessman from Kansas, read a sweet lonely heart ad, he would have had little idea of what awaited him. He had joined the Diamond Circle Club for a nominal fee and was enticed by the idea that he could find lasting love. Nannie was in her late 40s by now but could still lure a man. She certainly captured the heart of a man who was still handsome even though he was in his early 60s. He sent a letter to the club, requesting that his name and Nannie's be deleted from their list and thanking them for introducing him to 'the sweetest and most wonderful woman I have ever met.' They moved to Richard's home town of Emporia in October 1952.

At first, life seemed good for Nannie. She liked Emporia and liked Richard's generosity all the more. He bought her gifts and knick-knacks and, as a former salesman, knew how to talk up the prospects of the good life that lay before them. But if anyone should have known not to be taken in by first appearances, it should have been Nannie. Richard Morton was not the man he said he was. Far from facing a comfortable retirement, he was struggling with considerable debts and Nannie learned that he was also a philanderer. Richard, even though he had taken a new wife, still kept another woman in town.

Ever the cool head, by Christmas, Nannie was once again answering ads in lonely hearts columns, but neither her suitors or her errant husband knew about the letters she kept. This was a probably a sign that Nannie was ready to dispose of Richard and move on to the next victim, but her plans changed slightly with the arrival of her mother Lou in early 1953. Nannie swore that she had no part to play in Lou's death but the facts as they are known make her denials sound hollow.

Lou was dead within a few days of arriving at the daughter's house, the victim of a horrific stomach complaint. Her exhumation would identify a huge quantity of arsenic in her system but Nannie never accepted this. Perhaps it is worthwhile bearing in mind Brent E Turvey's understanding from his hours interviewing killers. He is a forensic scientist and criminal profiler who has spoken extensively to multiple killer Jerome Brudos, finding him a plausible and helpful interviewee. It took him a long time to realise a simple truth. Mr Turvey wrote: 'I learned an important lesson through that experience. The lesson was that offenders lie.'

The kind of casual lies and obstructions will be familiar to police officers but what Mr Turvey and others expose are psychological fissures in the minds of serial killers. On one level, they are capable of organisation and can conform to people's expectations. But drill deeper and it is clear that serial killers are unable to identify with others, to recognise pain or to show remorse. They are objects, there to be used. Lying and boastful behaviour has little to do with attempting to avoid justice. It is a device used on impulse, useful to support the sense of self at that moment in time.

Whatever impulse seized Nannie when caring for her mother, it was soon to arise again. Within a few months, Richard Morton was dead, displaying all the classic signs of arsenic poisoning and yet, once again, there was no official investigation. Nannie was ready to move on, to find her fifth and, as it would transpire, her final husband. With her mother, her sister, grandchildren, three husbands, and an elderly mother-in-law dead, this was a woman who should have shown signs of mental wariness and guilt. She was concealing the truth behind the many ghosts that Special Agent Ray Page believed surrounded her. Yet Nannie still walked with her head held high.

Photographs of Nannie at this age do show that she had aged. She wore thick glasses and her figure had thickened as the years had passed, she now looked filled-out and matronly. But her face is still remarkably line-free and full of character, and in the flashbulbs that surrounded her after her arrest, she glows.

Perhaps it was this girlish light that first attracted Samuel Luther Doss, a hard-working and proud resident of Tulsa, Oklahoma. He was 59 years of age and looking for a life partner when he met Nannie. Different from all her previous husbands, Sam did not drink or chase women and, although a solid character, he never sought to dominate those around him. He was God-fearing, conservative and was careful with finances. But Sam's settled ways did not enchant Nannie for long and when he criticised her for the hours she spent watching television and reading magazines with the fan on, he had inadvertently signed his own death warrant. As Nannie said during her confession: 'Well, what's a woman to do under those conditions?' For Nannie, it was simple. It was time to rid herself of her staid husband and move on. Detectives discovered that, indeed, she had entered her details on to yet more lonely hearts columns and was exchanging letters with a farmer from North Carolina. She had even sent him a cake.

Nannie was tried in Oklahoma the year after her arrest. Jovial throughout the lead up to her trial, when the press tried to provoke her she remained at her easy-going best. And yet there was a strong possibility that if Nannie were to be found guilty, she would be executed. With this prospect looming, the press goaded her as to what the State should do with her if she was convicted of killing Sam Doss: 'Why, anything. Anything they care to do is all right by me,' was her calm and smiling response.

But the press did not get the full trial that they had hoped to see. It was set for 2 June but in May Nannie decided to offer no contest to the charges before her and pleaded guilty. Since her arrest, Nannie had been seen by three or even four psychiatrists in an effort by the prosecution and defence teams to ascertain whether she was clinically insane. Of the detectives that had interviewed her, few would have believed that this Giggling Grandma was anything other than plain crazy. But the psychiatrists who saw her thought otherwise. Nannie did suggest that she had suffered a head injury aged around seven. Some reports suggested that the damage occurred whilst travelling in a train which braked hard and threw her forward, causing her to smash her skull. Other reports detail her pram being hit by a passing train. Nannie said that after the injury she suffered with blackouts and terrible headaches.

But after rounds of questioning, the psychiatrists involved arrived at the conclusion that Nannie's state of mind was clear at the time she killed Sam Doss. Oklahoma were prosecuting her for this crime alone as it fell in their jurisdiction. But it seems probable that when Nannie chose to kill, she always did so with a calm conviction.

Judge Elmer Adams wanted to ensure that Nannie understood what her change of plea would mean: 'You understand that all that is left is for the court to decide between a life or death sentence?' Judge Adams asked Nannie.

'Yes, sir,' she replied.

'You want to plead guilty?' continued the judge.

'I do,' she replied.

But when it came to sentencing, Judge Adams imposed a life sentence rather than the death penalty. Her composure unruffled, as she was led from the courthouse, Nannie turned to her daughter Melvina and said: 'Take it easy. And don't worry. I'm not.'

Nannie did spend the rest of her life in an Oklahoma State Prison. She died from leukaemia on 2 June 1965. One outcome that arose from her case was the push to pass a law requiring a medical examiner to determine the reason for death if an individual is not attended by a physician. The other certainty is that without the vigilance of young Dr W Dean Hidy, Nannie would have killed again. She had killed babies, children, men and women – there would have been no end to her casual killing if the autopsy on Sam Doss had not been requested.

As with many serial killers such as Rose West and Myra Hindley, Nannie took to prison life easily, soon settling in to a routine and the structured passage of each day. She showed no remorse for her actions. Indeed, as time wore on, her cheery disposition never dimmed. On the contrary, she took enjoyment from manipulating a new set of rules and relationships. Eventually she became one of the most senior of inmates and when a local reporter, a journalist from *Tulsa World*, asked about her life, Nannie quipped: 'When they get short-handed in the kitchen here, I always offer to help out. But they never do let me.'

3

MARYBETH TINNING

HUSH LITTLE BABY

'Now I lay me down to sleep,
I pray the Lord my soul to keep;
If I should die before I wake,
I pray the Lord my soul to take.'

FUNERAL PRAYER READ BY MARYBETH TINNING

Larry Daly, of the Daly Funeral Home, is a man who intuitively understands that his role is to take care of the bereaved as much as it is to attend to the deceased. He also knows that death is never easy and that it is particularly hard to bear if it is the loss of a child.

How do parents find the strength to bury a child? It was a question that Larry had been forced to ask himself. He and his family had suffered a terrible loss in 1971, when their five-year-old son drowned while out playing and not a day passed without his thoughts turning to his young son. As a professional, it was his duty to compose himself, especially now as he sat with Marybeth Tinning, assisting her with preparations for the funeral of her baby daughter, Tami Lynne.

Mr Daly knew the Tinnings well. He had first met Marybeth almost 15 years earlier when, heavily pregnant, she had asked for his help in arranging the funeral of her

49

father, Alton Roe senior. Mr Roe had worked at General Electric, the main employer in the town of Schenectady in New York State and had suffered a massive heart attack. Although rushed to Ellis Hospital, he died there a week later. Larry Daly was aware that Marybeth was a fragile young woman, trying to cope with bereavement before the birth of her third child.

But now, Mr Daly found that he had to dig very deep as he faced Marybeth Tinning. Over the years, she had come to rely on the Daly Funeral Home, she clearly appreciated their meticulous and sensitive approach and as she sat listening to the softly-piped music, she knew precisely what kind of setting she wanted to create for Tami Lynne's burial. As Mr Daly glanced up at the calm housewife, try as he might, he could not get beyond the disbelief and dismay he felt. Together, they were making preparations to bury her ninth child.

It was December 1985 and over the course of 14 years, every one of Marybeth Tinning's nine children had died. It seems astonishing now that any woman could give birth to eight children, and adopt another, only for them to die one by one, without any kind of alarm bell ringing. Nine children were dead. How was it possible?

But looking at the life of Marybeth Tinning, it does not take long for an even more incredible tale to emerge. It is a story of systematic flaws in officialdom and the story of a damaged young woman who would bring anguish to the lives of almost everyone she met.

At first glance, Marybeth would seem to have something in common with Annie Walters, a woman who callously killed newborns. But Marybeth's children were not all newborns when they died, Barbara was almost five years old, Joseph had just turned two and Michael was two-and-a-half.

These three Tinnings were children, not babies. But to unravel the mystery that surrounds the lives and deaths of all of Marybeth's offspring, we have to begin with the story of the youngest, a tiny newborn called Jennifer.

When Marybeth stood distraught in front of Larry Daly in October 1971, she was seven months pregnant with Jennifer. Marybeth's father had died and it was understandable that she appeared burdened with grief. Her relationship with her father had never been easy. Old classmates recalled watching a subdued Marybeth walk slowly towards the school bus, her head bowed under her father's stern gaze. He was difficult to live with but he was a hard worker, his job was tough, standing on one of General Electric's production lines and, although money was always tight, Alton provided for his family.

Later, Marybeth would complain that her father had been physically abusive, hitting her with a fly-swatter and locking her in her room for misbehaving. But this drew little sympathy from those who'd grown up with her in Duanesburg, a rural town on the outskirts of Schenectady. It was an ordinary working class neighbourhood where most children could expect a beating if they behaved badly and would say that it didn't do them any harm.

Sympathy seemed in short supply throughout Marybeth's childhood. She had a younger brother, Alton Junior, who she believed was favoured by her father and who didn't receive the punishments she did. They were never close but what made Marybeth's life that much harder was her failure to make friends easily. She cut a lonely figure in school, avoided by other girls for being just a bit too weird. Children can be brutal in their assessment of others and the hurt caused by cruel remarks can still be felt into adulthood.

The problem didn't seem to be that she was timid, it was more that she was unstable, shifting from withdrawn to furious if she felt she wasn't getting her own way. She would shout, dissolve into tears, sulk, threaten and invent stories to try and make herself the centre of attention. Needless to say, all children go through phases where they try and manipulate others but most learn that they have to learn to get along rather than dominate. School is as much about acquiring social skills as it is about learning how to read and write, but it was something Marybeth found difficult and she was excluded from friendship groups.

It cannot have been easy for Marybeth, she felt plain and unpopular and, increasingly, she switched off from events around her. She did not excel as a student either and although she talked about going to college, her teachers felt it was probably beyond her reach. Marybeth's self-esteem was battered both at home and at school, and her yearning for acceptance and approval lay at the heart of her every unhappiness.

But Marybeth was hardly the first girl to grow up unpopular at school and disgruntled at home. Many young women leave school and seize the chance to make a new start in life. Marybeth was probably hoping for change when she eventually found work as a nurse's aid, in the paediatric ward of Ellis Hospital in Schenectady. It was her first exposure to the pressures and difficulties faced in hospital wards and Marybeth watched as the human dramas unfolded. She saw nurses lend emotional support to parents as well as provide treatment and care to children. Parents with very sick children received enormous sympathy from hospital staff. Reserve and the careful etiquette of ordinary human interaction fell away as nurses, doctors, chaplains, relatives and friends all reached out to the grief-stricken. Watching this, it must have made an impression on Marybeth.

As a young adult, Marybeth still found it hard to make lasting friendships. She would either come on too strong, frantically hugging new acquaintances and overwhelming them with attention and gifts, or, she would avoid eye contact, use a girlish voice and even break down in tears when it was least expected. In short, Marybeth was a handful and many chose to rebuff her. Some felt sorry for her and she felt most at ease when people showed they were concerned. Those who did get to know her were always struck by how agitated she could be, wringing her hands and making up stories of being watched, followed or being the victim of malicious rumours. It is possible that Marybeth was suffering with manic depression from her late teens. She wanted someone to help, wanted someone to care about her and hoped for an end to her sense of loneliness.

Hope came when Marybeth was asked if she would take part in a blind date. As it turned out, Joe Tinning's arrival was something of a disappointment. He was a slightly built and painfully-quiet young man, two years younger than her. Marybeth was Catholic but Joe was from a staunchly Protestant family. But whatever Marybeth's initial concerns, they were nothing compared with the future problems for two dangerously mismatched people.

Joe Tinning was a good student and a hard worker who had secured himself a sought-after apprenticeship at General Electric. It should have been all he needed to set up home and raise a family. He was a little better paid than the men who worked on the line. But it wasn't to be. Because when Joe took Marybeth's hand in marriage, he had no idea that his new bride was a shopping addict. She spent obsessively, often buying the same item many times. One neighbour remarked that at a garage sale, Marybeth laid out item after item with the sales tags still intact. Consequently, rather than laying down a deposit on a home of their own, Marybeth and Joe stayed in rented accommodation for years.

Joe hardly ever challenged his wife's spending. When he did, neighbours reported rows but the raised and hysterical voice came from Marybeth. She admitted to one colleague that she kicked in a TV set in one moment of fury and Joe retreated further into himself. It was not in his nature to be outspoken. He was very uncomfortable expressing himself even with colleagues who had known him for years. Conversation with Joe amounted to no more than a few nods.

If Marybeth had hoped to be saved from her life with a severe and uncaring father, Joe's lack of emotional support left Marybeth tumbling deeper into isolation. Spending was one emotional boost and petty theft another. Her sister-in-law noted that money in her purse went missing after a visit from Marybeth and when the money that Joe had collected from his bowling club went missing, Marybeth went as far as to stage a robbery in their apartment. She was veering out of control, her husband was too withdrawn to challenge or help her and her fragile sense of self was about to shatter with horrific consequences.

Alton senior's heart attack could have been a chance to reconcile daughter and father but it wasn't to be. He spoke to his son, Alton junior, who was then unmarried, and asked that when he had a son, to please call him Alton. Marybeth was crushed that her father didn't even consider his daughter's unborn child fit for the honour. Alton senior did not reach out, he did not make his peace and when he died, his daughter was left with a poisonous mix of rage, fear and grief.

A lot of people, like Larry Daly, did rally round and try to comfort her, appreciating that Marybeth was in a precarious position so close to full-term. She took on her father's funeral arrangements while her mother's health was not good, but only later, after the trial, did some of the maternity staff reveal how unbalanced Marybeth appeared as she waited for the arrival of her baby. It was late December and Marybeth was convinced she would give birth on Christmas Day, that her child would be a boy and that it would channel her father's spirit. Staff knew about her recent loss and just hoped she'd move past her delirium once her baby was born.

Joe seemed detached but then he had a lot on his plate. The couple already had two children and this was to be their third. Barbara was four and little Joseph not yet two and although he had his parents, Joe senior and Edna Tinning to help out, it was a lot to deal with. Joe was quietly very proud of his two children and rightly so. Both had white-blond hair and were strikingly attractive. Marybeth liked to dress them well and took them out frequently. She enjoyed the compliments they received. In his son, Joey, Joe saw more than the family name living on, he had high hopes for his bright son's future. He could be the first Tinning to leave Schenectady and not fall into working for General Electric as he and his own father had. Perhaps little Joey would see the world and make it his own.

Joe hoped his wife would overcome the sadness she felt over losing her father, because she had a lot to live for. But, on 26 December, their worlds were turned upside down: Marybeth gave birth to a girl they called Jennifer and she was clearly unwell. Their baby died eight days later suffering with haemorrhagic meningitis and abscesses on the brain, having never left the hospital.

It is easy with hindsight to see that this was a tipping point for Marybeth. Losing the hopes she had harboured about giving birth to a baby boy born on Christmas Day were one thing, but this tragic turn of events was devastating. Joe found it difficult to reach out to Marybeth even now. He had grown up in a household that stoically accepted God's will and life's hardships. Coupled with his natural reserve, Marybeth was stranded in her mounting grief.

When she appeared again at the Daly Funeral Home, every member of staff was moved. A tiny white coffin was ordered and Marybeth asked for Jennifer to be laid in it in a white christening gown, the cask open, to receive the many mourners. It was a lovely service and heartbreaking for anyone that witnessed it. The outpouring of emotion comforted Marybeth but once the day was over and doors were closed, her relatives and neighbours trusted that with two other young children to care for, she would soldier on for their sake. no one could have predicted that within two months, Barbara and Joey would be dead.

It was only a fortnight after Jennifer's death that Joey was rushed into Ellis Hospital. His mother brought him in, saying he was suffering with fits and convulsions, choking on his own vomit. The team at Ellis stabilised Joey and he was kept in for observation for a few days and everyone was relieved that he quickly returned to perfect heath. He was sent home but within a few hours, Marybeth came back into the emergency room holding a limp Joey. He was dead.

She said that he had wanted to take a nap but that when she checked on him, he was blue and tangled up in a sheet. Staff were deeply saddened and a little perplexed, wondering if Reye's syndrome could be the reason for Joey's sudden death. Reye's starts with a high fever and vomiting but that mirrors many childhood illnesses. A link was found between aspirin and an increase in the severity of Reye's and doctors advised parents not to treat high fevers in children with aspirin. Untreated, Reye's can lead to respiratory difficulties, liver and brain damage. No autopsy was requested for Joey and his cause of death was given as cardio-respiratory arrest but that meant no more than registering the fact that the little boy had stopped breathing.

The news of Joey's illness was still being spoken of when Barbara was rushed to Ellis Hospital. It was 1 March and the emergency room staff was told that, like Joey, Barbara had suffered convulsions and was having difficulty breathing. The medical team revived Barbara and asked to keep her in overnight but Marybeth refused. Barbara was away from Ellis for only a few hours when she was returned, unconscious. They tried their best to resuscitate the little girl but she had lapsed into a coma and was pronounced dead the following day. Marybeth made an appointment at the Daly Funeral Home and composed her notice for the *Schenectady Gazette*.

An autopsy was performed and Reye's syndrome was again considered. Reye's can cause very sudden and serious illness and one of the symptoms is liver damage. Dr Thomas Oram was the hospital's chief pathologist and he summed up the dilemma faced at that time: 'When she died, no one thought of suffocation as a possibility. We know now that the anoxia caused by suffocation will produce a fatty liver. We did not know it then.'

In the first instance, the idea that a mother would deliberately harm her child in this way was simply not considered. Outwardly, Marybeth cared for her children, they were well-dressed and not suffering neglect or abuse. It was felt to be a terrible tragedy but very few expressed suspicions about Marybeth. In addition, pathology in 1972 could establish only so much. Reye's syndrome was not fully understood and there were enough characteristics shared with Barbara's autopsy results to convince Dr Oram of its likelihood at the time.

But there was talk. Neighbours in Marybeth's street were dumbfounded that two children who had been running around playing in the yard could be so quickly snatched away. Nursing staff talked too, concerned by what they saw when they watched Marybeth. She was dry-eyed and detached and looked away when spoken to. Yet no one offered Marybeth, a woman who had lost four family members in a few months, any kind of bereavement counselling.

Joe was still paying for the funerals in instalments when they decided to leave their apartment and rent elsewhere. Marybeth thought people were talking about her and it was hard to deny. They moved to Cleveland Avenue and Marybeth told Joe that she wanted to start fostering children. It was only three months since they buried their last child.

By late 1972, Marybeth had become a regular customer at Flavorland, a cafe and restaurant in a large shopping centre. Staff recognised her as she used to call in from time to time with Barbara and Joey and the waitresses thought the children well-behaved and very sweet. Seeing Marybeth now was difficult. She would sit, staring blankly, for hours and was clearly depressed. It surprised staff when she began to ask repeatedly if a position was available. At first she was turned down, the manager clearly not convinced that she was well enough. But her persistence paid off and the waiting staff rallied round, feeling sorry for this unfortunate woman.

It was the start of a long-term association with Flavorland and no one who worked alongside Marybeth came away untouched. She was unpredictable and sometimes short-tempered but she worked hard and her colleagues did their best to try and support her. Fairly rapidly however Marybeth's behaviour rattled the other waitresses. She would change her appearance almost daily, dying her hair and shaving off her eyebrows. She began to draw on eyebrows in thick pencil, often in bizarre zigzags. One of the senior waitresses spoke to her warning Marybeth that her customers were being put off. Once again, although her appearance was addressed, no one had the courage or skill to question what was boiling below the surface.

Reaction was mixed when Marybeth announced she was pregnant. Her colleagues wondered how stable she was but as she was approaching 30, they accepted that time was running out if she still hoped to have a family. Everyone hoped Marybeth's bad luck was at an end.

She needed to find a new obstetrician as her last, Dr Schwenk, no longer wished to treat her. Like a good many professionals who would come to deal with Marybeth, he had strong suspicions that she had a role to play in the death of Joey and Barbara but with no proof, all he could do was withdraw his services. Marybeth also chose not to have her baby at Ellis Hospital. No doubt her memories were too painful and Bellevue Hospital could mean a fresh start. Baby Timothy was born on 21 November and although a little underweight, doctors signed him off as perfectly healthy. He was soon seen in the neighbourhood and at Flavorland, a sweet little boy in a cute blue outfit, and clearly Marybeth was very proud of him.

On 10 December, Marybeth ran into Ellis Hospital with

Timothy dead in her arms. Thirteen years later, Marybeth would tell police officers: 'I put a pillow over his face.' But rushing into the emergency room, all staff could think about was their attempts to resuscitate the infant, a difficult task when a baby is not yet three weeks old. Marybeth said she had found her son in his crib and that he did not respond. The doctor on duty had not dealt with the Tinnings before and believed it was a case of cot death, or Sudden Infant Death Syndrome (SIDS), a catch-all diagnosis made in cases when it is impossible to ascertain why a healthy child has stopped breathing. The number of boys that die suddenly is greater than girls but it is very rare for SIDS to occur in babies less than a month old. No autopsy was performed and Marybeth was left to stage another funeral, again, with the casket open, toys placed around the baby and she read her favourite prayer:

Now I lay me down to sleep,
I pray the Lord my soul to keep;
If I should die before I wake,
I pray the Lord my soul to take

Joe's brother, Andy, had married a woman called Carol, who watched Marybeth closely throughout the service. Carol had two children from a previous marriage and could not imagine what it would be like to lose four children and sit through their four funerals. Carol's son was born with cerebral palsy and she remembers holding baby Timothy and thinking what a huge gift it was to have a healthy baby. Carol was badly shaken by the sudden death of Timothy and was deeply unsettled by Marybeth's unflustered calm.

Each person responds to grief in a different way. Some are

so shell-shocked by loss that they almost cease to function and yet Marybeth displayed an odd blend of emotions. At one moment she appeared utterly vacant and at the next, animated by conversation and enjoying her role as grieving mother, passing out sandwiches and coffee. Other mothers felt they would have to be buried alongside their children and could not host a gathering back at their apartments and chat away the afternoon.

In a little under two years, Marybeth had buried four children and those who knew them prayed there would be no more pregnancies, as clearly the Tinnings had a genetic abnormality that struck their children down. Joe's brother Andy urged him to think about a vasectomy and it was clear that although he said very little about his lost children, he was deeply saddened. Relations between Joe and Marybeth deteriorated and neighbours gossiped about the screaming fits Marybeth indulged in. Joe was a placid character but everyone has their breaking point. Marybeth spent as much as he earned and it was a grievance about spending that Andy expected to hear about when he met up with his brother. What he heard, however, shocked him. Joe said his food had started to taste bitter. Andy knew his brother was unflappable and would never make up a tale such as this. He urged his brother to think about leaving Marybeth but Joe said as a Tinning, he would never do that. He took the vows he made in church on his wedding day very seriously.

Carol wondered what her sister-in-law was capable of but knew how anxious Andy was not to alienate Joe. He wanted to stay close to his brother no matter how difficult Marybeth could be and as a couple they did turn to them for help in 1974. Carol's son suffered with severe asthma attacks and one afternoon, stranded at hospital, she asked Marybeth to pick up her son's prescription of phenobarbital, a powerful barbiturate.

Back at home with her son, Carol and Andy got a call in the early hours of the morning. It was Marybeth: 'Joe's dead!' She was screaming and clearly hysterical. The couple raced to the apartment and found Joe lying face down in the bathroom, unconscious, but Marybeth had not called an ambulance. That was left to Carol as Andy tried to revive his brother. Marybeth repeated over and over, 'I didn't do it,' as they waited for help to arrive. Doctors reported that the cause was a massive overdose of phenobarbital. Joe was lucky to survive.

Of the 70 or so tablets made up for Carol's son, none remained. Knowing something of the tragedy that surrounded the Tinnings, staff assumed that Joe had attempted to kill himself. Joe said he couldn't remember anything at all and despite Andy's attempts to intervene, Joe asked only that he be allowed to go home.

After that, a quiet Joe became even more withdrawn and over the next 11 years, trod very carefully around his volatile wife. The only one to challenge Marybeth directly was Carol. She was sensitive to Andy's concerns that the family did not tear itself apart but she found it hard to hold back. The issue of the money stolen from Carol's bag came up and she tackled Marybeth head on. Marybeth broke down and confessed and Carol urged her to get help.

They immediately drove Marybeth to the Catholic hospital St Clare's and asked to see a psychiatrist. It was late evening and Marybeth said she was going in to see a doctor but, as time ticked by, Carol wondered how long the initial consultation would take. She soon found out that Marybeth had not seen a doctor. In fact, she'd called Joe's parents and left with them through another exit.

Marybeth returned to Flavorland and the waitresses who had given her a baby shower for Timothy. There was a kind of acceptance amongst the women she worked with that Marybeth was 'unusual' and there was little appetite for more speculation about what happened to her children. The assumption was that the Tinnings weren't going to try for any more children and so it was a shock to one of the Flavorland waitresses when she took a break in the staff room with Marybeth and thought she looked pregnant. But worse was to come. When she asked if Marybeth was expecting, she looked detached and said: 'And God told me to kill this one, too.'

It is easy for people to talk in retrospect about their suspicions and even elaborate on their recollections for effect, but when journalist Joyce Egginton was told this account by a former colleague of Marybeth's she was in no doubt that the woman was being truthful and was haunted by what she heard. More than one waitress from Flavorland called social services about their concerns. But, as each of the Tinning children had death certificates signed off by doctors with reasons for their demise, social workers were in a difficult position, as they had to have some solid information on which to act. So the arrival of Nathan Tinning on 30 March 1975 was greeted with some anxiety at Flavorland – but surely nothing else could happen to another of Marybeth's babies?

Nathan was a typical Tinning baby, blond with big blue eyes and an inquisitive nature. The waitresses set aside their worries as it was obvious that Marybeth enjoyed bringing him to Flavorland and he was thriving. The Tinnings were renting a new apartment, this time on McClelland Avenue and there were other changes in Marybeth's life too. She moved to another Flavorland, to work day shifts. It was this Flavorland that she ran into on 2 September, pleading for help. Nathan had stopped breathing. Manager Michael Hovey pulled the five-month-old from the car and onto the bonnet, desperately trying to resuscitate him. Marybeth had not driven to an emergency room and it was the team at Flavorland who called for an ambulance. But the baby never regained consciousness. Marybeth said Nathan started to make gurgling noises in the car and that Flavorland was the first place she could think of to stop. A decade later, she would tell police that Nathan was crying and so she placed a sofa pillow over his face until he stopped.

The waitresses at both branches of Flavorland were stunned. Nathan had appeared healthy and alert. How could this happen? Marybeth returned to work. Time passed and with five children dead, Marybeth spent three years without children. Still only 35, perhaps she could have lived out the rest of her life in Schenectady, spoken of from time to time as 'that woman who lost all her babies'.

But Marybeth wasn't able to move away from the idea of motherhood and the fulfilment it gave her. Carol and Andy had decided not to have children together. Carol did everything she could for the son she already had, but it was hard to see him suffer and she feared that if she had another child, the chances were high that he or she could be born with cerebral palsy. A recessive gene that led to complications had been discussed amongst the medical staff that dealt with Joe and Marybeth. It was wise not to have any more children but Marybeth's thoughts turned to adoption.

By paying a private agency, Marybeth could avoid a lengthy adoption process. A fee of a few thousand dollars meant that she was in line to adopt a child in the autumn of

1978. A baby boy, Michael, was born on 3 August and delivered to the Tinnings' apartment. It was an exciting day for the couple but Marybeth had news that extended beyond the arrival of baby Michael. She was due to give birth again in late October and duly did on the 29th to a pretty baby girl they named Mary Frances. In less than three months, the Tinning household had grown from two to four. Marybeth had created another family.

Talk at Flavorland was intense. The babies arrived with Marybeth one morning and it was impossible not to be captivated by the little girl and boy. Mary Frances was a typical Tinning, with fair hair and blue eyes. Her adopted brother was handsome too but quite different in appearance. Marybeth said his heritage was Italian but most of the waitresses guessed that this was not the case. At least one of Michael's parents was Afro-American but Marybeth refused to acknowledge it. Once again, everyone hoped for the best as they watched Marybeth leave with her two children, and so when news came that Mary Frances had been rushed in to St Clare's emergency room, there was a shocked silence.

It was 20 January 1979. Mary Frances was three months old and at a key age if SIDS is to strike. Marybeth was holding her limp and unresponsive daughter in her arm and said that that was how she'd found her in her crib. The emergency team worked frantically to revive the baby and were very relieved when she began to respond. In fact, she quickly made a full recovery but doctors were not happy to let her return home. She was kept on the children's ward for two weeks, carefully monitored throughout and she seemed as well as any child at three months.

Marybeth stayed with her daughter throughout and staff watched her just as closely too. Many believed it impossible that a mother could set out to harm her baby. Clearly Mary Frances had been well cared for and the Tinnings had to have a rare genetic disorder that was interfering with the brainstem activity of their babies. Others were filled with doubt but had little proof. If there was a recessive gene causing difficulties in their offspring, then there would be a one-in-four chance that a child would inherit it. That meant, statistically, out of four babies, only one should have had the misfortune to inherit a faulty and dangerous disorder. The odds of every one of their six children displaying the affects of abnormal chromosomes, rather than just being carriers or not inheriting at all, was stretching probability and credulity.

Two of the nursing team reported their suspicions to the child protection unit and Marybeth was visited at the hospital by a social worker whose conclusion was there were no clear grounds for action. The doctors involved were sufficiently concerned to send Mary Frances on a long journey to a specialist hospital in Boston for exhaustive tests but nothing was found. Mary Frances would be sent home but with a sleep monitor which would sound an alarm if the her breathing ceased.

It was a month to the day that Marybeth first appeared in St Clare's with her daughter, when she reappeared and this time, as she ran in crying for help, the baby was in full cardiac arrest. Staff were devastated. Mary Frances was put on a respirator but the baby was brain dead. Two days later, the machines were switched off and Mary Frances was formally declared dead.

After another funeral service directed by the Daly Funeral Home, Marybeth went through the ritual that she always adhered to, removing all evidence that the baby ever existed. All clothes and toys and equipment were given away. Mary

Frances would be her last child, she told Joe's parents and, although bitterly sad, they felt it was the wisest course of action. Others wanted to ensure that Marybeth really was serious about her promise to stop having children and she assured all who'd asked that she had been sterilised. The one ray of joy throughout this sorrowful time was Michael. He was sturdy and cheerful and at least he was spared whatever genetic disorder was affecting the Tinning babies.

Marybeth clearly cared for Michael and yet her role as mother was not plain sailing. She was beset by paranoid fears that people were deserting her, fearing that she was plagued and that Michael would be taken from her, claimed by his birth mother. Those who knew her tried their best to reassure her but as well as worries about Michael remaining with her, Marybeth held a far more worrying trait. She refused to believe that Michael's heritage was black and her stubborn refusal to face facts put the little boy's life at risk. Michael developed a hernia and although its removal would be routine, medical staff wanted to check that he was not carrying sickle-cell anaemia, which is most common in those with an African or Caribbean descent.

If he was a carrier, the risks of complications during an operation would soar. The sickle-shaped cells can become trapped in the small blood vessels and oxygen levels can plummet. But Marybeth refused consent for Michael to be checked. They told her she was putting her son's chances of recovery in jeopardy but she would not be moved. Happily, Michael's operation was a success and he made a full recovery but for the staff at St Clare's, it was a worrying sign that Marybeth would put her concerns ahead of those of her children.

Fears about her attitude to Michael's health were fast

overtaken by a new development. Marybeth was pregnant. She quipped that the obstetrician who had performed her 'sterilisation' took her out to lunch and said that she'd waive her fee for the next attempt. She gave birth to Jonathan on 19 November 1979.

Not for the first time, Marybeth's colleagues at Flavorland were deeply worried. If Marybeth's children were cursed by a genetic inheritance, why would she risk another child's health? Most of them guessed that having her 'tubes tied' was little more than a lie. None of them organised presents for this new Tinning baby. All of them prayed for the best.

But Jonathan differed from Marybeth's other births. He was born premature, weighed less than five pounds and had complications. His testicles had not descended, the urinary opening in his penis was on the underside rather than the tip, and doctors surmised that it was likely that he had a kidney abnormality too. Jonathan was sent to the premature care unit where Marybeth stayed. The nursing staff were concerned. They were very experienced at dealing with mothers and knew that it was a distressing time yet Marybeth displayed very little emotion. One noted that Marybeth looked away and never smiled when Jonathan was brought to her but of course, all the staff knew about Marybeth's history.

One nurse who wished to remain anonymous later said: 'She would even say that everyone hated her because they thought she was doing something to them. She was weird. One of my first thoughts was that she was a witch.'

This statement was made by a professional health worker and it is clear how much Marybeth's demeanour was alienating those around her. Female staff and male doctors were increasingly divided about her. But those doctors who cared for Jonathan were not interested in the suspicions of the nursing staff. In the latest child they thought they had a clue as to the genetic abnormalities afflicting all the Tinning children. Jonathan's health problems were all corrected and after two weeks, he was judged to be progressing so well that he could go home.

He was eleven weeks old when Marybeth returned to St Clare's with him, unconscious in her arms. Incredibly, staff managed to revive him and he was kept in for observation but this was only the start of the intensive care staff assigned to the little boy. He was airlifted to Boston's children's hospital for specialist care and assessment. There his birth defects were found to be unrelated to this new health crisis. Jonathan was thriving. So much so, that he was sent home with a sleep monitor. It was only three days before Marybeth returned. This time it was too late for resuscitation attempts. Jonathan was brain dead and in a coma.

The hospital staff were devastated. Jonathan was kept alive artificially for four weeks, Marybeth remained with him and at one point expressed an interest in training to be a mortician. At the Daly Funeral Home, she had previously asked what qualifications were necessary to become an undertaker. Death was ever present to Marybeth, it dwelt within her and when Jonathan finally died on 24 March 1980, her thoughts turned to his burial.

Jonathan's autopsy proved inconclusive. Marybeth did not ask for his clothes to be sent to charity as she usually did with the death of her children. She said that her apartment had been broken into and Jonathan's clothes had been stolen. She imagined it was because someone hated her and wanted to punish her for having another child. But the tiny clothes were soon found, half a mile from Marybeth's home, scattered on an overpass of the highway.

Only Michael remained at home with Marybeth now. It is impossible to know what Joe Tinning was feeling. Staff at St Clare's were stunned by all that had happened but they were confident that Michael, a lively and inquisitive toddler, would be fine. As one nurse said: 'We called Michael her insurance card.'

If his health was good, it proved that there was a genetic fault line running through the tragic and brief lives of the biological Tinning children. Marybeth stayed at home caring for Michael but she was not without support. Joe's parents were involved in Michael's upbringing, often taking him off Marybeth's hands, as he could be too boisterous for her to cope with. Edna and Joe Senior were fond of Marybeth. They saw her as very fragile, almost a child herself. They grew closer still as Marybeth took the surprising decision to embrace their Protestant faith. Edna and Joe were very highly respected at their local church. They were good people and actively involved in the parish, particularly since their church had suddenly burnt down two years previously.

They were very fond of Michael and were worried when he had a fall and hurt his head quite badly. A social worker visited Marybeth to talk about safety in the home but despite some dizziness and loss of appetite, Michael seemed back to his indomitable self. So it was a shock when after Joe left for work, Marybeth called her sister-in-law to say that she could not wake their son. Her sister-in-law told her to get to ER immediately but Marybeth phoned her GP and asked when she could bring him in for an appointment.

Like many busy surgeries, they had an hour during which parents could bring children to be checked over. Marybeth gave no indication how poorly Michael was and waited over two hours to drive him to her GP. When she walked into the practice with the two-year-old in a blanket, the surgery nurse knew beyond doubt the boy was dead. She desperately tried to revive the cold and unmoving child while the ambulance crew raced to reach them. The nurse was devastated. She knew Michael and remembered how the little boy would walk into the surgery with his arms outstretched for her.

Marybeth was impassive. She had screamed for help when arriving at the surgery but now that she had reached St Clare's she was subdued. So was Joe. He'd arrived from work and staff could not help but notice that he did not embrace his wife. The cause of Michael's death was given as pneumonia and he was buried in a Protestant cemetery. Daly's made the arrangements as usual.

Schenectady's child protection hotline rang with more than a handful of calls from people who knew Marybeth but the pathologist had arrived at a medical explanation for Michael's death. There was little they could act on. Yet it was not that clear-cut. The pathologist found a patch of bronchial pneumonia on one lung, but he doubted that it was significant enough to overwhelm an otherwise healthy toddler. Nevertheless, in the eyes of any court, he knew it was sufficient for a defence team to show that illness was present.

Marybeth would have been relieved that a medical cause of death had been found but she was deeply unsettled by a rising tide of doubt that surrounded her. How was it that Marybeth was alone on the eight occasions that her children, biological and non-biological, had died – with the clear exception of the first death, baby Jennifer? Eight was enough for most bystanders. Even the medical examiner in Schenectady, Dr Robert Sullivan, signed off Michael's autopsy with the note: 'The family history is bizarre.'

It was too much for Marybeth and she wanted to leave

Schenectady. The Tinnings duly moved out of the town and back to Duanesburg, where Joe's parents lived. They'd offered to put them up until Joe had saved a deposit for a new home.

Duanesburg offered Marybeth the chance to recuperate from the trauma of losing eight children. Having tried a number of unskilled jobs, she became enthusiastic about the Volunteer Ambulance Corps, a vital rural community service in which Joe senior was a valued member. Marybeth worked hard in administration, but fellow volunteers found her difficult to befriend. It quickly became clear that Marybeth would invent stories where she'd be the heroine rescuing someone in a life-threatening situation. She talked about saving a woman who collapsed in a shopping centre when she went into premature labour. Marybeth single-handedly delivered the baby and wrapped it in the tin foil she had in her shopping bag. These stories were a transparent attempt to show that she should be admired and accepted but at the same time, Marybeth failed her medical technician exams and that left her only able to provide limited support for the units. A lot of volunteers who knew her background pitied her. She came over as childlike and desperately needing to be liked. It was heartbreaking to watch.

One of the volunteers was Reverend Burnham Waldo, a gentle and experienced priest who had counselled many of his parishioners. People turned to him as he did not rely on a few stale phrases about spiritual matters. He had a keen understanding of psychology and had helped parishioners who'd struggled with alcohol abuse and depression. The Reverend decided to try and help Marybeth.

At first Marybeth seemed to respond. She was ecstatic that someone was willing to talk and attempt to understand her world. Nobody had shown that level of care before. But it was too much. She lurched into an hysterical over-dependence on the Reverend, calling him in tears to say that there was an emergency at the ambulance station when the truth was she just wanted to see him.

Reverend Waldo spent hours with Marybeth and tried to get her qualified help, but he realised that her problems were simply too complex for him to handle. He attempted to curtail the demands Marybeth was making on his time but she became irate and responded by telling colleagues that they were having an affair. He met with her to calmly let her know that he was aware of the claims she'd been making and that it must stop and she had to seek psychiatric help. Nothing prepared him for the change he saw in Marybeth. It was more than anger. He witnessed her physically change and her eyes turn quite black. What stood before him, he later recounted chillingly, was someone 'with cancer of the human spirit.'

no one believed that the Reverend was having an affair with Marybeth but other rumours spread that were harder to refute. Marybeth had started to appear in bars and motels outside the town, her appearance radically altered and she did not try and hide the fact that she had been having an affair. Joe's response was to say nothing but to invest in their first home, a trailer outside Duanesburg. Marybeth didn't like it but it was all that they could afford. Within a few months, it burnt to the ground. Joe was back to square one and Marybeth asked to return to Schenectady.

The ambulance corps were relieved in the main. Equipment had begun to disappear and more than a few volunteers thought Marybeth had been involved but, again, there was no proof. To the dismay of some, Marybeth continued to volunteer for a further two years. Her role in the corps came to an end in 1984 when a trunk of equipment was found on a sports field. The trunk belonged to Marybeth but the equipment certainly did not, including ten infant plastic airways used to revive babies. Marybeth gave no explanation but she agreed to resign.

Marybeth took up a new job, this time driving a school bus. She was 42 years old and Joe must have imagined that their past tragedies were behind them. And so the shock must have been great when Marybeth announced that she was pregnant once more. She kept working until June 1985.

One of her new neighbours was pregnant at the same time, a nurse called Cynthia Walter and they became friends. Cynthia had no idea of the extent of Marybeth's previous losses. On 22 August, the local *Gazette* ran the news that Tami Lynne had been born to Marybeth and Joe Tinning. Waitresses at Flavorland where horrified. They were right to be. On Christmas Eve, the mailman wished Joe and his family a Happy Christmas but a subdued Joe told him that Tami Lynne had died four days earlier.

Tami Lynne was four months old and her health had been good. She differed from the other children Marybeth had given birth to in that she had a mass of dark hair. Marybeth fussed over her, dressed her beautifully and, to Cynthia's surprise, bought the tiny baby a mass of Christmas gifts. Cynthia's son, Aaron, was born a week after Tami Lynne and the two women faced the early weeks of motherhood together. Cynthia felt that she understood why Marybeth was spoiling her daughter. Marybeth had told her the sad story of how her only son died of SIDS as a newborn and that her daughter had been lost to Reye's. Cynthia felt the full weight of fear as she now held her own son and thought how terrible it must be to lose a child.

In the early hours of 20 December, Marybeth called and said, 'Get over here at once.' A shocked Cynthia, soon assisted by paramedics, tried to resuscitate Tami Lynne, but after reaching St Clare's Joe and Marybeth were told that it was too late.

Marybeth arranged Tami Lynne's burial with the Daly Funeral Home. The notice appeared in the *Gazette* and her daughter had an open coffin with soft toys placed around. Though the arrangements and service seemed familiar, this funeral was different from all the others Marybeth had organised, because it marked the beginning of the end.

Marybeth was planning to move house again, but a task force had been assembled as it was apparent from the autopsy that there was no clear medical reason why little Tami had died. Marybeth was questioned formally on 4 February 1986 by police investigators Bob Imfeld and Joe Karas. Marybeth was trembling and agitated and called Joe at work before agreeing to accompany the officers to the station to discuss Tami Lynne.

They had no warrant for her arrest. Marybeth went voluntarily. Once at police barracks at Loudonville, the investigators knew that psychologically, they had the upper hand. Marybeth was unsettled and struggled to remain focussed during questioning, unable to differentiate Nathan from Timothy and losing track of her train of thought. Joe was brought in separately and answered questions in a defeated monotone. It became clear that he would stand by Marybeth no matter what the investigators might find.

The police decided to use this loyalty to their advantage. They brought the couple together for the first time that afternoon and prompted Joe to repeat his simple but crucial intention to stand by his wife. The officers guessed that without Joe's support, Marybeth was far more likely to continue to lie about her role in the lives and deaths of her children. Asked again about Tami Lynne's last moments, Marybeth quietly said: 'I killed them. I killed my children.'

As the interview continued, Marybeth said that she had smothered Timothy, Nathan and Tami. She refused to accept that she had a part to play in the deaths of the others. It may have been a calculation on Marybeth's part. She knew she was in deep water over Tami. Joe's considerable loyalty was tested but she may have felt that as two of the youngest, Joe's bond with Timothy and Nathan would not have been as strong as those with toddlers Michael and Joe junior or his lovely daughter Barbara. That left Mary Frances and Jonathan and as they'd both had long spells in hospital, perhaps she felt that their deaths did not necessarily hint at her involvement. She may have thought that three was the limit if Joe could be expected to stay at her side.

The arrest and subsequent trial were a sensation. Prosecutors took the decision to only proceed with the case against Marybeth for the death of Tami Lynne. They felt it carried less risk than securing convictions for the other children. The forensic team wanted to exhume all bodies but straightaway they hit complications as the markers on Jennifer's and Timothy's graves had been mixed up. One of the other coffins had become waterlogged. Regardless of the fact that nine children lay dead, the safest course was to proceed with Tami Lynne's death alone.

Marybeth's trial did not begin until June 1987 and to the surprise of many, it looked likely that the prosecution could lose the case. Marybeth's defence team used a number of tactics. In the first instance, they said that Marybeth's confession had been forced from her under duress. Second, they brought an expert witness to the stand to say that Marybeth's babies were afflicted with Werdnig-Hoffman disease, a wasting condition that can lead to sudden fatalities. The prosecution team introduced medical experts to counter this but the jury were facing an avalanche of contradictory opinion. If sufficient doubt was created in the minds of the jurors, they could not convict.

The prosecution team was aware that they were losing the initiative as the trial was drawing to a close. Throughout, Marybeth had remained calm, cheerful and took endless notes, sitting next to her attorney. Her composure shattered one morning, however, when she spotted a young man in the courtroom. In a development worthy of any film or TV crime series, a man called Harley Spooner had contacted the prosecution team with a startling claim. He said he was tired of hearing 'all the bullshit' about Tami Lynne dying from a genetic disease. He said he knew it wasn't true as he was Tami Lynne's father.

Harley Spooner was a school-bus driver at the same time as Marybeth, but he was much younger and had a reputation for being something of a womaniser. He claimed that they'd begun a sexual affair but that he found Marybeth's emotional demands too difficult. He ended the affair but then realised soon afterwards that she was pregnant. She even brought Tami Lynne to the bus depot and he instinctively knew that the dark-haired baby was his own. In fact, she looked just like all the other babies he'd fathered by different women over the years.

To prove paternity, Tami Lynne would have to be alive and with the case winding down, the prosecutor did not have the time to introduce Spooner as a witness. But it was enough to bring him into the courtroom and see Marybeth's reaction –

clearly shaken, she asked to be led out of the courtroom, her baffled attorney asked for a recess and she was allowed to leave in order to compose herself. The prosecution team knew that any 'genetic' explanation for the death of Tami was a nonsense. She did not share genes with the other Tinning children. As it was, within days, Marybeth was found guilty and she was sentenced to a term of 20 years for the death of her Tami Lynne. Responsibility for the deaths of the other eight was left to speculation.

Joe, true to his word, had stood by his wife. But as she was taken away from him, those who knew him said that he looked like a weight had been lifted from his shoulders. Joe, like many others that had got to know Marybeth, could find no way to reach and help her. She was a profoundly damaged individual, very probably the victim of childhood abuse, who had grown into a woman capable of terrible harm. She desperately wanted children in order to stop the harrowing feelings of isolation and lack of self-worth. But as she quietly told police investigators: 'I mean, whatever I did just did not turn out right.' She felt a failure as a daughter and then as a mother. With the death of Jennifer whatever fragile sense of self she had seemed to collapse.

Marybeth could well have been suffering with postpartum psychosis, becoming overwhelmed by the idea that there was something wrong or bad about her child that then must be destroyed. Munchausen's syndrome by proxy was also raised as a possibility. Munchausen's was coined for the rare cases when people sought out medical help when none was needed. The proxy version involved even smaller numbers or women who harm their children in order to be the focus of sympathy and attention. Frequently, these women have long had a fascination with the medical profession.

Another disturbing thread came from Cynthia Walter's revelation that Marybeth confessed to once having an abortion at a time when it was illegal. Cynthia was shocked but Marybeth said: 'They made me do it.' It was before she knew Joe and she was not dating anyone at the time. The question remains, who impregnated Marybeth? Living at home and under her father's regime, if Marybeth had been sexually abused it would give an insight into the full extent of her mental collapse, whilst pregnant, at her father's deathbed.

Before giving birth to Jennifer, Marybeth was near delirium and in a frightening and destructive mood. Nursing staff allege that Marybeth attempted to induce the baby herself to ensure that it would arrive on Christmas Day. If that is the case, the risk of infection was high and could have resulted in the brain abscesses that killed Jennifer eight days later. It is a bleak and tragic possibility and would explain a good deal about the shattered personality that then went on to try, and fail, to mother so many others.

These are only theories and no one will ever know what occurred during the last moments before Marybeth raised the alarm when her children became unresponsive. Marybeth herself had ceased to be responsive to the real world many years before that. It is a tragedy for her, yet much more so for the tiny lives that she held in her hands, children that heard their mother whisper: 'If I should die before I wake, I pray the Lord my soul to take.'

4

MYRA HINDLEY

THE END OF INNOCENCE

'I didn't murder any moors, did you?'

MYRA HINDLEY IN A LETTER FROM HOLLOWAY PRISON TO IAN BRADY

It was only ever going to end in outrage. The tabloid headlines screamed out in indignation, victims' families conveyed their anguish and the wider public expressed its horror. And this was over a painting, 30 years after the crimes that convulsed the nation.

Artist Marcus Harvey had created a huge canvas, reproducing the infamous monochrome image of Myra Hindley, staring coldly and directly, mocking collective incomprehension. She is a monster. Black eyes heavily made-up, coarse, bleached hair and a smear of dark lipstick on the hard-set mouth. no one who has seen the original photograph will ever forget it. The pitiless menace of her stare, the viewer aware that it would have been the last face that those children saw before their lives were snuffed out. It haunts us still. And artist Marcus Harvey re-made the image, from hundreds of copies of a child's hand-print and exhibited it at the Royal Academy in 1997.

It was too much for public sensibility. Harvey would have known that he was playing with fire, after all he was born in Leeds in the early 1960s and would have grown up, as so many did, to fear the name of Myra Hindley, child-killer. Parents' eyes clouded in horror each time a story emerged in the press about Hindley's attempts to petition for freedom. 'The most hated woman in Britain' was, for once, a tabloid understatement.

One woman wrote to the papers to object to Harvey's picture hanging in the Royal Academy and she expressed what we all felt when she wrote that the painting showed 'a sole disregard not only for the emotional pain and trauma that would inevitably be experienced by the families of the Moors victims but also for the families of any child victim'. The author of those words was Myra Hindley.

Myra always knew how to wrong-foot people. She had a true gift for saying the right thing at the right time, she could read anyone, mirroring exactly what they hoped to hear. It was a talent that kept her alive in prison. After all, prisoners commonly give nonces a rough time, seeking them out for a beating and urinating in their food or on their beds. It is common knowledge that child-killers can expect no peace inside. Prison officers may even turn a blind eye if a cup of scalding hot tea is thrown in the face of a paedophile. What do you expect? It isn't a holiday camp. But it was for Myra.

Not only did she learn how to make friends with other prisoners, some of them became her lovers. Not only did she enjoy protection from prison officers, one even helped plan her escape attempt. Clever old Myra. Whilst her former lover Ian Brady deteriorated physically and mentally once jailed, Myra experienced a new lease of life. She sat her O-levels and her Open University degree, she sunbathed, she enjoyed cooking and gardening, she wrote poetry and she fell in love.

One of the things she came to cherish most was a walk on Hampstead Heath, spending time amongst the trees and flowers, breathing in fresh air and romping with the prison governor's dog. Lucky old Myra. She was enjoying simple things, things her five young victims never would.

It was Myra's ability to reflect what people around her wanted and expected that made her time in prison so fulfilling. It was a talent that brought everything to her – friendship, love, admiration, campaigners and a rare and dogged devotion. Myra could reflect light, but it was the same talent that also provided Brady with his dark and malevolent echo – bringing cruelty, torture, sexual perversion, deception and murder. That darkness was in Myra, festering below her quiet and assured surface. Perhaps that's why her choice of hair colour became so iconic; bleached white at the time of her arrest, she was soon pictured with the dark roots breaking through.

Pauline Reade, Keith Bennett, Lesley Ann Downey, John Kilbride and Edward Evans. These names are as familiar as the names of children we were at school with, a litany spoken whenever Myra's name was mentioned. Foremost in keeping the memories of the slain children alive was Ann West, Lesley Ann's mother. She exhausted herself in her campaign never to let people forget, she devoted what remained of her life to contacting the authorities, to speaking to the press, to reliving her anguish and, in time, Myra grew to hate the name Ann West.

Any attempt Myra made to reinvent herself, to show that she was worthy of parole and release, Ann West thwarted. She would not let the public forget what Myra and Ian did. Throughout the remainder of Myra Hindley's life, opinion polls showed that over 80 per cent never wanted to see her released. This was more than the grief of a mother, this was more than public outrage: Myra Hindley became a monster to us all for one reason alone – for a tape recording.

Without the recording, her fate would have been very different. Ian Brady was far from the first man to prey on children. Had he killed alone, he would merit only a few column inches after his arrest and his name would have been forgotten by now. Teamed with Myra, it was different. Mercifully, there are very few women like Myra Hindley. Women who lure children to their homes to abuse and kill them. Indeed, so atypical are female predators that they almost slip through the net.

Myra was one of those who almost got away with it. When investigating officers first talked to her, they thought she was surly, but not a killer. In fact, after talking to 23-year-old Myra, they let her go. Ian Brady was held in custody after what had proved an extraordinary morning, even by the standards of Manchester policing, but Myra was allowed to walk out of Hyde Police Station with her bleached hair, neat suit and her nose in the air. No wonder old friends and neighbours called her Miss Hoity-Toity, Myra clearly thought she was a cut above everyone else, but you can't hold anyone in the cells for that.

However, the arresting officer knew a little more about the true character of Miss Hindley, the secretary living at 16 Wardle Brook Avenue in a suburb of Manchester. He knew her for a liar. Because when Superintendent Bob Talbot turned up on the morning of 7 October 1965, saying that he had reason to suspect that there was a man in the house, the impassive young woman said: 'There is no man here.'

Yet Brady was there, lying on the sofa in the next room, composing a letter. Bob Talbot and another officer soon found him, pen in hand and naked from the waist down. Like Myra, he was unruffled by the arrival of the police, even though the body of Edward Evans lay upstairs, wrapped in an old sheet, waiting for burial.

Even when they found Edward's body, Bob Talbot and his team imagined that some sort of drunken fight had broken out, that Brady had gone too far and killed the 17-year-old accidentally. His girlfriend would have panicked and was trying to cover for him when the police arrived. It was a sad event but this was a new estate populated by people rehoused from the slum clearance programme, money was always tight and violence never far from the surface. A drink-related death would be far from unique but from the start the arrest hadn't been straightforward.

Superintendent Talbot borrowed the white coat of the local bread delivery man to disguise himself because he'd been told that Hindley and Brady both carried guns. In 1965, that was far from common and they had run checks that established that Hindley was a member of the Cheadle Rifle Club.

The warning about the couple being armed came in a garbled and panicked flood of information from a frightened young man who had dialled 999 earlier that morning. So incredible was his story that the police initially doubted there could be any truth behind it. But following procedure, they collected him from outside a phone box at around 6.15am, where he stood shivering next to his young girlfriend. The man was so terrified that the police constable had to coax him into handing over a carving knife and screwdriver before he was allowed in the patrol car.

One look at the young man told them that he was truly rattled and that was cause for alarm because this man was David Smith, a well-known delinquent and no stranger to violence. As well being caught housebreaking, Smith already had a conviction for causing actual bodily harm during one of his many fights. But now, something had scared Smith witless.

It was to prove only the start of the day's revelations. He was taken to Hyde Police Station where he gave his statement. The woman with him turned out not to be his girlfriend but his wife, 19-year-old Maureen Smith. The problem seemed to concern Maureen's sister, Myra, who lived with a man called Ian.

Maureen, or Moby as Myra called her, was close to her sister and always had been. Myra was older by four years and had always doted on Moby, even though they did not live together in Gorton. Once Moby was born, Myra was shipped out to her grandmother's house, a not unusual practice in the late 1940s. Granny Maybury and Myra's mother, Hettie, lived within a few doors of each other and both Hindley girls ran out of one back door and into the other. The red brick two-up, two-down terraces were a warren of family support for all the residents.

It could be a bit claustrophobic growing up in the tightly packed streets. Everyone knew everyone else's business but it also meant that children had lots of friends and lots of freedom, staying out until all hours. There would always be troublemakers, like David Smith, and there would always be people who would drink too much and get into scrapes but neighbours trusted each other and wouldn't hesitate to help each other out. If you were short of cash that week, someone would tide you over until payday. If you were sick, someone would knock on the door with a stew and a loaf of bread without waiting to be asked. It was a tough life but it was a tight-knit community and there was still a lot to smile about. Jobs were plentiful, youngsters could leave school on a

Friday and be taken on by one of the local textile factories by the Monday. There were plenty of ways to spend your pay packet. Everyone knew one another, doors were unlocked, the streets were safe.

Myra was popular growing up. She was a bit of a tomboy, bossy and self-assured, but she could be relied on for a spot of baby-sitting or dog-walking. Her life seemed like it would pan out as it had for girls of her background for generations. She left school at 15, found work, and no doubt would soon start courting a local lad and they'd get engaged and settle down. Once they could afford to find somewhere of their own, somewhere to raise kids, it would be within a few doors of her mum. It was a future that Granny Maybury must have dreamt of for Myra. She was close to Moby but it was Myra who was the apple of her eye.

There might have been a worry that Myra didn't get on with her dad but that was a common enough gripe at the time. Bob Hindley had been posted as a fitter with the Parachute Regiment during the war and Myra barely saw him from the day she was born, 23 July 1942, until he was demobbed at the end of World War II. Yet it was the same for everyone. Dads were absent and returned to homes where women were used to running things their own way. Bob Hindley soon found work as a machinist, he drank a fair bit and would raise his voice and lash out, but so did many fathers at that time. Besides, Myra could always run to Granny Maybury, and she frequently did, knowing that Granny always took her side. There is no evidence that Myra suffered prolonged abuse and neglect, and that sets her apart from other female serial killers.

As the years passed, Granny found herself swayed by Myra's opinions and her forceful personality. It must have been the case as Granny's old friends noticed in alarm that she allowed Myra's young man to live with them. 'Living in sin' was unheard of in Gorton at that time and although Ian and Myra kept up the pretence that they lived separately at first, by the time of the move to Wardle Brook Avenue, Brady was a fixture in the house and Granny made her excuses after tea-time. Effectively, she was banished to her own room. Brady had little time for the old woman.

They made a striking couple, Ian and Myra. They had met four years earlier at Millwards, a textile factory, where Myra was a secretary and Brady a stock clerk. Myra had already been through a few jobs, she had not always acquitted herself well and had been fired on at least one occasion for absenteeism and shirking work. She'd also proved to be manipulative, claiming to have lost her pay packet on one occasion. Her co-workers had a whip-round for her. It turned out not to be true. Few would ever feel happy to confront Myra, however, as she could be fierce and would give anyone who crossed her a mouthful of abuse.

Brady was different. He'd kept his head down at Millwards and was a diligent employee. He was not liked though: he was cold, aloof and had an air of superiority that failed to impress his co-workers. Four years older than Myra, he had only come to Manchester to seek out his mother. Brady had been born in Glasgow to a young single woman called Maggie Stewart, a tea-room waitress. She was later known as Peggy and had drifted in and out of Brady's life, eventually moving to Manchester when he was a teenager. Brady was raised by the Sloan family in the Gorbals, a rough tenement area of the city, and he was trouble from the start. He was a misfit, he rejected the Sloans and everyone around him, developed a fetish for Nazi memorabilia and was frequently caught thieving. He would torment pets and other animals. It was the courts that ordered him to leave Glasgow and start afresh with his mother in Manchester.

It was far too late by then to start again with a mind as damaged as that of Ian Brady. He had served time in Borstal for another theft and even though he left petty crime behind, he was retreating ever further into a fantasy world of violence and excess. He read *Mein Kampf* and the writings of the Marquis de Sade, using extreme texts to bolster his idea of himself as separate and superior from those around him. He claimed later to have already taken part in a murder but the police have no evidence of it. They did find detailed plans for bank robberies but, at that stage, both the claim of murder and a heist were important not because they were real but that they fed his splintering and antisocial mind.

He was a dangerous individual and might well have gone on to commit acts of violence anyway, but he really needed a conduit, someone who would listen to his rambling philosophies, his pseudo-fascism and his racist views. Someone who would look up to him, an audience to help him stage his depraved fantasies.

Enter Myra.

Myra adored Ian from afar. She wrote gushing entries into her diaries about how different he was, how dark and impressive his refusal to join in with the office banter was. She admired this gloomy Glaswegian, perhaps more so as he never paid her any attention. Ian was useless around women and his lack of confidence would have fuelled his anger. To initiate a conversation, he would have to feel in control, he was a man riddled with fear that someone might laugh at him. Myra would have tuned in and always appeared doe-eyed, in awe of him. It worked. On 22 December 1961, her diary entry was: 'Eureka! Today we have our first date. We are going to the cinema.'

If Myra had any notions that this would be a typical romance she was soon disabused. The film they saw was *Trial at Nuremberg*, exposing the horror of the Nazi death camps. Ian hooted with laughter when he watched footage of men, women and children being led to gas chambers. The images were unforgiving. Children pulled from their mothers' arms, an old woman mocked by an SS officer for trying to soothe her grandchild, a pile of emaciated corpses, a mountain of children's shoes rotting in the sun. Myra laughed too.

It was all Ian needed. Soon she was his disciple, she changed the way she looked, dressing in tight clothing, her hair white blonde, her look severe and Germanic. She read everything Ian told her to and parroted his views. He called her Hessie: there was a well-known pianist called Myra Hess and so at Millwards it was passed off as a reference to her. But of course, it was also a reference to Hitler's henchman Rudolf Hess and Myra and Brady delighted in their hidden, code-riddled world.

Their sex life soon took a darker and violent turn. Sadomasochism fascinated Brady and he took pictures of Myra wearing a hood, in crotch-less knickers, or with her buttock raised to show whip marks. Brady appeared in them too, hooded and naked except for a vest.

There was some irony in that Mrs Hindley chose the name Myra because it means 'purity'. By that stage of her life, any purity had gone. All those who knew her saw the changes, but she brushed off their every concern. She wasn't stupid however and she knew that Brady was more than 'different'. She even contacted an old school friend and handed her a letter. She said that it described how Brady had drugged her and she woke to find him on top of her. If she was to die, the friend was to hand the letter to police. But a few months later, she asked for the letter back and it was destroyed.

Was the letter evidence that Myra was under Brady's spell? Or could it be something else, perhaps a bargaining chip as the power began to shift in their relationship. It did shift. Brady came to rely on Myra. She could drive, he could not. A car would become pivotal as they moved bodies to the Moors. She joined the Rifle Club and bought the guns that they used to shoot on the Moors. She was the vocal one, Brady was too self-conscious to even buy a bus ticket. Myra did all the talking – her geniality would become vital as she groomed the children they would kill. Did Brady sense that his physical strength was one area of superiority over Myra? He could snap her neck. But the letter insured that if he did, he'd be exposed.

If it was a form of insurance, why did she get the letter back? In all likelihood, it was because the game they played became so bleak and woven with guilt that Myra was bound to Brady forever. She crossed over, she became a killer. After that, Brady toyed with Myra and she with him in a game that they would continue to play out over the course of their many long years in captivity. Each had the power to expose each other's secrets, right up to Myra's death. What bound them so tightly, for the next 24 years, was Pauline Reade.

Moby knew Pauline, they'd grown up on the same streets and she was in the year behind her in school. David Smith knew her too, Pauline was a year older than him and they had courted for a few weeks. Mr and Mrs Reade were hard-working and respectable and were relieved when their daughter broke up with 'good-for-nothing' Smith. Pauline was a good girl. She had a job since leaving school and always helped her parents around the house.

She had gone out on Friday evening, 12 July 1963. Like any other 16-year-old, she was excited to be going out to a dance and this was a popular one held at the Railway Worker's Social Club. Myra and Ian were yet to move to Wardle Brook Avenue and Myra was living in the house she grew up in, very close to the Reades. In fact, she knew the girl. Myra would have struck up a conversation with the teenager as she saw her pass, dressed in her pink dress and light blue coat. Perhaps she told Pauline that she'd hired a van for the weekend and about her plan to take a picnic up to the Moors. It was 7.30pm, still light at the height of summer, but they still needed to take blankets for their legs as the Moors were exposed and the wind could chill even summer air.

At some point, Pauline was persuaded to get in the van with Myra and Brady. They drove her up to Saddleworth, a huge moorland on the outskirts of the city. It stretched for miles, a place that was at once beautiful and desolate. Brady felt at home there and Myra did too. They had packed wine and whisky and, at first, it must have seemed a fun and spontaneous adventure. Did Myra tell her that they'd drop her back at the dance once the picnic was finished? Perhaps the van ride with Moby's sister seemed like a good idea, something to tell her friends about as not many people owned cars in Gorton. She must have felt grown up, dressed for a dance, speeding along the A road with the older couple at her side.

With a spade packed into the back of the van, there is no doubt that Myra knew this was no ordinary picnic. Pauline would never be seen again. The teenager was raped and murdered by the couple, who knew she would have to die. She knew Myra and she could not be allowed off the Moor. It was a ferocious attack. Her throat was slit, her skull fractured and even her spine was severed. Myra watched as the dead girl lay on a rug and Brady began to dig.

If they could get away with this, they could get away with anything. Pauline's parents waited anxiously for the police to locate their daughter but it was as if she'd disappeared into thin air. It seemed impossible: it was still broad daylight as she walked to the dance. How could there be no trace of her? But the only traces that remained were in the minds of the killers and in a snapshot Ian took as a memento. It featured a smiling Myra, standing at the girl's grave in the silent earth.

The murder bound Myra to Brady for many years, as they played a sinister game of cat and mouse from their respective prisons. Even incarcerated, the pair had never been charged with Pauline's death and they vehemently denied any involvement in her disappearance. It was a pact they held for years until Brady began to hint that further bodies were buried out on the Moor. He did so as his Hessie had long abandoned him, turning her attention instead to a string of lesbian affairs and her efforts to earn parole in the 1980s. By this time, Brady made it very clear that he had no interest in ever being released. It was in sharp contrast to Myra, who had converted to Catholicism, had radically altered her appearance and who would meet with anyone working to further her case for parole. Brady was angered by his former pupil. She paraded her remorse, stressed that she had been brainwashed by Brady and blamed the media for demonising her. Brady only had to mention Pauline Reade and Myra knew the game was up.

Plus Brady had another ace up his sleeve: Keith Bennett.

He would be murdered almost a year after Pauline but the 12-year-old's body has never been recovered. Brady's offers to walk the Moors with the police forced Myra's hand in 1987. It was the year that she would confess to both killings, bringing her bloody tally to five.

This was all to come. Back in late summer 1963, Myra felt only elation at the death of Pauline. Together the couple would talk about watching the girl struggle for life, they would laugh and relive their abuse. They had more than their memories: they had the photographs they had taken at Saddleworth, something they could return to. Ordinary snaps acting as a code for them alone; under these feet lies the body of a mutilated child.

The fact that the police were clueless delighted them. As the year played out, Joan and Amos Reade came to the slow realisation that their lovely daughter might never return. They had their son to focus on caring for but not knowing where Pauline was became unbearable. If only they had insisted that Pauline walk to the dance accompanied, they thought, if only she had stayed in with them in their neat and cosy home.

Joan kept a vigil, refusing to lock the back door in case Pauline wanted to walk in, as she always had. It destroyed Joan. She was placed on antidepressants but as the years of uncertainty and pain stretched ahead of her, it proved too great a burden and her mental health collapsed. By the time Myra saw fit to confess, Joan Reade was in a mental hospital, a ruined shell of the women who had once been a good neighbour and loyal friend to all in Gorton.

Other mothers, other families, would be destroyed by Myra and Brady. Far from satiating their appetite for abuse and death, Pauline had only revealed the depth of their hunger. As

Christmas approached, Ian was becoming agitated. He found it a difficult time of year, perhaps remembering the childhood he'd spent as an outsider, the bastard without a father. He wanted a distraction. He wanted a 'happening' as he would come to call their murders.

Those who knew 12-year-old John Kilbride always remembered his smile. He was a bright lad, the eldest of seven born to Patrick and Sheila Kilbride, an Irish family living in Ashton-under-Lyne in Manchester. John had carried out all his household chores and was then free to go to the local cinema on Saturday 23 November. Once the film had finished, he and another friend hung around the market stalls running errands for the stallholders to earn a few shillings. The last time his friend saw him was near a stall. He'd hopped on a bus home but John hadn't finished with the task he'd been set. As the bus turned the corner, John went out of sight and would not be seen alive again.

Myra had been busy that morning. She had to take the bus to a car hire place called Warren's Autos. She said she'd return the Ford Anglia the next day. She was true to her word but the owner was less than pleased. The car was mud-splattered, as if she'd driven through a field. He grumbled but Myra said nothing and with her weird black clothes and hostile stare, the manager knew he was wasting his time complaining to her.

A massive search operation was launched for John Kilbride. Thousands of flyers were sent out and the local press carried his picture but as before it seemed as if a youngster had simply vanished. Some of the impact of his disappearance was lost, as the day before the abduction John F Kennedy was assassinated in Texas. Although it happened thousands of miles away, the story was huge news across the globe.

The Kilbrides were lost to grief, ultimately the stress of losing their child to the Moors Murderers would break Sheila's and Patrick's marriage. It took a few minutes to end the life of 12-year-old John Kilbride but it seems that no stretch of time can bring an end to the grief his family endures. Even with grandchildren at her feet, decades later, Sheila still cries herself to sleep over her first-born, her strong, smiling boy.

To Myra, the child was no more than fuel for her and Brady's fantasy life. Something else to remember, another reason to drive up to the Moors to sit and watch and take pictures. But again, it wouldn't be enough. Over the course of one year, the attacks on Pauline and John had set a rhythm to their killing. Christmas and summer. Seasonal peaks that triggered something within them both and an impulse they cared not to contain. It was 1964 and the year would prove to be their most depraved.

Keith Bennett was the same age as John Kilbride. It was 16 June when he set off to his grandmother's house where he stayed every other Tuesday. He was also the eldest child, one of four, and his mother Winnie Bennett was expecting again. At seven months pregnant, she was looking forward to the new arrival and hoped they'd all cope. It would be a busy household with five children and Keith's stepfather Jimmy Johnson. The first indication that something dreadful happened came with a knock on the door the next day. It was her mum asking where Keith was. Winnie's heart froze in confusion: this should have been Mum dropping Keith off on the way to work, not asking where he was. Gertrude Bennett had waited for Keith the evening before and when he hadn't shown up, she thought Winnie must have forgotten that it was his night with her.

The Bennett family began an anxious search, one that has continued to this day. Despite Myra's confession in 1987, too much time had passed for her to pinpoint where Keith had been abused and buried.

At the moment he disappeared, it marked no more than the start of a busy few months for Myra. As well as moving out of Gorton and to Wardle Brook Avenue, Moby had become pregnant and married David Smith. She was 18 and David only 16 but they found themselves taken under Myra and Ian's wing. Myra would pick them up in her car and they would drive out to the Moors. She noticed that Ian was unusually chatty around David. He was keen to impress the boy with all his thoughts and views and David provided a ready audience, taking at face value much of what the older man had to say. To a large extent, David had always been an outsider too, disliked for the trouble he brought and it was the first time he was applauded for his antisocial behaviour. Ian said they should plan a bank job together. David agreed. Myra was more than a little jealous, Moby was too naive to see it but she sensed Ian was physically attracted to David.

David was caught up in the couple, he liked the fact that they couldn't care less what people thought of them. But while he was a bit of a rogue, as soon as Moby became pregnant, he knew he'd have to do the decent thing and marry her. Myra and Ian didn't believe in marriage: they thought it a pathetic restraint imposed by society. David thought that was pretty cool. But as rebellious as David was, he had no idea that Ian's and Myra's views about living outside society's rules had gone beyond setting up house together. He had no inkling that they were preparing to introduce him to the full measure of their dark and destructive world.

By Christmas, Myra's house, No 16, was how she wanted it. There was a red carpet in the living room, pink walls and imitation brick wallpaper around the fireplace. In her bedroom, she had a new patterned headboard and spotted wallpaper. She was pleased with the finished look. Granny Maybury's dog, Lassie, had puppies and Myra picked one out for herself. She adored the dog she called Puppet. Everything was almost as it should be – except Christmas was always a difficult time for Ian.

Lesley Ann Downey had enjoyed a lovely Christmas with her family in Ancoats. She was 10 and Christmas had brought all she'd hoped for: a little sewing machine, a nurse's uniform, some games and a doll. Her mum Ann was expecting a baby and on Boxing Day the children went out to the funfair so Mum could rest. It was a great day out for all the local children, including Lesley Ann's three brothers and it wasn't just kids who enjoyed the rides. Myra and Ian were there too.

Lesley Ann was last seen standing by the dodgems, smiling as she watched the brightly painted cars smash and whirl about under the flashing lights. That was the last time she was seen. Evidence of her final hours was found in a suitcase, locked away in the lockers of Manchester Central station. The ticket that corresponded to it unlocked more than the luggage. It was the key to the whole case and revealed to the police, prosecution and public the truth about Myra's character. It shone a light into Myra Hindley's and Ian Brady's depraved and pitiless world and it would become central to the most notorious and sensational trial the UK had known. Without it, Myra would have walked away, her name forgotten.

David Smith was at home with Moby when Myra called for him. It was quite late, 11.30pm, and she said that Ian had some miniature bottles of wine for him, that he was to come to the house. When they got near, Myra told him to wait on the pavement opposite until the landing light flicked on twice. Myra wanted to make sure that Granny Maybury was tucked up asleep in bed. David waited, the signal was given and he walked through the same door that Superintendent Bob Talbot would the next day.

Ian led David into the kitchen and then went back into the front room with Myra and closed the door. As David began to pack away the bottles, he heard a scream. At first he thought it was a woman's voice, it was high-pitched. Then came another scream and another. David was rooted to the spot, unable to process what was happening. It was Myra's voice that broke through his daze: 'Dave, help him!'

David burst through the door of the living room and struggled to see what was before him. The room was lit only by the flickering TV set, the sound off. There was a boy of his own age with his head and shoulders on the sofa, his legs slumped onto the floor. Standing over him was Ian. The lad was screaming and Ian raised his right hand which held a hatchet. The lad faced upwards and then nothing happened for a second or so. The scene was frozen, Myra at Ian's side, David still in the doorway. Then Ian's arm swung downwards and David heard the hatchet smash into the left-hand side of the lad's head.

The boy was still able to scream out and made a desperate attempt to break free from Brady but it was too late. The blows rained down on him with increased savagery, Myra stood so close that one blow grazed her face. The boy was on his stomach, on the floor and he was hit in the neck, back and head.

Brady stopped. He looked around and even in the dimness, it was clear that the boy's blood had reached as far as the wall opposite. Brady picked up an electrical flex and wound it around the young man's neck. He pulled on it tightly until the gurgling noises coming from the boy ceased. 'It's done,' said Brady. 'That was the messiest yet.'

David was ordered to help with the clear-up. There was even blood in the budgie's cage. The task took a long time. Myra and Ian smoked and David was handed some wine to drink. His mind was racing. He was convinced that if he protested about what he'd seen, he'd be next. Myra came in with all the materials she'd need to prepare the body for disposal. They decided to leave the body in the spare room until morning and as they struggled to lift it, Ian quipped, 'Eddie's a dead weight.'

Myra was convulsed with giggles and David was ordered to help carry the body upstairs whilst Myra held Granny's door shut. Back downstairs, the couple relived what they'd done, prompting each other with memories of the terror in the boy's eyes as the axe was raised. Myra was still wearing her blood-soaked slippers which David could see as she'd rested her feet up on the mantlepiece. It was then that David heard them joke about the Moors. They tried to get him to join in with their banter and David tried to appear as relaxed as they did. He was waiting for his moment to leave, trying to assess how to say that he was ready to leave, without causing them to doubt him. It was 3am when he stood up and made his goodbyes.

He wouldn't recall the walk back to the flat or remember how much he shook once he got into bed with Moby and began to sob. She cried too when he told her, but she was absolutely clear about what they had to do. They were to get up, walk to the phone box and call the police. Moby loved her sister but she did not hesitate when faced with her distraught husband and his account of what he saw. It made no sense to her, it could not be true but if there was anything in it at all, the police would have to know.

Back at No 16, Ian moaned about having twisted his ankle. In his frenzied attack, he'd damaged it and Myra thought it best to take a day off work and rest. He was writing his note to his manager at Millwards the following morning when the police entered the living room.

Detective Chief Inspector John Tyrell was the man who would receive praise from the judge in court for his diligence. Once arrested, four days after Edward Evans' body was discovered, Myra yielded nothing. She was tougher than Brady, plus her lover said, 'The girl had nothing to do with it.' Myra's stone-faced attitude and Brady's careful and fastidious manner was their undoing. Something wasn't right about that woman and Tyrell also guessed that Brady was such a meticulous note-taker that there was more to be found.

They stripped the houses where Myra and Ian had lived but found little, so Tyrell went back to No 16 where Brady's notebooks had turned up with his coded messages: 'PB', 'GN' and 'ALI'. Among Brady's lists they also found the name John Kilbride. They were aware of the hunt for the boy which was being coordinated from a neighbouring constabulary and they passed on the information to the officer in charge of the case, Detective Chief Inspector Joe Mounsey. David Smith had made incoherent accusations of 'other deaths'. Could there be something in it?

Tyrell found a white communion book, an old gift from Myra's aunt, on a shelf and wondered if PB might mean Prayer Book. Holding it in his hands, he found a piece of paper jammed into the spine of the book. A luggage ticket.

The two suitcases were handed over to Superintendent Bob Talbot. He found strange paraphernalia such as a black wig, a rubber hose, pornographic pictures, Nazi writings, bullets and a cosh with the word 'Eureka' written on it. It was unsettling stuff. There were also any number of notebooks, more photographs and a couple of tapes. The pictures were shots of the Saddleworth Moor, obviously an obsession for the couple. Bob Talbot turned over endless shots of the bleak, featureless landscape until he reached a photograph of a girl taken in a bedroom somewhere. She was naked except for striped socks and brown-buckled shoes. There were nine pictures in total. They showed a girl kneeling in prayer, lying on the bed, standing with her back to the camera, holding her arms out wide. The terrified face was that of Lesley Ann.

Bob Talbot felt a wave of sorrow. This poor young girl. Where was she now? He was distracted by thoughts of how this would be broken to the family when he decided to play the tapes. Perhaps he should finish going through everything before talking to the team about the photographs and how they would handle the next session of Brady's questioning. The tape spooled and played. Some radio programme about the rise of fascism, Brady ranting 'Sieg heil,' some music and a sketch from the *Goon Show*. It played out almost until the end when there was an abrupt change. There were noises from inside a house somewhere, Brady's voice gruffly telling dogs to get out of the way, doors shutting, footsteps, and then, unmistakeably, a woman's voice. The voice was that which had greeted him at No 16, the voice of Myra Hindley.

There was another voice too. That of a young girl and she was screaming.

Bob Talbot sat pinned in his seat, horribly aware that it was a record of a young girl's suffering and there was nothing he could do. She was crying, she was struggling to breathe and Myra could be heard to say, 'Hush. Put it in your mouth and keep it in.'

The girl pleaded with her, sobbing, and Myra said, 'Shut up or I'll forget myself and hit you one. Keep it in.'

The child was retching. She had been told to call her abductors 'Mum' and 'Dad'. She sobbed, 'Can I just tell you something? I must tell you something. Please take your hands off me a minute, please. Please, Mummy, please. I can't tell you... I can't tell you. I can't breathe. Oh...I can't – Dad – will you take your hands off me?'

She asked what they will do with her. Brady said he just wanted to take photographs. 'Put it in,' Brady said.

She struggled, through her tears she tried to resist. She asked to go home, saying she has to see her mum because she was supposed to go out with her. Brady's voice was heard again: 'Put it in. If you don't put your hands down I'll slit your neck. Put it in.'

The girl had pleaded for them not to undress her, she said her neck hurt and Myra snapped, 'Shut up.' The girl retched.

The tape whirred on. Brady is grunting, Myra again said: 'Put that in your mouth... packed more solid.'

The girl sobbed and said that her mum was waiting for her, that she had to be home by 8 o'clock. She whimpered. Myra's voice was muffled and the recording ended. Country-style music faded in, followed by footsteps, then 'Little Drummer Boy'.

It took only 13 minutes for Bob Talbot to sit and listen to the recording but he knew as he looked at his office walls that something had changed in him forever. All the officers that listened to the tape were shattered by what they heard. Those that were fathers found it hardest of all. Typing out a transcript was one thing, to hear Lesley Ann suffer proved quite another. Years later, one of the detectives was at a party when 'Little Drummer Boy' began and he had to walk out, he was physically ill.

Talbot realised this altered everything. The woman who had been on the periphery of the investigation was now at its dark heart. She was not a dozy girlfriend trying to cover for her man, she was a sexual sadist who preyed on children.

The detective also knew that he would have to play the tape to Lesley Ann's mother, to identify the voice of the child. She arrived at the station, the police ashen-faced and hardly daring to look at her. They were in shock and they were upset but what would it mean if you had to listen to the sound of your child being tortured? Ann did just that. She had to sit and listen.

It would have been better for her if she had never known what happened to her daughter in the last few minutes of her life. Because what unfolded was far worse than anyone could have imagined. Ann was shattered. For her, the torture was just beginning: never again would she know peace. The terrible anguish of hearing what happened, of not being there to stop it, not being able to reach out and help her little girl, broke her. She lost the child she was carrying and it seemed that she would not survive. She was dragged through the next few months because she had to care for her other children but did so as a shell of the woman she once was.

Eventually, she remarried and became Ann West, the name Hindley would dread. Ann was clear. Her's was a life sentence and she vowed that as long as she lived, no one would be allowed to forget what Myra Hindley did. She was true to her word.

The search had begun on the Moors. The police who

volunteered had no idea that Saddleworth would become infamous, that this was just the first of many desperate searches as the years unfolded. Brady had taken scores of photos and the place was vast. Essentially, it was a perfect burial ground as it was impossible to search. Help, when it came, was from an unexpected source.

Pat Hodges was the same age as Lesley Ann and she had been groomed by Myra. She had been coaxed into her car any number of times and taken to pick up Ian and drive to the Moors for picnics. Most shockingly, she had been driven up there on Christmas Eve, two days before the brutal abduction and murder of Lesley Ann.

It will never be known why the couple chose to drive the girl safely back home, untouched. Pat's voice was captured on tape however and heard months later by Bob Talbot. It was Pat discussing the recent disappearance of Lesley Ann, Myra asking her a few questions about the missing girl. Pat had no idea that she was being taped. But ten months later, Pat was able to lead them to the place where Myra and Ian would park on the Moors. Some 150 policemen started digging over the earth at a stopping point that Pat recognised. The search team were hopeful as the area did correspond to a code in one of Brady's books: WH for Wessenden Head.

There was a strange mix of emotion on a dig. Wanting to find a body, excitement rising as a bone was discovered and then disappointment when it became clear that the discovery was no more than an old sheep bone. But then it hit them, any excitement was misplaced: they were looking for a dead child. Late in the afternoon, a blue coat was pulled from the earth. A pink cardigan and tartan skirt. Lesley Ann was uncovered. She was naked, her clothes piled next to her and her string of white beads, a present from her brother that Christmas.

Myra was under arrest now, not for Lesley Ann's murder but for the death of Edward Evans. The tape of Lesley's abuse was played to her and it was the only time her stone-faced silence cracked. Her temple throbbed and she pulled a handkerchief to her face. She cried but the detective noted her tears ended as quickly as they had began. She then snapped back into her flat-voiced denials. 'I didn't do it, Ian didn't do it. I suggest you talk to Smith.'

The huge irony of landing blame at the feet of David Smith will not have escaped her. If it wasn't for Smith, she and Ian would still be at No 16, planning their next 'happening'. It was Ian's stupid fault. He was so caught up in bringing the boy along, in making him his new disciple that he had made a mistake. Smith hadn't been ready.

The search continued. The photographs Brady had taken were key. One, in which Myra hugged her dog Puppet and looked down at the ground, proved the vital link to the next discovery. On the opposite side of the road from where Lesley Ann was buried they found the remains of John Kilbride. He lay face down, his trousers pulled down to the knees and his underpants knotted behind his thighs. The picture of a smiling Myra was taken on top of his remains.

While the search continued for other bodies, with over 400 sites ready for excavation, the police prepared their case. They had enough to put them away for life and it became their sole focus. The committal procedure was scheduled for 6 December 1965 and it would change British law. Until then, the prosecution had to present its evidence in full to a magistrate before the case could be recommended to go before a crown court for full trial. The evidence heard that day included the tape of Lesley Ann's last few minutes alive and Ann West had to give her statement at the magistrate's court. When she ended by turning her rage on the bleached-haired and impassive Myra Hindley, few could blame her. It caused a media storm. Press descended on Hyde from around the world and the nation was convulsed with outrage as witnesses made their statements. It made it impossible for a future jury to not be touched by the coverage. After this case, the prosecution no longer had to present full evidence to a magistrate's court. It would be the safest route to avoid prejudicing juries in future.

Myra arrived at Chester Crown Court four-and-a-half months later in a smart suit with a notebook clutched in her hand, looking the part of a demure secretary. She'd put a lilac rinse through her bleached hair, just one of a dozen or so transformations that she would embark on over the next few years. She and Brady denied murdering Edward Evans, John Kilbride and Lesley Ann Downey. They attempted to suggest that Edward was murdered because he made sexual advances on Brady and that the other two children left their company intact. Their defence teams also tried to lay the blame for their deaths at David Smith's door. Both he and Maureen testified against the couple. At that stage, Brady was still protective of Myra, happy to soak up the charges. They wrote loving letters to one another and had applied for a marriage licence, believing that they would then be entitled to spend time together. Their application was turned down. Myra continued to write to Brady, unaware that the secret code they used in correspondence had been broken by police. By taking the first letter from each sentence, they noted that Myra had spelt out: 'Smith will die and Maureen too.'

Myra performed well when questioned, she appeared mentally tougher than Brady and she blocked the prosecution's attempts to force an admission about the part she had played. It was Brady who slipped up. He was painting a fiction for the jury, suggesting that he had taken obscene pictures of Lesley Ann, that Myra knew nothing of his scheme until the girl was in the house and that the ten-year-old left as she arrived, with David Smith. Myra had gone along with this invention, saying that she was caught shouting at Lesley Ann only because she 'was embarrassed and wanted it over with quickly'.

But as Brady was cross-examined, he made his blunder. When asked what happened once he'd finished taking the photographs, he said, 'We all got dressed and went downstairs.' We all got dressed. It was a slip that the judge brought to the jury's attention before they left to deliberate on the evidence they'd heard. On 6 May, the jury returned their verdicts: guilty.

Myra Hindley became prisoner 964055 and started a new chapter in her life. Brady began his slow descent into paranoia and insanity that ultimately led to his removal to a high security hospital. Ann West commented that at least he'd had 'the decency to go mad'. It is a remark that is significant for two reasons. First, Brady had committed crimes of cruelty and horror – beyond our ordinary understanding – and a diagnosis of 'madness' helps us comprehend how such a thing could happen. Second, it was a statement that highlighted Myra's status – the merry prisoner.

Reports would trickle out saying that Myra was depressed or that she was in anguish, but there were too many other reports of her affairs and friendships to create an impression that she had finally faced up to her crimes. Indeed, her affair with prison officer Pat Cairns, who pleaded guilty at the Old Bailey in 1974 to planning an escape attempt with Myra, did nothing to allay the fear that Myra was a highly manipulative individual willing to use any means necessary to further her own ends.

Yet her conversion to Catholicism and claims to be a political prisoner, did garner her a group of admirers and campaigners who urged that she be considered for release. The most notable was Lord Longford. He believed that Myra had changed. He was a devoutly religious man who felt that as sinners each of us is worthy of redemption. He did not hear the remarks Myra made when she mocked him, particularly the irritation she expressed to her lovers if she was called away to meet with the 'old bore'. All he heard was her earnest Catholic repentance. She gave Longford what he wanted: she always had the talent to design her message for her audience and in doing so she tarnished the old man's reputation irrevocably.

If the assertion that Myra remained unrepentant and manipulative sounds implausible, if it appears like yet more of the demonisation that Myra complained about from the British press and public, it is worth noting the journey that Carole Callaghan took. Carole arrived in Holloway shortly after Myra, serving time for her part in an armed robbery. She was tough and streetwise, and although she and Myra were never lovers, they became very close friends. Carole protected her, acted as lookout so she could conduct her many affairs in privacy and became convinced that her friend could not have had a part to play in the death of the children. She'd been in South Africa at the time of the trial so only heard Myra's sanitised version of events.

Once out of prison she remained a devoted friend, writing to Hindley, sending gifts, running many errands and defending Myra's reputation at all times. When Joan Reade made yet another attempt to find out what had happened to her daughter, Carole recalled Myra passionately denying any involvement. Myra was entirely convincing when she talked of Joan as 'that poor woman', someone that she would never leave in such turmoil if she had the power to help her.

When Myra did confess, in February 1987, to the deaths of Pauline Reade and Keith Bennett, it was too late for Joan Reade. She was in a mental asylum, lost to grief. Myra confessed because she wanted to get one up on Brady, who had begun to talk to the press about the other murders. She hoped if she got there first, it would help in her attempt to gain parole. For Carole Callaghan, the news was a terrible blow. She said that when she heard, she realised that she been conned for 20 years. She added: 'Now I know that I have given a lot of my life to defending lies. It hurts, especially when I think of the families of Pauline Reade and Keith Bennett.'

Myra never got her way, not in the end. She died in prison on 15 November 2002 and was cremated in Cambridge five days later. Nobody from her family attended. Ann West wanted life to mean life but she had not lived to see the day. Exhausted by years of grief and campaigning for families who had lost children, she died after a long battle with cancer and was buried next to her daughter in 1999.

One member of the public did gain access to Hindley's funeral. She left a message expressing the outrage of many in three simple words: 'Burn in hell'.

In some ways, Myra was right. She had been demonised. Talk of hell, of demons, of evil, tracked her until the end. It can't be coincidental that she reverted to Catholicism, a faith that resonates with themes of sin but also of redemption. Yet even those who hold no religious views find it difficult to avoid the concept of evil in the case of Myra Hindley. Unlike other serial killers, she was not rooted in an early cycle of sustained and dehumanising abuse that led to isolation and a retreat into a violent fantasy world. She was a late and an entirely willing recruit. She knew the difference between right and wrong. She watched as children pleaded for their lives. She did not act out of madness, out of delusion or pain: she chose to torture and abuse because it pleasured her. For that, she will never be forgiven.

One 13-minute tape recording changed our idea of the evil women are capable of. It also obliterated the days of unlocked doors, tight-knit communities and the idea that children could roam the streets around their homes in safety. We all cried when we heard of Lesley Ann's pleas to go home. She never would, and knowing what became of her changed us all. It was the end of innocence.

5

ROSEMARY WEST

AN EVIL KINDLING

'YOU WILL ALWAYS BE MRS WEST, ALL OVER THE WORLD.'

FRED WEST IN A LETTER TO ROSE

When 17-year-old Caroline Owens saw the grey Ford car moving slowly towards her that December night, she thought little of it. Caroline had noticed Fred and Rose West earlier in the day when she was walking through Gloucester and it didn't surprise her that they pulled over and Rose struck up a conversation.

Caroline hoped that there would be no ill feelings as she had recently moved out of the West's house having decided that her job as a nanny to their three children wasn't working out. She'd told the Wests she was leaving but didn't tell them that it was because the setup at No 25 Cromwell Street had unsettled her so much. Caroline wasn't easily ruffled, she was one of 15 children cared for by her mother and stepfather so she was used to hectic households. She knew the house had lodgers on the top floor and that the Wests had plenty of friends that came and went but it was Fred and Rose who proved too much.

Fred talked about sex continually. He made bizarre references to abortions and operations he'd carried out and made leering remarks virtually every time he spoke. Rose wasn't an ordinary housewife either. A plain woman with large and thick glasses, she'd walk around the house in see-through or revealing clothing and white schoolgirl's socks. The lodgers talked openly about their sex sessions with her. Caroline even felt that Rose was making suggestive remarks to her, but it was a comment Fred made about their eight-year-old daughter, Anne Marie, that caused Caroline the most discomfort.

Her father casually remarked that Anne Marie had lost her virginity and looked a little surprised when Caroline asked him what on earth he meant. Fred stammered through a tale of how the little girl had fallen off her bike and had impaled herself on one of the handles. It wasn't the first time that Fred had tried the story out, testing out the listener's reaction.

When the Wests offered her a lift home, Caroline thought it would be a good way to show that there were no hard feelings. As Fred headed into the countryside with Rose and Caroline in the back seat, he knew that he was not driving to the girl's home town. He watched in the rear-view mirror as his wife started making advances on the girl and it made him smile. Rose was always feisty when she was pregnant and he knew they were in for a good night. Driving up to a field, he noticed that Rose was getting nowhere in her attempt so he swung around, told Caroline that she was a bitch and punched her until she blacked out.

Caroline came round to find her arms tied behind her back. She was being held on the back seat and Fred was winding masking tape around her mouth, making it impossible to scream and very difficult to breathe. Rose was laughing. Fred restarted the engine and turned the car back to Gloucester.

Caroline guessed that they were pulling into Cromwell Street and knew that at the top of the road, outside No 25, it was badly lit and she'd be easy to force inside without anyone knowing. She hoped that a lodger or one of the children would discover them and call the police.

Fred hauled Caroline into a first-floor room and locked the door. She looked around and saw a sofa, a mattress and Fred with a knife, leering as he came towards her. They forced her to undress, leaving her only her shoes. Fred cut and pulled the tape from her mouth and even apologised for slashing her face before Caroline's mouth was stuffed with cotton wool, the tape reapplied and she was blindfolded. She was pushed on the mattress where she struggled to breathe.

Soon Caroline felt a hand enter her vagina, probably Rose's, she judged from the long fingernails. Then Fred's rough workman's hands pushed into her and she heard him say: 'She is big inside, but the lips are too fat. They will get in the way of the clitoris.' Caroline remembered Fred's boasts about his operations and fear gripped ever tighter.

Rose held her legs apart and watched as Fred thrashed Caroline's vagina with the buckle end of a belt, saying he wanted 'to flatten' her clitoris. The pain was unbearable. She struggled to breath as Rose began to perform cunnilingus on her and Fred stood behind his wife and had sex with her.

When Rose at last left the room, Fred vaginally raped Caroline. It was quick and Fred hurriedly asked Caroline, 'Not to tell Rose.' He was crying. Eventually, Rose returned and the couple went to sleep, leaving their victim still bound. Caroline tried to get out of the first-floor window but it was hopeless. When a visitor came in the room to talk to Fred, the terrified girl tried to raise a scream but Rose held a pillow over her head. Caroline saw a change in Fred after that. He was not weeping and snivelling but was enraged and yelled that he would 'bury [her] under the paving stones of Gloucester', with the 'other' girls.

Later that morning, Fred's mood shifted again and he began to ramble apologetically that it was Rose's idea that they 'get' Caroline and how it was just what Rose was like when she was pregnant. Caroline had endured a night at their hands and was desperately trying to think of a way to escape. She was allowed to talk and was smart enough to go along with Fred's mood. She then began to suggest that she was happy to reconsider her decision to leave No 25. She said she would move back in and take up her old role as nanny. Fred was pleased. Why didn't Fred let her start by cleaning up now?

He untied her and let her take a bath to scrub the tape marks from her face. Rose watched as Caroline vacuumed and played with Anne Marie and baby Heather, after which she made Caroline a cup of tea and said that they would go to the launderette together that day. The three of them set off in Fred's Ford and while he went looking for somewhere to park, Caroline told Rose that she was just nipping around the corner for cigarettes and would see her later. She rushed home. Caroline's mother was shocked to see her daughter's bruised face and knew that something terrible had happened. When she'd heard enough, the police were called.

When the case finally came to court early in 1973, 31-year-old Fred West and his pregnant 19-year-old wife weren't imprisoned. They walked away with nothing more than a £100 fine. By pleading guilty to the lesser charge of assault, Caroline was spared a court appearance but she had little idea that the couple would be able to walk away so easily.

Caroline said: 'It made me feel like I wasn't worth anything,' and she faced many years of depression and despair as she tried to rebuild her life.

The Wests felt they'd enjoyed a lucky escape and they were very pleased to get back home to No 25. They were off the hook. Now, though, things would have to change. They couldn't afford to have any more girls go blabbing to the police, that much was certain. And it was this terrifying and cold logic that would mean that no other girl would be able to talk her way out of the house at the dark end of Cromwell Street. The court's leniency, the oversight of social workers and the police now left the Wests free to commit horrific acts of savagery for years.

The murders that would take place in the unassuming English town had echoes far beyond the UK. The case has gained international attention and residents around the street that the Wests lived in have grown weary of the number of visitors asking for directions to the house. People have read about the discovery of nine bodies, the dig for more in surrounding fields and the tales of gruesome torture orchestrated by the couple for over 20 years. The council demolished the house and created a public walkway. They removed all the rubble to prevent trophy hunters taking away pieces as souvenirs. Keeping trophies was something that Fred understood very well.

Removing particular bones from his victims was one of Fred's practices. Initially, it presented a puzzle to the forensic teams at work as they struggled to rebuild the remains of the victims found. It became clear however that each of the corpses had bones missing, specifically centred around the hands, wrists and feet. Occasionally, Fred would remove larger bones, such as ribs, kneecaps or shoulder blades – up to 80 at a time. He amassed hundreds of bones. None have been recovered.

Why did this married couple turn to torturing and sadistically killing, not just girls they lured from the street, but their own children? There is no one simple event in the early lives of these two people, no tipping point that transformed two ordinary youngsters into monsters, yet there are enough indicators at the outset that set them apart.

Fred West was born in September 1941. His was not a remarkable background. His parents were from poor rural stock in Much Marcle and Fred watched them struggle to maintain a basic standard of living. In other ways, Fred's childhood was ideal, as he grew up surrounded by green fields filled with wild flowers and had woods and streams to explore. Life as an agricultural labourer, the future that awaited Fred, was nonetheless hard and Fred would have been under no illusion as he watched his father droving cattle.

Fred was the eldest of six and by all accounts, spoiled by his mother. Daisy had lost her first child at full-term and so Fred was especially precious to her. He had inherited his mother's features, growing to have an unforgettable and simian look.

His brother John was born a year after him and they were the closest of the West children when they weren't fighting. John looked more like father Walter and took after him in terms of physical strength. He regularly beat up Fred, asserting himself over 'Mummy's boy', in part out of jealousy of Daisy's devotion to the other boy.

Rumour had it that Daisy sexually abused Fred from around the age of 12. But former Detective Superintendent John Bennett, who would lead the investigation into the

Wests and questioned those who knew the family well, said, 'There isn't anybody alive who has ever said that.'

Daisy may have been soft on Fred but there is no evidence that her relationship with her son was incestuous. There is speculation about Walter, however, which still persists. Years later, Fred would say that his father sexually abused young girls and that he saw it as normal. Fred may well have been attempting to present his behaviour as unexceptional, blaming his father for his later crimes, and whilst this is typical of serial killers to look to everyone but themselves when it comes to explaining the horror they inflict, many continue to believe that Walter had a part to play in shaping Fred. His one maxim was, 'Don't get caught.'

Fred was not bright and struggled a great deal at school, regularly being mocked by classmates for his slowness. By the time he approached his teens, Fred was also known for his clumsy and aggressive attempts to molest girls. This in itself should have raised an alarm but the girls who grew up with Fred just learned to keep a wary distance. He left school at 15 and began work as a farm labourer alongside his father and was soon joined by his brother John.

Fred decided that a motorbike was what he needed to impress the girls he knew attended a youth club in the nearby town of Ledbury. At 17, Fred bought a James motorcycle and it was whilst heading home one night in November of 1958 that he ploughed into a girl on a bicycle heading the other way. Fred was taken to hospital in Hereford, was seriously injured and did not regain consciousness for a week. The accident left him with a permanent limp and facial scarring but his family would later say that the biggest impact it had was on Fred's temperament. He would suffer severe mood swings and showed increased levels of aggression.

Less than two years later, during an attempt to grab a girl at the youth club, he toppled off a fire escape. He landed headfirst and was hospitalised again, although he was only unconscious for one day on this occasion. His family believe that these two events resulted in brain damage.

Head injuries are often factors put forward in trying to understand the physical make-up of serial killers. As serial killers act in a way that suggests an inability to control behaviour and emotion, it would be convenient if that registered clearly in their brain physiology. Whilst some serial killers appear to have sustained brain injuries, such as Henry Lee Lucas, who was convicted of 11 murders having received several beatings at the hands of his brutal mother, others such as John Wayne Gacy complained of black-outs, migraine and fits, and yet postmortems revealed normal brain function.

Whatever the truth about Fred West's injuries, by 1960 he was engaged in a sexual relationship with a 13-year-old girl. It led to a trial the following year after the child became pregnant. Police questioned West, almost 20 at this point, and he showed no remorse. When he was pushed over allegations that he molested other young girls he angrily stated: 'Well, doesn't everyone do it?' The case against him collapsed, as the girl would not testify, but it was enough for Fred's family to disown him for some time.

Fred was at that point already involved with a girl named Catherine Costello, or Rena. By 16, Rena was already known to the police as she came from a troubled background and had appeared before magistrates for petty theft. Rena's life was difficult but once she met Fred West, she would lurch from one sad episode to the next and ultimately become one of the couple's victims.

Rena was from Glasgow and had only visited

Gloucestershire in an attempt to get her life back on track. She put up with Fred's sexual demands when they first met in the summer of 1960 and later, on her return in 1962, Fred was keen that they should see each other again. By now, Fred had a conviction for shoplifting and Rena was known to earn money as a prostitute. She was also pregnant after a brief affair and Fred would later boast that he tried to abort the child. The omens for the life of Rena's unborn child were already grim. Fred was openly hostile from the outset and the baby, Charmaine, would come to see the very worst in human behaviour in her brief life.

Fred and Rena married in November 1962 and the couple travelled to Scotland. Before long, Rena turned to prostitution again and Fred took to inventing stories about himself as a gangster running a ring of call girls. Those who knew Fred knew to expect tall tales. Fred had long struggled to distinguish reality from fiction. One of the few verifiable facts to emerge from his time away from Much Marcle was that Rena had a second child in 1964, a girl that looked much like her father, and she was named Anne Marie. Fred was said to be thrilled to have a daughter with Rena and he clearly favoured her over Charmaine, but that did not stop him fathering other children whilst in Glasgow. There were two other children that are documented but Fred would later insist that the real number was 42.

Rena and Fred had a volatile relationship, they broke up for a while and Rena took up with another man, John McLachlan. Rena told John about Fred's frequent outbursts of violence, particularly if she turned down his insistent need for sex. McLachlan intervened on one occasion and noted that Fred had no desire to fight another man, he preferred to beat women and children – he was a coward.

Fred worked selling ice cream from a Mr Whippy van and without doubt the opportunity to speak to young girls appealed to him. Rena also introduced other girls to Fred, among them a teenager called Anna McFall. She was from a broken home and was mourning the loss of a boyfriend who'd died in an industrial accident. She'd visit their flat and it was not long before Fred was making lewd remarks to her. This didn't deter Anna, neither did the sight of Rena's two baby girls being left in a bunk bed with the middle section fenced off with wooden slats. The children were expected to stay penned there for hours at a time, particularly Charmaine.

In 1965, Fred hit and killed a small boy while driving his ice cream van and, driven by fear of reprisals, he decided to head back to Gloucester with Rena, the children, Anna and another girl, Isa McNeill. Fred found work in an abattoir and the family moved in to a caravan. It was a short-lived arrangement, as the relationship with Rena grew more explosive and she called John McLachlan to ask him to collect her and the children. McLachlan duly arrived and Rena and Isa made to leave. After a struggle, Rena left her young daughters with Fred. To Rena's surprise, Anna also announced she'd stay with Fred and act as nanny to the girls. Anna had fallen for Fred.

Anna was only 16 years old when Fred began his affair with her and he soon tired of Rena's daughters so he dropped them off with Gloucestershire Social Services. The girls would be shunted from one set of foster parents to another and then back with Fred for the next five years. It wasn't until 1966 that Rena reappeared in Gloucester, where she was arrested for theft. A young WPC, Hazel Savage, acted as a police escort to Rena and had little idea that 28 years later she would hear the name Fred West again.

In the spring of 1967, Anna told Fred that she was

pregnant. Fred began to panic. Perhaps Anna was pressuring him to divorce Rena, perhaps he hoped to be reunited with his wife and saw Anna as a threat, it is impossible to know. All we do know is that Anna was last seen in July 1967, heavily pregnant. She would not be seen again for almost 30 years, until forensic scientists painstakingly rebuilt her skeleton and that of her unborn child lying at her side.

That wasn't all that was found. Anna had been bound with a dressing gown cord with her hands behind her back, probably as a form of torture as well as restraint. How Anna had died could not be established. She could have been strangled but Fred would later tell a prison visitor that he'd stabbed her during an argument. What was established was that Fred had dismembered his pregnant girlfriend.

Working for an abattoir, Fred paid a good deal of attention to the work they carried out. He watched how limbs were removed from carcasses and it probably meshed with the idea that he had of himself as someone who could carry out operations. The reality would have been different. A human corpse is not easy to move and manipulate. Even when there is no pulse, the blood loss he would have encountered would have been substantial. Wherever Fred was when the dismemberment of Anna took place, the floor would have been thick with blood and it would have taken a good deal of time to remove signs of what had taken place. Fred was happy to take his time.

Forensic study showed that when he removed Anna's legs, he had done so methodically and with a sharp knife, he did not act in a frenzy. He placed sections of Anna in black plastic bags and rolled them in a sheet. He may well have removed her unborn child at that point, as this would fit with his obsessive interest in terminations.

He removed bones from the hands and feet of his former lover too and these were not found with the rest of the body. What drove him? One theory is that by dismantling Anna, he had complete dominance over her and keeping mementos provided him with a sexual thrill. Rena and other women who had sex with Fred would relay certain details about his psychosexual predilections. He was not well-endowed, he would not indulge in foreplay and could not become aroused unless he attacked his partner with a sudden ferocity. Sex would be very brief, often resulting in Fred appearing to fit or black out, which could indicate a form of brain damage. He harboured both sexual insecurity and aggression, sex to Fred was devoid of physical comfort or tenderness. His fantasies grew more extreme, as the only satisfaction came when a victim was rendered powerless by his sexual rage. He was a highly dangerous individual, someone who had raped young girls, was capable of torture and had broken all taboos when he elected to murder his lover and unborn child. Yet this was only the beginning.

Fred was already known to the police because of ongoing criminality: petty fraud and handling stolen goods. There is no doubt that he should have come to their attention again as, since he was a sexual predator with a below average IQ, he would have made mistakes and he would have been caught. It is highly doubtful that he would have got away with his crimes for a further 30 years if he had worked alone. But some time after burying Anna in one of the fields that he ran through as a boy, he met someone who would transform his world. Fred would grow from dangerous misfit into someone whose name would become a byword for the worst acts of sexual depravity. He met Rose.

Looking at pictures of 15-year-old Rose Letts, it is hard to pick out the features of the woman who would become infamous: the drab, bespectacled and overweight Rose West. Back then, she was slim, pretty and had the kind of large and attractive brown eyes that made you want to take care of her. But Rose had known very little care.

Rose's mother shared the same name as Fred's, Daisy, but whereas Mrs West was a large and robust-looking woman, Daisy Letts was timorous and prone to depression. Whilst working as a house servant in Devon, she had the misfortune to meet Bill Letts, a man who hid his schizophrenia well enough to continue a career in the navy but who inflicted every kind of misery on his growing family.

Bill was violent and controlling, making a series of impossible demands on his wife and children. The house had to be spotless for his return and if he discovered anything that did not meet his exacting standards, beatings followed. Daisy would have to hide her bruised and blackened face from her neighbours and the children crept around him in silence. His explosive temper was impossible to navigate and the children would have to watch as Bill dragged his screaming wife by the hair and pulled her backwards down the stairs.

After the birth of their fourth child, a boy, in 1952, Daisy suffered severe and prolonged postnatal depression. With no improvement the following year, she was given a course of electric shock therapy. ECT can lead to memory loss, personality changes, fear and anxiety. But what is truly alarming is that Daisy underwent her treatment while pregnant. Rosemary was born a few months later on 29 November. The family noticed that from the very start, this baby was different from the other Letts children.

Rosemary wasn't a demanding baby, which at least allowed

Daisy to set her down and attend to her household chores. But Daisy noticed that Rosemary would obsessively rock herself, a rhythmic and constant motion that the other children would complain about. Watching her youngest, Daisy tried to see what it was in a rocking of her head that Rose found so comforting, her head swinging from side to side, with an absence of expression and no light in her eyes. It made little sense and it was unsettling, often continuing for hours.

The signs were there in many ways. Mothers can't help but notice how a baby's progress compares to others. By the age of one, parents can already tell if a child is bright and inquisitive and Rosemary was slow. Today, it's probable that health visitors would pick up on the developmental milestones that Rose was failing to achieve but in the 1950s all Daisy could do was watch and at least be happy that her daughter was such a pretty baby.

Rose's siblings soon dubbed their sister 'dozy' Rosie. She could not take part in their role-playing games. She simply did not have the mental alertness to join in with their imaginative play. They also noticed that although they found Rose's passive and absent ways irritating, Bill did not. It seemed surprising at first because on the surface, Rose appeared to be the most vulnerable of them all. It is easy to imagine Bill loathing this vacant child but the opposite came to be true.

Bill found Rose amusing. This stunned the other children who had endured a regime of terror and had to keep their wits about them at all times if they were to avoid a thrashing. Yet the clues as to why Bill favoured Rose lay in her slowness. Rose would never try to outwit her father or conceal anything. His paranoia simmered below a brittle surface and he mistrusted his family as well as neighbours and the outside world. And there was another, much darker side to Rose's passivity. She became useful to Bill.

Rumours had spread that Bill Letts had an unhealthy interest in young girls. Someone even openly called him a pervert in the street and it sent his paranoia into overdrive. For a man who frequently moved his family due to a misguided idea that a neighbourhood was 'getting' at him, for someone who had a furious temper and who was openly hostile to children, it was curious that he chose to open a youth club. This was while the family was living in Northam. Accusations of inappropriate behaviour soon followed and were enough to persuade Bill that he and his family needed to move, but the relocation to Plymouth would not prove permanent.

Meanwhile, Rose was growing up, struggling in school and was often bullied for her learning difficulties. She would tell lies and cause annoyance through her lack of common sense. Other children found her easy to manipulate. So did Bill. By the time Rose was ten, it was likely that Bill was sexually abusing her. This has never been proved but before Rose reached puberty she was displaying sexually provocative behaviour, walking around the house naked, standing in front of her father without her clothes on and talking about the babies she'd have, signs that suggest that she had already been exposed to sexually-inappropriate behaviour. Then she turned her attention to her younger brothers.

Rose's relationship with her two younger brothers was a mix of mothering and bullying. She was frustrated at not being able to control them as she wished. Graham and Gordon put up with dozy Rosie's attentions but when Graham was ten and his sister 13, he became confused by a new turn in her behaviour. They shared a room as the house was crowded but Rose would get into his bed naked and she moved from hugging to masturbating him. He was too young and too unhappy to be able to talk to anyone in the family about the abuse and it continued until Rose left home at 15.

Rose was not driven out of her parents' home. Unlike the other Letts children, she was not subject to her father's savage beatings and, oddly enough, was even spared Bill's taxing list of household chores, such as scrubbing the toilets with bleach four times a day. What made Rose leave the house was her newly-formed passion for a man who chatted her up at the bus stop as she waited to get home from work in a bakery.

This man could talk the hind legs off a donkey and had even taken to getting on Rose's bus just to sit next to her. He had the bluest eyes Rose had ever seen and she felt sorry for him. He was much older than she was and clearly a man of the world, but he was left to cope with two young daughters as his wife, who was no good, had run off and left them. Rose drank all this in. She had always enjoyed attention from older men and she thought what a good idea it would be if she were to move in to his caravan and become a nanny to his daughters. Fred said that would be great.

Rose took Fred home to meet her family. He was chatty but the more he talked, the more Daisy and Bill were convinced that he was as slow-witted and as prone to lying as their youngest daughter. Bill took an instant dislike to him, calling him a dirty gypsy, and was infuriated by Rose's smiling dismissal of his objections. He sensed, rightly, that Fred and Rose had begun a sexual relationship and there may well have been more than parental concern at work. Fred was taking his place in his daughter's bed.

Later, Rose would talk of being raped on two separate

occasions before she met Fred but it is impossible to verify if she was telling the truth or merely fabricating in the hope of mitigating her later horrific acts. There were many rumours about Rose. For example, her brother-in-law was convinced that she would have sex with truck drivers that stopped at the café he ran with Rose's sister, and whatever the actual facts of Rose's sexual experiences, it is certain that Fred was not her first.

This enticed him all the more as Rose was not repelled by his insistent urges and his increasing appetite for extreme and sadistic sex. Rose did not mind that Fred tied her up, hit her and, just as significantly, did not mind hitting and humiliating him if he requested it. Fred had a lifelong obsession with other sexual deviances such as coprophilia and being urinated on – something the police would also discover on video. Here was a giggling 15-year-old girl, totally compliant and ready to push his fantasies ever further.

Fred must have been excited by all that Rose represented, but there were storm clouds gathering. He had continued to thieve and handle stolen goods, ever convinced that he could escape punishment by presenting a tale or two. The patience of the courts was running out. Bill Letts would not let Rose go without protest either and he told social services that Rose was having underage sex with a man 12 years her senior.

Had he spoken to his sons, Bill Letts would have been yet more infuriated to learn of talk that Fred was not the only man Rose was spending time with in the caravan. She was working as a prostitute at Fred's request, learning that the money was useful and that it excited Fred to hear and watch her entertain other men. Rose was still 15 and it was only right that social services took her into care, a home for teenagers.

Then there were the other girls in Fred's family:

Charmaine and Anne Marie, still suffering at his hands and intermittently being placed with carers until he once again felt ready to haul them back to wherever he was lodging. These vulnerable girls were never given the help they needed to escape from a life of degradation. They may have had hopes that life with Rose could be different. She could only be kept at the home until she reached 16 and, perhaps then, they could set up home as Rose had talked about.

Fred probably had his hopes too but first he faced a 30-day jail sentence in Gloucester for his ever-growing list of petty thefts and failure to pay fines. Rose bided her time, waiting for Fred's release and any protestations her father had were silenced entirely when it was discovered that she was pregnant. She was advised to terminate but had no intention of following anyone other that Fred. Her family gave up on her. This was a turning point for them all.

It was 1970, Rose was 16, Charmaine was seven and her half-sister Anne Marie was six. Fred was approaching 30. Rose wanted to stay with him and gave birth to a daughter in October of that hectic year. Fred had moved once more, this time to a flat in Midland Road, Gloucester, the town where he and Rose would remain. Rena had made another appearance, no longer to check up on Fred but to see how her girls were. Whatever she found when she saw Rose, it was enough to convince her not to take her daughters away with her. Yet life was to take a turn for the worse as Fred was imprisoned once more for theft and fraud. He would spend a total of ten months in jail from November.

Rose was visited by her mother, who found her and the children living in squalor. Rose was not coping and was ill-tempered whenever challenged by Charmaine. Anne Marie was far more passive and perhaps Rose saw something of her younger self in this quiet girl. Charmaine, however, saw through Rose and her attempts to behave like a grown up and the smart little girl was also learning to endure beatings from this new stepmother. Rose's mum summed up her attempts to care for Charmaine and Anne Marie succinctly when she said: 'It was like a child looking after children.'

Letters survive from Fred's term in prison and they are revealing. Fred is barely literate, his attempts to construct sentences are woeful and they meander much like his speech did. His attempts to spell mirror his accent, he wrote 'cuming' for coming and 'agen' for again. Rose's letters are more coherent but are more chilling to read. Two lines in particular give an insight into the life Charmaine endured: 'Darling, about Char. I think she likes to be handled rough.' Some of this handling had resulted in a visit to casualty for Charmaine in March of 1971. By the end of June and before Fred was released from prison, Charmaine was dead.

Rose fended off questions from the school, from her neighbours and from Anne Marie by saying that Rena had picked her up. no one contacted Rena or made any concerted attempt to find the eight-year-old and it would be 23 years before her body was found. The burial was all Fred's handiwork, a task he faced once he was released on 24 June. What went through Fred's mind when his girlfriend told him where to find the small body, waiting in the coal cellar? It is impossible to know. All forensics would establish once Charmaine's remains were uncovered, buried in the back yard of the Midland Road flat, was that there were bones missing – some fingers and toes and both kneecaps.

Rose had joined Fred. They were both killers now. Perhaps Rose had lashed out in a fit of temper and accidentally killed the girl in her care, it is not clear as it is not something that

Rose will comment on. But the fact remained, accidental or not, both had blood on their hands. Yet even at this point, the madness could have stopped. Rose could leave Fred and gain distance from the corrosive effects their 'love' was having on them and the innocents around them. And she did.

Rose appeared at her family home, with baby Heather, telling her parents that her relationship was over. Bill was still angry but was dumbfounded when Fred knocked at the back door, calling out to Rose, 'Come on Rosie, you know what we've got between us.' Indeed she did and after a few hours, her parents allowed her to leave. It was unlikely that Daisy could offer Rose sanctuary and as Bill had done so much to damage his daughter, it would be fruitless to have expected them to intervene and, in doing so, change history. But when they closed the door on Rose, they helped their daughter walk back to a life of prostitution, torture, child abuse, abduction, and murder.

There can be no doubt that there was a bond between Rose and Fred and it was a bond that would endure until Fred chose to take his own life after his arrest and imprisonment. Prison was never going to be a place where Fred could exist for long. During his brief stays at Her Majesty's pleasure, he had been badly intimidated by other male prisoners. Fred was a coward and he also knew what he could expect as a lifer convicted of offences against children; as a 'nonce', his life would always be under threat from prisoners who view abusers as fair game for violent retribution.

Rena was to make a reappearance late in 1971. She came down from Glasgow to see her daughters and there was no sign of Charmaine. There would be little point in pretending that Rena had been an ideal mother: she was a prostitute, a thief and an unstable woman who had driven away from

Gloucester without her daughters. But she was still mother enough for worry to cut through the fog of her sad life and to try to find Charmaine. Fred fobbed off Rena with a few excuses for the girl's absence but it was clear that this could not go on indefinitely. Ultimately, Fred lured Rena into his car with a promise that he'd take her to see Charmaine. Rena stood little chance when Fred turned on her, strangling her and, as her life ebbed away, she must have wondered if this was the same fate her eldest daughter had met.

Again, Fred chose a field that he knew well, Letterbox Field, to dispose of her body. First came the grim task of dissecting her body and this probably took place back at the flat he shared with Rose where Charmaine was buried. In the grave, the forensic team would find a narrow chromium tube, probably used to restrict breathing (an obsession for both Fred and Rose) and a small plastic boomerang, a child's toy which could well have been used to sexually abuse Rena.

Fred would have taken his time dismembering his wife's body. Her legs were severed in such a way as to reveal that it was done with a precision that hinted at Fred's obsession. Her left kneecap and a collection of 35 other small bones were kept aside. Rena was buried in several plastic bags and would lie undisturbed for 23 years.

What is surprising about Fred and Rose as a couple is that they made little effort to hide their voracious sexual appetites, Fred's continual brushes with the police, or Rose's prostitution, and they openly made sexual suggestions to anyone who spent any time with them. But neighbours took the view that this was as far as their peccadilloes went and social services did not figure in the lives of the vulnerable West children.

In 1972, Fred and Rose married at Gloucester Register

Office. Fred casually lied about his status as a bachelor and they looked to the future. Rose wanted to move out of the flat. It is doubtful that she was plagued with guilt over Charmaine, buried at her back door, but what interested her most was her burgeoning career as a purveyor of sadomasochistic sex and her growing client list. She wanted somewhere where she could have her own rooms to work out of, somewhere that Fred could rig up with peepholes, listening and videoing devices. They found the ideal wreck to renovate in No 25 Cromwell Street.

It was a large but fairly ordinary semi-detached house at the top of a downmarket street, notable because it had a garage unlike the other houses in the row and was next to a Seventh-day Adventist Church. At the back it had a long but narrow garden which backed on to ground that was unused except as a car park for a nearby college. Fred relished the work he could carry out over the four floors, including the cellar. He was known to be an enthusiastic builder.

They had to take in lodgers to cover the mortgage and soon a couple of young men moved in upstairs, happy that the cooker and sink Fred had installed on the first floor meant that they did not have to share facilities with the Wests. They shared something with Fred though – Rose. On the first night they'd moved in, Rose climbed into bed with one of the 18-year-olds and they both regularly slept with her throughout their tenancy. Fred didn't mind, his fascination as a voyeur was growing and all he asked was that Rose make her cries during sex louder.

It was into this unconventional set up that one of the lodgers introduced Lynda Gough. She was 17, wore glasses and like Rose, had also struggled with learning difficulties at school. Unlike Rose however, she was a simple soul. She dated one lodger and when he rejected her, started to see the other. She was desperate for a boyfriend and a regular life. She was impressed by Rose and welcomed an opportunity to work for the Wests, as a nanny, as Rose would need an extra pair of hands now that her daughter, Mae, had arrived. It was a key year for another reason. During that summer of 1972, Rose and Fred decided to begin sexually abusing Anne Marie.

Fred had been at work on the cellar. Rose led her eight-year-old stepdaughter down the steps into the cold room, illuminated by a single bulb. Fred had installed a lock on the door and Rose turned the key. Her father, wearing only a pair of shorts, said he was going to help her, as all fathers should. Anne Marie saw there was some things on the floor. A roll of tape, some cloths, a Pyrex bowl and something she wasn't sure about but would come to know as the years passed – a vibrator. She began to cry and Rose laughed, telling her that she was lucky, that they were making sure that when she had a husband, she'd know how to satisfy him and keep him. Rose pinned Anne Marie down, straddled her and sat on her face as Fred raped his daughter. Her hands were bound and her screams were muffled by the gag of tape. She watched as her father pulled matter from her and dropped it into the glass bowl. She thought it looked like red frogspawn.

Afterwards, Rose chatted to her breezily and said that it was what happens in all families and not to make a silly fuss unless she wanted to be beaten. Anne Marie's internal injuries meant that she had to be kept off school. And it was only the start of the abuse Anne Marie would suffer as the years passed.

It was at this time that Rose and Fred met Caroline Owens, the girl they would abduct and sexually assault. The same year that detectives went to Cromwell Street to interview Rose and found her hostile and dismissive of Caroline's account of what happened. 'Don't be fucking daft. What do you think I am?' she demanded of DC Kevin Price, only to later admit to what had taken place when the police discovered a button ripped from Caroline's coat in their Ford. It wasn't until January 1973 that the case came to court but once Rose and Fred walked away with a fine, Anne Marie knew what to expect.

Rose would take her down to the cellar, waiting for Fred to come home for lunch. In the meantime, she'd tie Anne Marie to a metal frame Fred had installed. When she lifted her skirt, Anne Marie saw that her stepmother was wearing a belt adapted to hold a vibrator. First, she gagged her and then beat Anne Marie with the belt as she waited for Fred. He arrived pushed for time, needing to get back to a building job. He ignored his daughter's pleading and raped her as she hung there. Once he left, Rose repeatedly abused her with the vibrator and then walked away. It was some time before she cut her down and put her in the bath, warning her to keep her mouth shut.

Her school failed to see that they were dealing with a traumatised child, her parents had walked free from court, and so it is not surprising that Anne Marie felt alone and abandoned – and wondered perhaps if it did happen in every family?

'I made you,' said Fred, 'I can do with you what I like.'

There has been some suggestion that statistically, those who are abused as children are more likely to become abusers. It can be a consequence of the long-term damage that abuse causes and some victims feel drawn to re-enact what they suffered, a twisted impression that by becoming the abuser – the one with the power – they can erase the sense of powerlessness and pain that tormented them. But the numbers of abused who become abusers is small. Survivors of abuse are more likely to suffer depression, fractured relationships, alcohol and drug abuse, all symptoms of a damaged psyche trying to cope with feelings of shame and distress.

Many will sympathise with adults who suffer addiction after a childhood of abuse. But sympathy has its natural limit. It stops when the abused choose to abuse. To deliberately inflict pain on the vulnerable for your own ends, to increase human misery when you know the price it exacts, is unforgivable. This is the point where compassion melts away.

People like Rose West stand outside our understanding of what it means to be human. Not only did Rose repeat the abuse she may have endured, she amplified it. Her need to abuse others became impossible to satisfy. She may have known fear growing up, but once mistress of a household, she orchestrated horror and degradation on an unimaginable scale. And Lynda Gough was her next victim.

The Wests had spent time with Lynda, slowly ensuring that the teenager came to trust them. Rose had even been to visit her mother, to let them know that if Lynda accepted their job offer, now that Caroline had left, she could rest assured that she'd be well looked after. Rose knew how to charm. Rose was a mother after all, five months into pregnancy with her first son, Stephen. With a growing brood, Lynda thought she'd have plenty to fill her time.

Lynda would have turned 20 in April 1973, but it is likely that she did not live to see her birthday. The sequence of events that led to Lynda's death will never be fully known but she would become the first woman to be buried at No 25 Cromwell Street.

What is known is that her face was almost entirely

obscured with tape, dehumanising her and causing her to struggle for air, both aspects that excited the Wests. She was tied in a style that her tormentors were picking up from the extreme pornography they enjoyed, she was reduced to a sexual toy, unable to defend herself from the pain they took their time to inflict. And watch. As serial killers, the Wests would have no flicker of remorse or recognition of the pain that they were inflicting. Lynda was merely a canvas for them to act out their dark fantasies.

A clue about the dysfunction of Fred's mind came after his arrest. Although often coy about why he removed bones (Fred probably didn't have a firm idea why he kept them), he did reveal why he removed Lynda's head after he'd dismembered her legs and removed her hands, feet, her breastbone and several ribs. He said: 'I wanted to make sure she was dead.'

This sounds absurd. He and Rose had tortured Lynda until she died. He had dismembered her corpse. How could he have any doubt about whether she was alive? But his remark does echo those made by other serial killers. There is a gap, an absence in the psychological make-up that allows them to see others as human. American serial killer Richard Macek not only used to kill young girls but he would often then indulge in necrophilia. He told forensic psychologist Dr Helen Morrison: 'I can't tell if people are alive or dead unless they stop fighting me.' Dr Morrison came to the conclusion that his necrophilia was not sexual but 'an effort to resolve his confusion about the line between life and death.'

Rose and Fred did not see their victims as human beings and they were soon preparing to kill again. Lynda's mum knocked at the door of the Wests' house a few weeks after failing to hear from Lynda. Rose stood in the doorway and calmly said that she'd left to find work elsewhere. As she said this, Mrs Gough noticed that she was wearing Lynda's slippers. Rose said they had to let Lynda go as she'd hit one of the children. As far as Rose was concerned, the door was closed on her and her daughter forever.

Lynda's parents continued to search for their daughter, even contacting the Salvation Army but crucially, not the police. In fact, the Wests would also manage to kill Anna McFall, Charmaine Costello and Rena Costello without friends or family formally registering them as missing.

Rose had refined Fred as a predator. She didn't want to risk snatching a girl off the streets. It is likely that Fred had used abduction before he'd met Rose as several unsolved rapes involve descriptions that match Fred. But Rose knew that the safest way to secure girls was to befriend them so she turned her focus to the nearby Pines Children's Home. Carol Ann Cooper lived there and was typical of the 15-year-olds residing in care. She was from a broken home and after her mother died she spent some time living with her father but it didn't work out. Rose tuned in to her unhappiness and said she understood, as she had also spent time in care.

Carol boarded a No 15 bus from Worcester on 10 November 1973, just after 9pm, and it was the last time she was seen alive. When her remains were discovered years later, her head was found encased in tape, made to look like the sadomasochistic rubber masks Rose had seen in her magazines. Her limbs were also bound and she would have found both breathing and any movement almost impossible as she was toyed with by the Wests. By now, Fred had installed hooks in a ceiling beam to allow Rose to watch as he hung girls there. It isn't known how long Carol had to endure her suffering. Pathologists found a deep stab mark on her skull, possibly a result of a blow to kill her.

Unconsciousness would have been a mercy as Fred proceeded to remove her legs, hands and feet and then severed her head above the fourth cervical vertebra. Her remains were then shoved into the three-foot-deep pit that had been dug on the right-hand side of the cellar where it was found 20 years later. Unlike Lynda, Carol had been registered officially as a missing person but the police focused their search in Worcester, as there was no evidence to suggest that she had been taken 30 miles away to the house in Gloucester.

Within weeks, the police would be approached again about a missing woman. It was a case that the police and the media took notice of as the student, Lucy Partington, had no reason to disappear, in fact she had everything to live for. Lucy was from a privileged background, was intelligent and very popular and in her final year studying for a degree in medieval English at Exeter University.

She had just enjoyed Christmas at home in Gretton, a Cotswold village. A lot was expected of Lucy: her father was an industrial chemist and her mother an architect. Her uncle was the writer Kingsley Amis and her cousin, Martin, would also grow to be a renowned writer. Martin Amis would go on to talk about his horror over Lucy's fate in his book *Experience*, but it is Lucy's sister, Marian, who has written most movingly about her sister and her disappearance in an essay called *A Shining Silence*.

Lucy had been visiting a disabled friend and had left after 10pm with her application for the Courtauld Institute of Art, where she hoped to carry on her studies after graduating. The letter was never posted. As Marian wrote: 'This is where, for me, it all goes into slow motion. The moment when Lucy, satchel swinging on her shoulder, hurried through the darkest of nights. There was a national power cut due to the fuel crisis. She was intending to post the letter before the bus came. The moment when Lucy's life met its opposite.'

It is likely that Lucy missed her bus and worried about disturbing her friend's father should she have had to knock on their door and request a lift. Rose and Fred probably came along with their car and when Lucy saw Rose's smiling and homely face, decided to accept their offer of a lift.

Fred may have punched her into unconsciousness, as he did with Caroline Owen. No one saw the couple force Lucy into the cellar at Cromwell Street. No one witnessed what followed next: she was gagged, stripped and bound and so much adhesive tape was applied that it formed an oval mask with only the smallest holes allowing some air to enter through her nose. Lucy could have remained alive in the cellar for as long as a week as the Wests tortured her.

One official record of Fred's movement that week shows that he went to hospital on 3 January with a deep cut to his right hand that required stitching. Lucy had been abducted on 27 December. Had Fred injured himself whilst dismembering Lucy's body? Twenty years later, the pathologist noted that as well as disarticulating her legs, Fred had removed a total of 64 bones, including a shoulder blade, something the pathologist noted would be difficult to achieve if you were not medically trained. Did Fred struggle with its removal and in his frustration cause himself an injury? Lucy was buried in the cellar and life at Cromwell Street carried on.

By spring, the Wests felt the urge to kill again. Therese Siegenthaler was a 21-year-old Swiss student studying sociology and living in Lewisham, in south-east London. Therese hoped to see more of Britain and Ireland and in

April 1974 set off to hitchhike to Holyhead and catch the ferry to Dublin.

In an interview some two decades on, Fred called her 'Tulip'. He and Rose listened to her accent and thought she was Dutch. Therese was another to be gagged, this time with a brown scarf and she was tied up, raped and killed. Fred got to work as a butcher and removed her legs, a collarbone, 24 finger and toe bones and 14 bones from her wrists and ankles. The rest of Therese's remains were placed in a hole in the cellar, which was later covered by a fake, built-on chimney.

Therese's family reported her missing but although the London police were sure that something untoward had happened to the Swiss student, they had no way of knowing which route she had followed on her way to catch a ferry in north Wales.

Rose West arrived in casualty in August of that same year with a deep cut to her right hand, the cause of which has never been explained. Rose has never admitted to playing any part in any of the murders that took place at her home, but it is possible that there were further victims between Therese and the next known victim, Shirley Hubbard.

Shirley was 15-years-old and went missing on 14 November 1974. She had travelled to Worcester as part of her work experience, the town where Fred and Rose had earlier abducted Carol Ann Cooper. Trying to get home that evening, she met the same fate as Carol Ann. Many years later, Shirley's remains showed evidence that the Wests' methods were becoming more and more extreme. It is not uncommon for abusers to increase their levels of brutality as the satisfaction they gain from previous techniques becomes exhausted. The search for sexual release becomes harder to attain and it is the victims who have to pay a higher price.

The tape around Shirley's face was so thick it looked like an enclosed mask. A plastic tube with a diameter of only a centimetre was threaded through the mask and into one of Shirley's nostrils, her only access to oxygen. This extreme form of bondage would at once dehumanise the frightened teen and increase her torturers' sense of power and excitement as they watched the girl struggle to stay alive. It can never be known how long Shirley remained tied up and abused, the terrifying realisation ever present that she might not live through her ordeal. Eventually, she was killed and her body taken apart. Fred threw her decapitated head into a hole he'd prepared beneath a wall decorated with Marilyn Monroe wallpaper. Fred kept 23 of Shirley's smaller bones.

It is almost impossible to imagine ordinary life continuing at No 25 Cromwell Street but it did. Fred was employed as an odd-job man and general builder locally, with few complaints other than his habit of stealing odds and ends off building sites and his crude attempts to chat up any women he came in contact with. The West children went to school, although they were not allowed to bring friends back home to play or to go and visit their friends' houses. Lodgers came and went, carrying on with their lives with only the occasional grumble that Fred would build ceaselessly, improving the house and extending it sometimes long into the night. From time to time, one of them would complain that an unpleasant smell was evident but Fred would say that it was probably a dead rat under the floorboards somewhere.

One former lodger was 18-year-old Juanita Mott, again from a broken home but making her own way in the world. She moved into a bungalow with her friend Jennifer, who was preparing to get married. Juanita promised to look after Jennifer's children during the ceremony, but disappeared without a word. Jennifer knew that her friend would not let her down in this way and feared the worst and yet no one reported the missing teenager to the police. As she was someone who had lodged with the Wests, enquiries should have made at No 25 Cromwell Street. Instead, Juanita was bound like a struggling animal and had a noose around her neck. She was then buried alongside the other girls in the cellar. She was found with more than 80 bones removed from her body and the mark of a hammer blow on her skull. Rose's and Fred's need to see pain, fear and humiliation in their young victims was escalating.

All of the girls they abducted shared certain characteristics. They were petite and shared a physical similarity to the young Rose West. It is known that serial killers take their time to select their victims and Rose was driven by a sexual attraction to these young women.

One girl in care, a 15-year-old, described how Rose lured her into friendship over a series of months. At first she saw No 25 Cromwell Street as a place of refuge. But Fred and Rose locked her into a room one afternoon where she saw two other young girls tied to beds. Fred and Rose sexually abused all three, anally raping them with a candle and vibrator. It is probable that one of the other girls was 12-year-old Anne Marie. The girl from the care home stated with absolute certainty that Rose led the abuse, laughing at the girls' terror, summoning and instructing Fred in what act to commit next.

'This is fun,' said Rose, finding one girl paralysed with fear. 'I like the stiff ones.'

It isn't clear why the 15-year-old was able to escape with her life. As Rose and Fred were adept at killing and disposal of bodies by this point, Rose must have taken a calculated guess that the teenager before her was so wracked with shame and fear that she would not be able to tell anyone what had happened at her friend's house. And she was right. It was only when police began making extensive enquiries in the 1990s that she was able to reveal something of the true nature of the relationship between Rose and Fred.

It had been a long time since Rose was the timid teenager Fred had first met at the bus stop all those years ago. She controlled him now and he was learning to duck her furious temper just as his children had. Like her father, she was hysterically strict about her children's household chores and would beat them on a whim. Anne Marie bore much of the brunt of her anger and regularly had to be kept off school because her injuries were impossible to hide. But her actions went far beyond a regime of physical punishments.

Rose encouraged Fred to make a device for Anne Marie to wear, a belt with an upturned vibrator attached that looped through her legs. Anne Marie was forced to insert it and walk around the house whenever Rose wished. She found it funny and would take photographs of her stepdaughter's humiliation.

Anne Marie was also introduced to Rose's clients before she was 13. Rose felt there was good money to be earned.

Rose's regime of prostitution, torture and abuse would have continued indefinitely but a challenger arrived and upset her world. At first it seemed good that Shirley Robinson had entered the Wests' home. In 1977 Shirley was only 18 but had been working as a prostitute for some time. She'd moved into 25 Cromwell Street and had sex with Rose and Fred separately and both at the same time; it seemed that they had found an ideal new playmate.

That same year, Rose became pregnant by one of her Afro-Caribbean clients. In the adverts Rose placed in contact magazines, she specified that she was available to West Indian men or 'coloured men' as they were one of her sexual obsessions and, oddly, Fred approved of the pregnancy saying 'they' were 'better breeders'. Rose was looking forward to the birth of her first mixed-race child when Shirley announced that she too had good news. She was expecting Fred's baby.

Rose gave birth to Tara on 9 December 1977. Shirley's baby was due on 11 June 1978 and Fred made a mistake. He had enjoyed the attention Shirley had lavished on him and joked in front of lodgers that Shirley was his 'next wife'. Rose was enraged and made it clear that enough was enough. The last time anyone saw Shirley alive was in early May. Her baby was almost full-term but Fred disposed of her and his unborn child with the same callous disregard that he had shown Anna McFall a decade earlier. Mother and baby were thrown into a pit he'd dug in the garden, near the back door.

Twenty-eight of Shirley's bones were missing and, somewhat inexplicably, there was no trace of her hair. It is likely that Shirley had been scalped, as well as decapitated, perhaps in an effort to remove all signs that she had ever been a person in her own right. Anyone who enquired about Shirley was told that she'd moved to Germany and was very happy and that she'd had a baby boy. At least some of that would have been true as there was every likelihood Fred knew the sex of the child. Satisfied that the threat to her domination over Fred and the house had been removed, Rose returned to prostitution and kept a predatory eye open for the next victim.

Alison Chambers was naive to an extent rarely found even in the stream of waifs and strays passing through Cromwell Street. She listened in rapture to Rose's description of a 'farm' that she and Fred had in the countryside. Alison had

Above: Annie Walters (*left*) and Amelia Sach (*right*), known as the Finchley Baby Farmers, killed an untold number of young children who had been put up for adoption by their desperate parents. They were executed at Holloway Prison on 3 February, 1903. It was the only double hanging of women in modern times.

Below: Grandmother Nannie Doss, 49, chats gaily with detective Harry Stege before being finally charged with murdering her husband, Samuel Doss, in their home town of Tulsa, Oklahoma in 1954.

©*PA Photos*

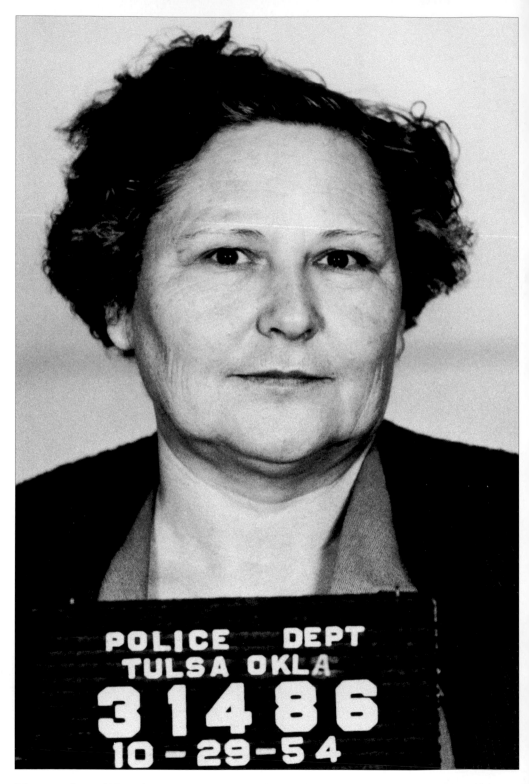

The mugshot of Nannie Doss, taken on 29 Oct, 1954. Doss signed statements saying she caused the deaths of four of her five husbands by putting liquid rat poison in their food and drink.

Above: Convicted mass killer Rosemary West, after appearing at Gloucester Magistrates Court in early 1995. She has since stated that she is ready to spend the rest of her life in prison and expressed her wish to apologise to her daughter, Ann Marie, for the abuse she suffered.
©*PA Photos*

Below: The paved walkway on the site of Fred and Rose West's former home at 25 Cromwell Street in Gloucester, which was opened for public view in 1997. ©*PA Photos*

Above left: Myra Hindley and Ian Brady posing for a self portrait on the moor where they buried their child victims.

©*Rex Features*

Above right: Hindley's now infamous mugshot.

©*Rex Features*

Below: Hindley and Brady arriving at Chester Crown Court in 1966.

©*Rex Features*

Marybeth Tinning is led to Schenectady County Court by Sheriff Bernard Waldron, 1 October 1987. She received a twenty years to life sentence for smothering her infant daughter with a pillow.   ©*PA Photos*

Above: Sara Aldrete, 24, speaks with reporters after her arrest in Mexico City, 7 May 1989. Her companion, Adolfo de Jesus Constanzo (not pictured), was the leader of a satanic cult responsible for killing at least 15 people in the Matamoros area of northern Mexico.

©*PA Photos*

Below: Forensic investigators wait outside the house rented by serial killers Paul Bernardo and Karla Homolka (*inset*). In February 1993 the couple were arrested for kidnapping, raping and killing several young girls in Ontario, Canada. Homolka served 12 years in jail for her role in the murders.

©*Rex Features / PA Photos*

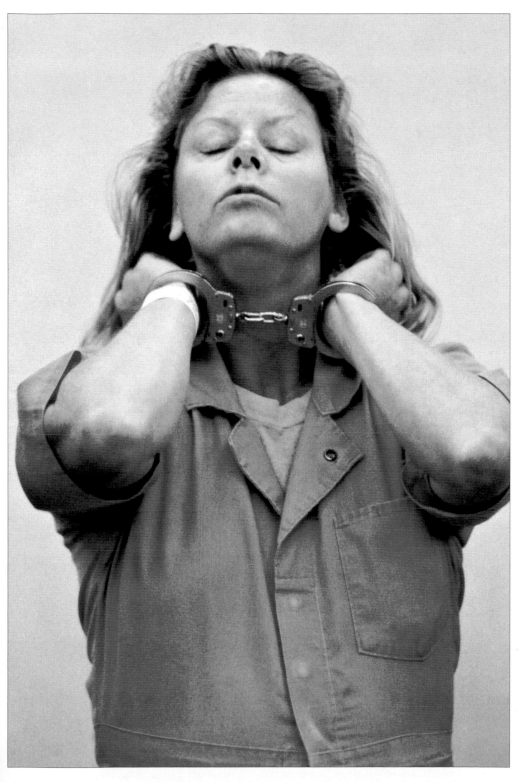

Above: 'We have evil in us, all of us do. And my evil just happened to come out because of circumstances.' Aileen Wuornos, who killed seven men, was executed by lethal injection on 9 October 1992.   *©Rex Features*

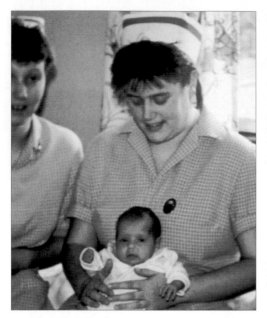

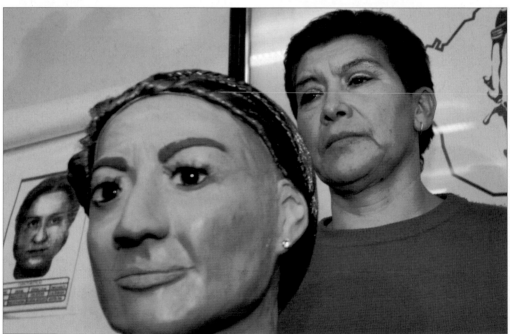

Above left: Beverly Allitt photographed on the children's ward where she worked.

©*Rex Features*

Above right: Allitt outside Grantham Magistrates Court after her appearance for the murders of four children and injuring nine others. She was given 13 life sentences.

©*PA Photos*

Below: Juana Barraza, 48, next to a bust the Mexico City police used in the search for a serial murder suspect, January 2006. Police said Barraza matched the profile of a suspected serial murderer known as the Old Lady Killer – except that she is a woman, not a transvestite as authorities previously believed. ©*PA Photos*

talked of her desire to live on a farm. Just before her 17th birthday, in August 1979, Alison ran away from the care home in which she stayed. She never made it to the farm she dreamt of. Gagged with a purple belt, she was raped and killed, her remains joining those of the other girls on the property, a graveyard of unimaginable horror.

Alison was reported missing as so many youngsters are year in year out. But the police knew this was a girl who had run away from care before and what was more, her mother, back in Swansea, had received a letter from Alison around the time of her disappearance, talking about life looking after five children for a good family. It was a family that had disposed of another vulnerable girl. They seemed to be unstoppable, yet Rose's own vulnerable child would prove their undoing.

Heather had watched and had seen too much as she grew up at No 25. Unlike Anne Marie, she wasn't a troubled pupil failing at school, she was diligent and her teachers had high hopes for her. No doubt Heather saw her GCSEs as a possible escape route out of her parents' house.

Fred disliked Heather. She could watch him at a distance with a blank look yet he felt it held disapproval and Fred was easily unsettled. She was smart and she took to guarding her younger sister when she went to the bathroom and asked the girl to do the same for her. There is no doubt that Fred intended to inflict on his other daughters what he had on his first-born, Anne Marie. Heather was dogged in her determination to avoid Fred and both her parents began to mock her and wear her down with accusations that she was a lesbian. But no matter how vigilant Heather was, there is no doubt that her parents abused her.

The house was filling up. Although Anne Marie had

escaped at the first opportunity, moving in with Chris Davies, a window cleaner, Rose had another two daughters in quick succession. She gave birth to Rosemary junior in 1982 and the following year a girl she named Lucyanna, both mixed race. Raising her large family seemed to fuel Rose's anger rather than divert it. She would beat the older children mercilessly, both Steve and Heather bearing the brunt of her rage. They were made to strip, were tied up, cut and repeatedly punched. Both tried to run away but after sleeping rough for short spells, had to return home in defeat.

It is shocking to think of these children so exposed to abuse without any figures in authority intervening. No health visitor called in to see the newborns, no teacher noted that Heather would not change for sport, too ashamed of the welts she had to hide on her body and no concerns were raised by the police officers who made visits to No 25 over Fred's persistent thieving. A later enquiry would note the number of mistakes made by the authorities. In the 1980s, there were wide gaps in the systems of the social services and the police and a determined abuser would know that.

Anne Marie and Chris Davies married in 1985 and it can only be wondered what her mother was thinking during the family celebration. Was she remembering the 'preparations' she'd put in place for her stepdaughter from the age of eight? Heather begged her sister to take her away with them but Anne Marie was a defeated soul and feared her parents too greatly. In 1986 Heather sat her exams, fully aware of how well she needed to do if she was to escape Cromwell Street and she broke down, admitting to a friend that her father was sexually abusing her. Her friend pleaded with Heather to tell her mum what was happening. That glimpse into the shattered life of Heather West is almost too hard to bear. The one person who should have laid down her life to protect her was at the root of the horror in her life. All hope was bleeding from Heather and her friend never saw her again.

She feared turning 16 and despaired of ever finding a route out of the house and into any kind of normal existence. What could she do? Fear caused Heather to retreat into depression. She had made a frantic attempt to secure work outside Gloucester, a job that would include accommodation, but paralysis over her situation was gripping her as sure as Rose's attempts to physically beat her into submission. The tension in the house spiralled ever higher. Rose and Fred were faced with a daughter who knew full well what they were, a girl bright enough to cause their perverted world to implode. She wasn't like Anne Marie, a tragically betrayed child who still loved her father. Heather was a tinderbox.

Heather's application to work at a holiday camp in Devon was unsuccessful and her sobs were heard throughout the night. It was significant that siblings and lodgers could talk only vaguely about the many times they'd heard her scream, 'No, Daddy, no', but they each remembered this night clearly. It was the sound of a girl defeated and it was probably the last night of her life.

The children came back from school to be told that Heather had left, that she'd gone off to the holiday camp after all. Five years would elapse before some of the truth emerged. Both Fred and Rose had been at home that day. Rose has never revealed what happened and Fred made various remarks about an argument and that he might have killed her, strangled her, when he was annoyed that she was looking at him in a surly way.

This was what the forensic team found: Heather had been buried in the back garden, naked, her hands tied with rope, her limbs dismembered and she'd been held face forward when decapitated. Her kneecaps were removed as were her hands and feet and her fingernails were ripped out. Her fingers were not placed in the black bin bags with the rest of her remains. Fred said he was thinking about making a fish pond and that day, he asked his son Steve to help him dig a hole. A day or so later, Steve noticed it had been filled in. Fred said he and Rose had changed their minds.

It would have gone on indefinitely – but one young girl spoke out. She was only 13 and was not officially named. It was 1992 when she told a school friend that she had been to No 25 and that Fred and Rose had raped her. It was a staggering allegation and although the youngster at first begged her friend to tell no one, they found the courage to talk to a local police officer together. The case was opened and it was a stroke of fortune that it landed on the desk of Detective Constable Hazel Savage. She remembered Rena and the name 'Fred West' from almost 30 years earlier. Thankfully Hazel Savage was a tenacious investigator and she would become an object of pure hatred for Rose.

Early on Thursday 6 August 1992, the police arrived at No 25 Cromwell Street. They had visited before to catch Fred fencing stolen goods or evading vehicle tax and sometimes to check for drugs in his lodgers' rooms. But this time they had a warrant to search for evidence of child abuse. Rose was hostile from the outset but watched impassively as the police removed box after box of pornography, vibrators and sadomasochistic equipment. At 9.05am, she was arrested on suspicion of aiding and abetting in the rape of a minor and for obstructing the police. The police did not locate Fred until 2.15pm. He was arrested for rape and buggery of a minor.

DC Savage needed to build a picture of life at No 25 and

do so quickly. When talking to Anne Marie the next day, what emerged was far graver and more horrific than anything the experienced officer could have imagined. DC Savage wanted to talk to all family members. It was not long before she realised that three were missing: Rena Costello, Charmaine Costello and Heather West. The remaining West children were taken into care.

Rose was questioned about Heather and her story veered from outright denial to patchy accounts of giving her money to run away and later receiving a few phone calls over the years. She explained that she had kept this quiet from Fred as she and her father didn't get on. But now that the police were finally and fully engaged, it was becoming clear that Heather West was no longer alive. There was no record of her having worked or claimed social security and experience alone led them to suspect that Rose was lying when she gave her account.

Rose was released on bail whilst Fred was held on remand and their trial date for the rape of the 13-year-old girl was set for 6 June 1993. But before the case could even be heard, the young girl no longer felt able to face the Wests even by video link and the case collapsed. Twenty years earlier Fred and Rose walked away from court and they did so again. But this time the authorities would not turn their back on No 25 Cromwell Street.

Social services concluded an investigation into tracing Heather and reported back to the police. Hazel Savage had heard the other West children joke that if she wanted to find Heather she should look under the patio. It was covered with crazy paving that took the form of coloured squares of concrete and the children would say: 'She's two up and three across.' Suddenly it didn't seem so funny. The children themselves were free to return to their parents after the rape case collapsed but none of them did. Only the eldest, Steve, would visit his parents. Rose's response was to plan having more children.

Wednesday 23 February 1994 would become known as Day One. The police applied to Gloucester magistrates for a search warrant for both the house and garden at No 25. Steve was with Rose early the next day when the police arrived. When she was told that they were going to begin excavating the garden, he heard Rose scream: 'Get Fred!'

The call to Fred's employer was made at around 1.30pm but Fred disappeared for over four hours: time that would remain unaccounted for. When he returned, he could see work on the garden had begun. It was the next day, when Hazel Savage was questioning an angry Rose, that Fred said he'd speak to the police outside the house. Once inside a police car, he confessed that he had killed his daughter. He told them they were looking in the wrong place and that he wanted them to stop digging. But the excavations continued. What the police teams found went far beyond the domestic incident they thought they were dealing with – far beyond anything the UK had seen since the Moors Murders three decades earlier.

The work was painstaking, not only that of digging through Fred's attempts to fill over the remains of the victims with concrete but also that of reassembling the corpses and then attempting to identify them. In just two weeks, the remains of nine women, including Heather, were found. Fred was mentally disintegrating and would indulge in rambling but only partial confessions. Rose was silent.

The police moved their search to the flat Rose and Fred shared in Midland Road where the pitiful remains of

Charmaine Costello were found. Fred continued to co-operate and made every effort to say that Rose knew nothing but by now, other children were coming forward. An 11-year-old girl and a younger boy told police of Rose's sadistic assaults. Still, all Rose would say was that she knew 'nothing'.

Fred directed police to the fields where he had buried Rena and Anna McFall and the investigators began to realise that there were long gaps in both Fred's and Rose's violent episodes. It was probable that further vicious and fatal assaults took place but it is less likely that the full extent of their crimes will ever be known. Fred talked about letting the police know about 'one a year', realising that he would never be freed and that talking to the police would at least ensure him some time outside to identify where he had buried the victims' remains.

Rose and Fred would meet on only two further occasions, in June and December 1994, when they were formally charged with the murders. During both appearances, Rose refused to have anything to do with Fred. She would not take his calls or reply to his childlike pleas for love. On New Year's Day 1995, Fred West was found hanging from a noose made from his prison bed sheet. Rose was placed on suicide watch. It proved unnecessary. She stood trial for the murder of ten women, including her daughter Heather.

Rose denied any involvement but even if her hands did not go around the throats of those terrified young women until she squeezed what little life was left out of them, she was equally culpable. The court case was a sensation. It took the prosecution over a day-and-a-half just to outline all the police had found and even the most hardened of journalists found the case difficult to stomach. BBC news reporter Jackie Storer has since said: 'There were lots of times when I remember thinking: There can't be anything else, I have heard the most evil things I am ever going to hear. But there would be.'

On 22 November 1995, the jury found Rosemary Pauline West guilty of ten counts of murder. She remains in prison to this day, denying that she is a killer. She regularly makes the news, stories such as a 'romance' with a British rock musician who played with the band Slade, or the 'deliberate poisoning' of her pet hamster are leaked to the press. There will always be a fascination with Rose as the public can never forget the emotionless housewife they saw in the dock during that bleak November, listening impassively as accounts of her depravity were heard.

Without doubt Rose is loathed and feared as much as a child abuser as for her part in any murder. She seems to break every natural code we believe women are born with, an innate desire to nurture young life, not use it and destroy it through cruel sexual gratification. But perhaps the clue to unlocking a mind capable of such cruelty lies precisely in the idea of use.

It is doubtful that Rose was capable of recognising the humanity of those around her – perhaps her mind was irrevocably damaged during her mother's ECT treatments, or perhaps, with two mentally unstable parents, the genetic dice were loaded against her ever functioning healthily. Perhaps her father's abuse was the final environmental factor that allowed Dozy Rosie to emerge as such a damaged child.

Meeting Fred was decisive. The evil in Rose Letts flourished like an aggressive cancer once they were together. They encouraged each other and gave full vent to their lack of humanity. They tracked the vulnerable together and viewed the terrified children and women at their feet as nothing more than flesh to use.

Even now, the human cost of the Wests' depravity does not stop accumulating. Anne Marie tried to take her life on more than one occasion and has changed her name. Fred's brother, John, committed suicide in February 1997. Steven West was jailed for seven counts of sex with a minor in 2004 and in 2007, Rose's brother Gordon, now a homeless drug addict, was jailed for theft.

So many of Rose's victims do not have family able to speak out on their behalf, to try and communicate the weight of their loss. Little Charmaine knew nothing but cruelty in her brief life, other girls felt abandoned by their broken families with too few being sought for after their disappearance, others cannot articulate what their loss means. Lucy Partington's sister, Marian, has tried to show us what impact the disappearance of a loved one can have. She wrote, 'Somewhere inside I became disconnected from the past and disabled by the future.'

Mercifully, very few of us will ever know the trauma of losing someone to extreme acts of cruelty and violence. But we understand pain and the burden of grief, we understand what is meant when Lucy's sister talks of how sorrow can disable. Each of us should be grateful for the burden of loss. Because it is what sets us apart.

Although alive, Rose understands nothing about love and nothing about grief. Her lack of humanity kindled unimaginable pain and it is something we can never share, no matter how much we learn about her. For that, we should be thankful.

6

BEVERLY ALLITT

NURSING EVIL

'There may be nothing in it but if there is,
it's bloody horrendous.'

CALL MADE TO DETECTIVE SUPERINTENDENT STUART CLIFTON

If you know the story of Hansel and Gretel, you will remember Hansel left a trail of breadcrumbs so that he and his sister could find their way home. They'd been led deep into the forest by their evil stepmother and Hansel hoped that once the moonlight picked out the white crumbs scattered along the dark path, it would lead them safely back. It remains a haunting image, playing on our primeval fears of darkness and abandonment and it was a tale Beverly Allitt would have listened to as a child.

In the story, the breadcrumbs led from darkness to light but the trail works in reverse too. You can be led into darkness, if you take the time to trace what has been scattered on the way. And there were many, many clues thrown out by the real persona that lay behind nurse 8811817E, 21-year-old Beverly Allitt.

In the first week of April 1991, staff at the intensive care unit at Queen's Medical in Nottingham knew that something was terribly wrong. There was a good deal of talk and it is little wonder as in the space of a few weeks, Queen's Med had been sent four children from a neighbouring hospital in Grantham. All four had recovered as rapidly as they had collapsed and while that was good news, the pattern was puzzling. The children were clearly caught up in something over at Ward 4, the children's ward at Grantham.

A children's ward would expect to call out the crash team no more than once or twice a year, yet they had been summoned to 14 respiratory or cardiac arrests involving eight children in just six weeks. The specialist team at Queen's Med knew that something was very wrong but they did not share their concerns with Grantham. This lack of inter-agency communication allowed, as it has in other cases, a serial killer to continue unchecked. It was the kind of institutional blindness that would have a devastating and lasting impact as Beverly Allitt's dark psychosis flowered. By the time she was brought to justice, four children were dead, three narrowly survived attempted murder and a further six suffered serious assault.

When the news broke that there was 'an angel of death' at work in a hospital in Nottinghamshire, it quickly made national and then international news. It was the true stuff of nightmares. Should a child ever need to spend time in hospital, parents become painfully aware that their little ones are beyond their help. It is terrifying but they trust the judgement of doctors and nurses. They trust that everything is being done to help their child. The idea never occurs that someone is waiting to pick out a defenceless child and inject them with drugs. Drugs that would stop their heart, paralyse their limbs and flood their fragile lungs with liquid.

And shielded by that trust, Allitt was able to act out her every fantasy.

It began on Valentine's Day 1991. It was a Friday and Beverly Allitt learned that she had been hired to work on Ward 4. She had been working at the Grantham Hospital ward over the last few weeks and was due to start full-time on Monday the 17th. She had been turned down for other positions within the hospital but Ward 4 was desperately short-staffed and Allitt seemed the best choice in the short term: there was a lot of short-termism in the NHS and ward managers felt as if they were fire-fighting one crisis after another a good deal of the time. The post for a registered sick-children's nurse had been advertised, but Grantham Hospital hadn't received a single reply. Even posts such as chief pathologist could take up to two years to fill.

Funding was hard to come by and there was a continual shortage of money for vital equipment. Wards had to borrow and beg amongst themselves for basics such as incubators. The bureaucracy was vast and yet simple paper trails, like those tracking blood samples and results, regularly broke down.

The staff were overworked but they remained deeply committed to their patients. When nurses complained, it was about the ongoing changes within the NHS, not their role as carers. There was particular resentment towards the internal market which was trying to get hospitals to function as 'streamlined businesses'. Despite management memos about 'clients' and 'service providers', nurses knew that their 'market' was caring for the daily influx of sick children and their anxious families. No 'business model' could alter that.

Ward 4 had a sound reputation for caring for children, but many felt that the reorganisation meant that no one took direct responsibility for it. The staff there came under the jurisdiction of a manager more than 25 miles away in the town of Boston and complaints that travelled up and along the chain of command often fizzled out before they could make any impact. To make matters worse, the two consultants working on Ward 4, Dr Porter and Dr Nanayakkara, could rarely get through a meeting without disagreeing. Dr Porter was the older of the two, quieter, an introvert and not used to being consistently challenged by the more abrasive Dr Nanayakkara.

Most admissions to Ward 4 were not suffering with life-threatening conditions. If they were, then the children would be sent to the ICU at Queen's Med, not the general children's ward at Grantham. But they still dealt with serious conditions: babies with bronchitis and children dehydrated from gastric bugs and in need of careful attention. Into this world stepped Beverly Allitt. She was unhappy.

She had applied to specialise in children's medicine at Pilgrim Hospital in Boston but had been turned down. She'd missed some 126 days of her nursing course through sickness over the previous three years, but now seemed fine. She'd worked hard since the New Year and was eager to please. no one guessed that Bev was unhappy. After all, Big Bev was loud and brash, she would be the one who would clown around at social events, always 'good for a laugh'. no one knew that Beverly dealt with stress very badly. In fact, she had been turned down by Pilgrim Hospital the week before she was due to start work at Grantham and she sensed that something would happen, something would erupt. She could never contain all she felt.

Liam Taylor was admitted to Grantham Hospital on Thursday 21 February, suffering with bronchiolitis. He was only seven weeks old and despite being generally in good health, a common cold had taken a turn for the worse. His GP was not unduly worried but, being cautious, recommended admittance to Ward 4 to allow him a quicker recovery. His parents, Chris and Joanne Taylor, had an older son, Jamie, and so knew how ill children could appear only to rally again within an hour or so. They wanted the best for their new baby and so settled Liam in for the evening and went to collect his big brother. When they left, Liam was in the care of Nurse Allitt.

It took moments. Moments to look down at the child in the cot and decide. Bev was left to administer a feed, Liam was too congested for a bottle feed so he had a tube inserted into his throat for food and another inserted into his arm, for antibiotics. It was only around 5pm but it was quiet. Bev had what she needed and watched calmly as the tiny body in front of her began to react to the poison that was flooding his system through his antibiotic tube. He was lurching into a cardiac arrest, his body arching and convulsing as he fought for breath. A minute passed. Bev emerged from the cubicle, yelled out for assistance and then stood back.

A resuscitation team is always on standby somewhere in the hospital. They were paged and told where to go. It was a gathering storm that thrilled Bev, who knew what she'd unleashed. She stood at the back of the cubicle and shook as the scene unfolded, doctors battling to understand what was afflicting the baby, shouting out frantic instructions, the whole team acutely aware that every second mattered. His heart had stopped but why? Had he choked on vomit? That was what Nurse Allitt said, something about him vomiting violently and then gagging.

Their efforts paid off. Somehow, they had managed to

revive the baby, although he was weaker than they must have realised. Yet it was extraordinary that a baby at that age, born in good health, should suffer a heart attack. Dr Nanayakkara believed that pneumonia must have moved to his lungs and ordered a series of tests.

Chris and Joanne were devastated when they saw their son. They had left him kicking and smiling in new baby clothes, fully confident that he'd be home again in a day or so. Now he was wired up to monitors, motionless and grey, unrecognisable. They did not leave his side but it took until later the following day before Liam opened his eyes and lit up with recognition when he saw the anxious faces of his parents looking down at him.

They wondered if they should ask about transferring Liam to Queen's Med but Bev brushed the idea aside, saying that the ICU were always too busy to care for each child as her ward could. Bev had hovered around Liam ever since he 'went off' on her, his parents were grateful that she was on hand and happy to answer their questions. Jamie was staying with a friend – they would not leave their youngest son again. That evening, they were led to the parents' room where they were told to try and get some rest. It is never easy to snatch sleep in hospitals but eventually, exhaustion took hold. It was just before 5am when Chris was shaken and told that Liam had suffered another collapse.

Dr Nanayakkara was baffled. The baby was wired up to a monitor for a condition called sleep apnoea – problems in breathing in sleep – but no alarm had rung. Liam had seemed to make a full recovery and yet here was the doctor standing in front of two parents in deep shock. He had to tell them that Liam had suffered another cardiac arrest, that his heart could well have stopped for over an hour and although he was now breathing, it was highly probable that Liam would be left with severe brain damage.

In fact, Liam was still convulsing. His limbs seemed to be reacting to an invisible force and although he was alive, his parents knew as they held him, that their little boy was beyond their reach. His tiny frame was damaged beyond repair and his suffering was more than they could bear as the hours passed. They wanted the invasive treatments to end. They just wanted to hold him and try to come to terms with the fact that his future had been so brutally snatched away. Liam was cradled by his parents to the very end.

The ward staff were upset that the little boy had lost his fight for life. They talked about what had happened in quiet tones, many expressing sympathy for Bev who had only just qualified and was the one who had to raise the alarm. Bev seemed fine though and the workload of the ward forced the staff to keep busy and trust that it would the last misfortune they'd see for quite some time.

Dr Nanayakkara struggled to understand what could have happened to Liam Taylor. He attributed his collapse to 'probable septicaemia' but this was rejected by the coroner, who did not appreciate the appearance of 'probable' on a death certificate. The consultant pathologist, Dr Terry Marshall, then carried out an autopsy. The eight-week-old boy was perfectly healthy but for one thing: the tissue in his heart had been almost entirely destroyed. The cause of death was given as a myocardial infarction – a heart attack. Dr Nanayakkara was unhappy. Eight-week-old babies don't have heart attacks, not without sign of congenital or structural defects or a serious infection, but with the death certificate supplied, Liam's body was removed for cremation.

Not all of Beverly Allitt's victims were babies. Tim

Hardwick was 11 years old when he was admitted after a series of epileptic fits. Epilepsy was only one of Tim's health complications. He had been born with severe cerebral palsy, was unable to speak and was very weak, weighing less than three stone. Tim was frail and virtually mute, something Nurse Allitt would have observed. He was as helpless as a newborn.

It was Bev who raised the alarm late on the afternoon of Tim's admittance on 5 March. One of Bev's colleagues, Mary Reet, came when Bev shouted and found Tim ashen and motionless. Mary ordered Bev to call for the crash team, Tim had gone into cardiac arrest. Dr Nanayakkara attended with the team as every effort was made to restart the boy's heart. They tried injecting adrenalin, they tried bursts from the defibrillator but after 30 minutes Dr Nanayakkara instructed the team to stop. They had failed.

The pathologist felt the death had to be a result of epilepsy. He'd noticed tiny bleeds in the lungs of the deceased but with the boy's history of ill-health, concluded there had been a natural death partly as a result of his severe epilepsy. Dr Nanayakkara was plagued with doubts, he and everyone on Ward 4 knew that the boy had not had a fit for more than four hours. It could not have been a fit that led directly to his heart failure.

March was an unhappy month on Ward 4. Nursing is a stressful job at the best of times and a loss is always hard to take. They asked questions of Bev, as she was unlucky enough to have found Tim. It all seemed too much to take in. Bev was getting used to being the focus of attention now and would explain how both children had 'gone off' on her. Heads were shaken and commiserations made.

Bev liked being asked to talk about what had happened.

Those who knew her as she was growing up would have recognised the way in which she liked to be at the centre of things. If she sensed that limelight was slipping away, she'd embellish her stories or simply lie to try and regain it. It was something of a joke, she'd even been labelled 'the Fable' by one lad and it stuck, if used only when talking about her behind her back. It was hard to detect fact from fiction with Bev. She wasn't unpopular however, although she could wind people up.

Years before, Bev had always had to have the latest things before her school friends did. If they said that they were saving up for a particular item of clothing, they could guarantee that Bev would buy it first. She'd flaunt it in front of them. She had money to spend.

Maybe she had a comfortable existence, but not everyone envied her home life. More than a few thought her dad was a creep who would always make smutty remarks and try to hug them, even if it was clear that it made them uncomfortable. There were rumours about Bev's dad. Her friends could feel sorry for her but Bev seemed to zone out when he was around. Not that she wasn't aware of what was happening around her, on the contrary, she could show a mean streak. One friend found maths a bit of struggle but worked hard and eventually managed to score well in a test. As the maths teacher praised her, Bev casually piped up, 'Oh, is that the one I did for you?' She knew people's weak spots and knew how to hurt.

The team on the ward didn't see this side of Big Bev. They liked her, even if one or two grumbled about the fact that when the crash team was in action, she did nothing but stand there, motionless. Others rallied to her defence. She was newly qualified and a crash is terrifying no matter how experienced you are. Bev was doing okay. The staff knew that medical teams had to protect one another, it was part of the territory. There was an us-and-them mentality that helped to shield everyone from a stressful environment that the outside world simply didn't understand. Bev understood.

When Kayley Desmond collapsed in the early hours of 10 March, everyone's heart went out to the little girl. She was only 15 months, but Kayley's short life had been vexed by illnesses. She'd been born with a cleft palate, was struggling with feeding and had missed developmental milestones. Kayley seemed in constant pain, emitting a high-pitched whine, and doctors suspected that she was struggling with some sort of brain damage. She had been to Grantham Hospital any number of times and had been admitted on this occasion with a chest infection. Bev asked for help with an antibiotics drip and when fellow nurse Lyn Vowles came into the cubicle, she could see that all was not well. Kayley had stopped breathing. A frantic attempt was made to revive Kayley: getting oxygen into her lungs was the priority. It looked like they would fail to revive her when a dose of aminophylline kicked in and Kayley's pulse picked up. The decision was made to transfer the girl to Queen's Med immediately. Bev volunteered to go in the ambulance.

Kayley made a good recovery, particularly in light of all her other health complications. In face, she made an immediate recovery, much to the relief of her parents and staff at Queen's Med. Yet, although Kayley had arrived safely, her X-rays had not. They had been ordered in an attempt to see what was at the root of Kayley's collapse but had been mislaid. It was unfortunate as, if they had been examined properly, a dark and tiny air bubble would have been identified just under the toddler's right arm. Another clue was lost.

In a little over two weeks, Kayley was joined at Queen's Med by another emergency admittance from Grantham, a five-month-old baby boy named Paul Crampton. He seemed to be suffering with sudden hypoglycaemic slumps, as if he was diabetic. It was severe enough to induce a coma. His parents kept a heartbreaking vigil as their once lively and alert young son repeatedly slumped into unconsciousness, grey and inert, his eyes rolling to the back of his head. The medical team struggled to revive him, administering dextrose in a desperate attempt to raise his blood sugar levels.

Despite the extreme anxiety, his parents were clear-headed and questioned how the boy could become seriously ill so quickly. He had no history of diabetes and their suspicion was that the wrong drug had been given to their baby. They thought the hospital could be covering their backs by not admitting what had happened.

Some of the staff on the ward had concerns about the true cause, as Paul showed every sign not of an infection but of a system flooded with poison. Had there been a mix up? One nurse was so unsure she even told Paul's parents, 'If I were you, I would move Paul from here.' It seems an extraordinary acknowledgement that something dreadful was preying on the children at Ward 4 in Grantham. But they simply didn't consider the idea that a malicious individual could be responsible.

On 28 March, Dr Porter arranged for a transfer to Queen's Med and the focus moved to the possibility of a virus infecting the ward, seeping from the air ducts perhaps. In truth, there was a virus, but its origin was human. It had ravaged the mind of Beverly Allitt and was urging her to find it a new and savage outlet on the ward.

Tracy Jobson was also a nurse at Grantham but she worked in the intensive care unit. Tracy was on the rota for the crash team and had even attended Ward 4 over previous weeks. More significantly, Tracy shared a house with Bev. They lived in a semi on the outskirts of Grantham and, although Tracy had a boyfriend when the two first met, she now shared Bev's bed. Tracy was happy with her lot, they had a nice home and had bought a kitten that Tracy adored. Bev would tell her about all the mysterious crashes on Ward 4 and Tracy's suspicion was also that a virus must be responsible for the children's rapid deterioration. She felt Bev was coping well and was pleased. Bev had taken so much sick leave that it had looked at one point as if she'd struggle to qualify and find work. Ward 4 had been her salvation. The extra weeks she'd put in there meant that Bev's tutor would finally sign her off as a qualified State Enrolled Nurse. Big Bev patrolled the ward, watching and waiting.

So much had happened lately but Bev knew that it couldn't end, not yet. She sat and watched as five-year-old Brad Gibson was admitted. He was a little boy with a big character and was there because his GP wanted antibiotics administered by drip to help check the development of a chest infection. His mother, Judith, didn't like hospitals, but she appreciated that fact that once Brad had received his antibiotics intravenously he seemed like his old self. Judith sat with him as he drifted off to sleep and she tucked him into his hospital bed for the night. She had to return home to care for her two older children but felt quietly confident that Brad would be home in a day or two. She decided that they'd all celebrate a late Easter together. It wasn't to be.

Judith was called in the early hours of the morning and asked to come to the hospital. By the time she and her husband had arrived, the crash team was struggling to resuscitate their little boy. His heart had stopped quite some time earlier. The chaplain was called and Judith wondered how she could tell her sons that their baby brother had died.

Despite all the anguish that swept through Judith's mind, nothing prepared her for the sight of her small son lying stripped on a hospital bed, wired to machines and drips. Into his narrow chest, eight vivid burn marks were proof of the shocks that had to be administered as staff struggled to restart his damaged heart. The team had worked for over an hour and, although Brad was stabilised for the present, Judith was warned that the crisis was not at an end. Brain damage was highly likely but it was impossible to guess how much he had suffered.

Brad was transferred to Queen's Med and back on Ward 4, one of the nurses, Catherine Morris, was explaining all that she'd witnessed to her colleague, Margaret. Brad had complained repeatedly that his arm hurt where the drip was placed but still, it made little sense as to why he had collapsed so suddenly and dramatically. As they talked over what could have happened, Bev entered the room to say that there was something wrong with Henry Chan. Henry was a two-year-old admitted with concussion after he'd fallen out of bed and now he was crying.

Margaret and Catherine walked up the ward together, still in conversation. They could not hear Henry crying. In fact, as they entered his cubicle, they heard nothing at all as the toddler was blue and lifeless. The crash team was summoned. They revived Henry yet, as he sat wearing an oxygen mask, his mother was horrified to see his system collapse and his face become a vivid and violent blue. She had to watch as her son's back arched and he shook with convulsions, medical staff streaming into the room in another desperate attempt to stabilise him.

Nurse Allitt, positioned at the back of the cubicle, watched too. Catherine noticed Bev, about whom she already had doubts. She had seen Bev during other crises, standing in a slightly vacant way, dropping equipment and failing to assist. It irritated her but she was distracted by the fact that the junior doctor on duty stated that Henry's collapse was due to febrile convulsions brought on by his head injury. Catherine was an experienced nurse and knew that febrile convulsions were preceded by very high temperatures. She knew the doctor was wrong. Henry's temperature had been normal.

The young boy was strapped onto a stretcher and Bev climbed into the ambulance, making the now familiar journey to Queen's Med. Henry would make a good recovery and, once again, doctors at Grantham were puzzled. The tests they'd sent off seemed to be producing nothing to indicate what virus was responsible for so many dangerous setbacks. Staff at Queen's Med flagged up their concerns at their weekly meeting. Brad Gibson's quick recovery made his heart attack all the more suspicious.

Staff reasoned that the drug prescribed to clear his airways – salbutamol – must have been injected by mistake. Salbutamol should have only been given through a nebuliser, a device which releases a small quantity of the drug as a mist through a mouthpiece. If injected, salbutamol could overwhelm even a healthy heart. That might explain Brad's complaints about pains in his arms too.

If incompetence was at the root of Brad's collapse, the long-term injuries were only now becoming apparent. Although awake and alert, Brad could not use his legs properly. His parents were doing all they could to help their son but had to watch as the once energetic boy now pulled himself along on his hands and knees, clearly still in pain.

Any conclusions Queen's Med were drawing were not shared with Grantham and back on Ward 4, a new crisis was unfolding. Becky Phillips was a twin, nine weeks old and had been unwell since her premature birth that January. Born weighing only three pounds, both Becky and her sister Katie were in and out of Ward 4 to monitor any complaints. Their parents, Peter and Sue, had great faith in the hospital, to the extent that they'd asked one nurse to be godmother to the twins. Becky had been admitted with a gastric bug and she'd struggled to keep any milk down but after a couple of days, Dr Nanayakkara was happy enough for her to be discharged.

There had only been one hint that all might not be well, although it was not thought of as significant at the time. Bev had told another nurse that she thought Becky had been 'cold and clammy' before her feed but, after a final examination by Dr Nanayakkara, the smiling girl was taken home. It was during the first night home that Becky stopped breathing. Her parents were thrown into panic and rushed back to Grantham, where Becky was snatched from them and taken to a resuscitation room. As her parents stood crying, their daughter's life slipped away and she was declared dead at 3.45am on the morning of Friday 5 April.

Back on Ward 4, it was too much to take in. Seven children had been struck down in seven weeks and three of those children were dead. no one, no matter how experienced, had encountered anything like that. Perhaps Legionnaires' disease was contaminating the ventilation system? Perhaps one of the nurses or doctors was carrying a virus? Perhaps they were unaware of the fatal consequences of an adult illness on the young? The ward was in shock and gripped by a sense of failure, even as they all agreed their sense of despondency paled when compared to the grief the families faced.

Every heart sank when Katie Phillips appeared on Ward 4. It emerged that Becky's twin was only there for tests to avoid whatever it was that struck her sister. As her parents sat at Katie's side, they learnt that a postmortem on Becky concluded that she had died from Sudden Infant Death Syndrome (SIDS). Yet the pathologist also noted that the blistering on Becky's heart was unusual.

It was Bev who cried out to say that Katie had gone blue. Her parents had left her bed to plan Becky's funeral and Bev slipped into the cubicle. How long had she watched the sleeping child? Was the decision made before she made her way to the cot or did it emerge as she looked at the sleeping baby, wired to a sleep monitor? The monitor would have to be gently dislodged, the last line of defence safeguarding tiny Katie from Big Bev.

'Cardiac arrest, Betty,' Bev called out to Nurse Asher and once again, Bev was right. The baby's heart had stopped. The crash team went through their motions once more, a sickening familiarity weighing on them. They willed the girl to respond, none daring to look at each other in case their fear showed.

They managed to reach Katie, managed to massage her back to life and more tests were taken, more X-rays requested and once again, Ward 4 was pitched into a state of high alert. But not high enough.

Just two days later, Bev was motioning to Nurse Lyn Vowles, holding Katie in one hand, clutching her against her shoulder and hooking her finger towards Lyn with the other. Katie's face was scarlet, her breathing had stopped again.

The team revived her once more, two days after her first collapse, and the request was made for a transfer to the hospital where she was born: Nottingham.

While the call to Nottingham city was being made, Bev and Lyn were alone with Katie. Bev had an accident. She sprayed some substance or other into Lyn's eyes, who jogged from the room to wash it out. She was still within listening distance of the room where Katie lay when she heard Bev shout for assistance. Katie had started to fit, her body rigid as she fought to take in oxygen. The police were asked to escort the ambulance to Nottingham. It was doubtful that the baby would see out the night.

As Katie was driven away, she was journeying to safety but her parents had no inkling of this. All they could feel was the crushing certainty that they would lose a second child. Only days earlier, they had worried how they could explain to Katie as she grew up, how she had lost her twin. Now that imagined future seem to mock them. They were going to lose both girls.

Katie's X-rays would have at first glance revealed nothing, no signs of pneumonia overwhelming her lungs or evidence of infection or a defect. The evidence they captured was of a quite different kind and not visible to an untrained eye. They showed ghostly shadows, almost like cobwebs, tracing across Katie's nine week-old ribs. They were fractures. Despite the elasticity of a newborn's bones, Katie had been held so tightly that her tiny ribs had shattered. The X-rays were returned to her hospital file.

Everyone was rocked by the events of the previous two months and many involved with running the ward tried desperately to think of ways to stem the rise in life-threatening emergencies. Some suggested they close the ward until they could get to the bottom of the virus plaguing the children, or at least contact GPs and quietly inform them to direct children elsewhere. Something had to be done.

'Once again I find it necessary to express my concern about the staffing levels on Ward 4 during the period of night duty,' wrote one of the Ward's Sisters, Jean Savill, in a letter to her superiors. She had sat at the bedside of Katie Phillips for two nights and the child had slept soundly but, with three other wards to take care of, she had eventually been called away. The following afternoon, Katie had collapsed once more.

Jean knew the ward was short of staff and equipment but she had not even had a reply to her letter when the next crisis hit. Michael Davidson, a-six-year-old, had been accidentally shot with an airgun pellet and was on Ward 4 to recuperate. It was Tuesday 9 April and Michael had been recovering well when an IV drip was inserted and he went into arrest. He was revived but Jean Savill was confounded when she heard about Michael's sudden decline. She asked Dr Porter if he could compare the notes of all the children who had collapsed and see if there were any common factors. Slowly the veil was beginning to lift.

A consultant from Queen's Med contacted Dr Nanayakkara and expressed the opinion that Becky's SIDS could not explain what had been happening to Katie. A second postmortem on Becky was recommended. Her parents agreed.

Hundreds of miles from Grantham, another clue to the deaths was picked up. Robert Henley, a specialist at the Department of Medical Biochemistry at the University of Wales at Cardiff, reached for the phone. He wanted to talk to Dr Porter. Mr Henley did not usually make calls but when he saw the results of a blood sample taken from little Paul Crampton, he did not hesitate. One of the tests assessed the level of insulin and while a healthy sample would return a reading of around 15 milliunits per litre, Paul's sample contained more than 500 milliunits. It might have been more, but that was as high as their equipment allowed them to measure.

On Friday April 12, Dr Porter suggested the lab had to be wrong. Paul was not being treated with insulin. Mr Henley was sure that the results were correct and the two men eventually reached a compromise. Queen's Med would send another sample of Paul's blood to Cardiff for testing. More time was lost. Two weeks had elapsed since Paul Crampton's collapse.

By the following day, Ward 4 was busy with new admissions. Eight-week-old Chris Peasgood and five-week-old Christopher King were both having difficulties. Chris had a chest infection and Christopher was struggling to keep any feeds down. Their mothers stayed on the ward with their boys. Bev saw Chris' mother, Creswyn, sitting anxiously. She looked careworn and Bev knew she smoked so she stepped in to suggest that she take a moment to have a cigarette break. Creswyn was returning to the ward when a panicked nurse told her that Chris had suffered a cardiac arrest. It didn't seem possible and Creswyn was lost in despair. Even after being revived, Chris' lungs failed to function independently and the fear was that if he had another attack on his way to Queen's Med, he'd be lost. Bev climbed inside the ambulance, setting off with the very ill baby at her side.

When Dr Porter arrived back after the weekend he was told that Chris had to have choked milk into his lungs. Paul Crampton's results were on the doctor's mind but Chris' setback seemed of a very different order. Perhaps Paul had been incorrectly injected with insulin – all medical staff were fallible. But he felt it wise to wait for the second set of results before raising the alarm and prompting an investigation.

By Tuesday, Dr Porter would be greeted by more bad news from the ward. Christopher King was struggling for breath and was relapsing once he came off emergency oxygen. A gastric complication was one thing but now the child was inexplicably fighting for air. He was grey, limp and unresponsive, his lungs would not fill and his heart was on the verge of collapse. Ward 4 knew that they were at the edge of their capabilities and, once more, the emergency ambulance was sent to ferry him to Queen's Med.

Nurse Clare Winser couldn't help but notice something. When Christopher 'went off' it was Bev who was with him, saying that she was preparing his feed, yet Christopher's gut complications meant that he should not have been given milk. Clare didn't like Bev, she didn't like the way she'd stand like a spectator with that distant smile on her face when the many crises hit the ward. But what could she say? Not liking someone was hardly grounds for causing trouble on the ward.

Bob and Hazel Elstone knew nothing of the tensions, of the unhappiness and the shattered nerves plaguing the team on Ward 4. All they knew was that their seven-week-old baby Patrick was poorly with gastroenteritis and that the ward was the best place for him, somewhere he could be monitored and not be at risk from dehydration. He was a handsome boy with big brown eyes and he would smile broadly, but seeing his little form in the hospital cot was heartbreaking. Oddly enough, like Becky, Patrick was a twin too. Bev would have seen this on Patrick's notes and she was there on that Thursday, helping Patrick to settle in. She was also there at 4pm in the afternoon and, within minutes, walked back down the corridor to look for Mary Reet.

'I think Patrick might be in trouble, Mary,' Bev said and once again, she wasn't wrong.

Patrick's breathing was shallow and he looked very pale, Mary acted promptly, feeding him oxygen and the baby rallied. She remained with him over the next few hours, anxious that Ward 4 should not lose another child. Blood tests were taken and monitors for oxygen and apnoea (problems with breathing while asleep) were set up. Patrick was checked over once more.

All seemed well and Bob and Hazel came in with Patrick's twin, Anthony. They walked into a scene of devastation. Patrick had collapsed once more and they thought they'd lost him. He was rushed to Queen's Med and the parents were advised to baptise Patrick as the outlook was poor. But the boy was fine after a night in Queen's Med, as were Christopher King and Chris Peasgood, who, within a few hours, was yelling at the top of his lungs. It was a pattern: children were being admitted to Queen's Med after arrests without prior symptoms.

Dr Porter was considering the possibility of meningitis. Sister Moira Onions finally got the two consultants together and asked them what action could be taken. The two men were still at loggerheads. Dr Nanayakkara said he would compile his own report. The bureaucracy of hospital life inched forward, but progress was too slow to protect the most vulnerable: reports were being written, letters composed, some phone calls made, Dr Porter went to a conference, blood tests were waiting for analysis.

Clare Peck arrived on Monday 22 April, the day the two

consultants agreed to work on their reports. She was a jolly, 15-month-old baby, but her asthma was a source of worry to her parents. She had suffered an attack and this time wasn't responding well to the nebuliser and so Dr Porter asked for a chest X-ray. He decided that the best course of action would be to treat the asthma with a shot of aminophylline. An IV (intravenous drip) was set up and Bev was left alone with the child as a junior doctor left to calculate the dosage. Bev stood next to Clare and looked down at the baby's blonde curls. It took nothing, moments, a switch in Bev's thinking and in less than five minutes, Clare had stopped breathing, her back arched and her face was a vivid blue.

Dr Porter was summoned and he worked over the next half-an-hour to stabilise Clare. He was shaken and felt that Queen's Med would a better place for the child. It was, and as he began to explain why to Clare's parents, Bev jogged out of the treatment room shouting, 'Quick, quick, she's gone blue again!'

But Clare would not be resuscitated again. The team fought with everything at their disposal: adrenalin, calcium chloride, dextrose, electric shocks and more adrenalin. Everything was employed but nothing could reach her. Clare died in her mother's arms and Dr Porter was heard to say in anguish: 'This should never have happened.'

All the doctor's years of experience cried out to him. When he fought for Clare it was not asthma he was battling, he knew it now. He had fought a poison that roiled through the child's system and nothing he did could prevent it taking the toddler's life.

He composed himself, talked to Clare's parents but revealed nothing of the suspicions that were causing him such distress. He re-entered the treatment room to draw blood samples from the dead child. He'd always been a rational and scientific man and now he intended to use science to uncover the malice that stalked his ward. Dr Porter asked for immediate analysis from the pathology laboratory. The lab found huge levels of potassium and called Ward 4. They did not get through to Dr Porter and he would later be adamant that he never received news of the call. They sent the results up to the ward but they went missing. To add to the mishaps, the lab lost its own printouts.

A postmortem decided that asthma was the cause of death and Clare's cremation was arranged. Dr Porter was wrong-footed and had little idea of his next step when the team at Queen's Med called with an ultimatum. Call the police or they would.

It now seems extraordinary that a hospital ward could drift from crisis to crisis with no one in authority able to stop the horror unfolding. Yet staff on the ground simply could not see what was in front of their eyes. Their judgement was clouded by inherent trust and the need to do their best for their patients. But Bev watched everything and knew just what steps to take. She had moments of pure clarity. But her time was running out.

On 26 April, a child's cot was set ablaze. Luckily all the children on the ward were out of harm's way but the hospital fire officer concluded that it had been set deliberately. Bev removed the ward allocation book, which recorded the names of the nurses on duty, plus the time and the names of the patients they were caring for. The book could trace Bev's presence, a trail that would lead to the realisation that no child collapsed when Bev was off the ward.

On 30 April the police were contacted by Grantham Hospital manager Martin Gibson. The task of investigating the events on Ward 4 fell to Detective Superintendent Stuart Clifton. It would prove a mammoth undertaking.

As the Detective Sergeant who carried out the initial interviews with Dr Porter and Dr Nanayakkara told them: 'There may be nothing in it but if there is, it's bloody horrendous.'

The paper trails of evidence, the conflicting medical opinion and the man-hours for sifting through hundreds of statements needed a rare tenacity and focus. There were potentially 15 victims, four attempted murders and four deaths with little or no evidence to hand. Luckily, DS Clifton's team were experienced and persistent enough to get to grips with the investigation. They found that the systems that should have been in place had broken down. The key to the cupboard containing medicines such as insulin had gone missing at some point in mid-February. That meant there was no record of who had accessed the cupboard and when.

Tracking the samples doctors had taken from the children also proved to be tricky. Some had simply been mislaid, others mis-labelled and it would take weeks of sifting through the pathology laboratory find them. One, a vital sample from Paul Crampton, was found in Boston Hospital.

But slowly police began to assemble a time-line of events and the painstaking process of TIE (Trace, Interview and Eliminate) was set in motion. Clearly, not all children suffered in the same way and their background health issues clouded what could have caused them to collapse. Paul Crampton registered high insulin levels but Clare Peck did not. There was still a long way to go. But a picture started to emerge from the time-line pieced together – one name always present, one on-duty nurse, one voice ringing out at the point of crisis.

Bev Allitt was arrested on 21 May 1991. The house she shared with Tracy was searched and the ward's allocation book was found at the bottom of her wardrobe. She was taken in for questioning and police officers were amazed how easily she responded to questioning. She was relaxed, almost to the point where she mocked their line of enquiry. She had answers for everything: yes, the allocation book was in her room as she'd borrowed it to help write her diary.

DS Clifton knew that they were in no position to charge her. She was released on bail. The police had hoped that the arrest would rattle Allitt and prompt her to confess and her unshakable calm proved to be something of a setback. A sense of urgency grew when the medical expert leading a review of all samples gathered from the children, Professor Marks, called to say that he had results from Paul Crampton's insulin reading. Initially, the lab at the University of Wales in Cardiff had arrived at 500 or more milliunits per litre and indeed, it was more, it was 43,167 milliunits.

Paul Crampton had been deliberately injected and they could narrow the time-frame for such an injection.

And results came through for Liam Taylor's apparent heart attack. His heart had stopped, but the conclusion was that it was a case of asphyxiation or poisoning through barbiturates or insulin.

Becky Phillips' blood had also been examined. She had 9,660 milliunits of insulin in her system. It was slow-acting insulin that could have taken up to 12 hours to act and, of course, Becky had been at home when she had collapsed. Her parents did not know where all the medical evidence was leading but they did know that the police where investigating and they were unhappy about it. They still had great faith in the hospital, all their other children had been treated there over the years and they felt that the staff were being unfairly persecuted. It was nonsense and they said as much as they sat and shared a cup of tea with Katie's godmother. She'd just called in to take Katie out for a treat.

Katie was dressed for a trip out in her buggy and Sue and Peter waved goodbye as she and her godmother set off. Bev waved back and said she'd be back soon. Bev was super with Katie, always calling in and checking on their daughter.

The press were constantly running stories on the investigation. If there was any foundation to it, they knew it was going to be huge. Tabloid journalists went to any lengths to feed public hunger for information. Staff on Ward 4 were not going to speak to any reporters but that didn't stop the press. The first thing was to identify who worked on the ward. One trick was to send flowers in from a 'grateful former parent/patient' and then watch who left the hospital holding them. All the Ward 4 staff were hounded, including Bev and it was proving too much for Tracy. She asked her mum, Eileen, if Bev could move in and her mum gladly offered to help. They all liked Bev.

It was only 15 minutes or so since Sue Phillips had closed the door when it was thrown open: 'For God's sake, Sue, call the doctor!' Bev was standing with Katie's buggy, her daughter was convulsing, her face red and contorted. Time went into slow motion for Sue. She was screaming and could not believe it when she saw Bev, the attentive godmother and nurse, calmly walk away. Katie was rushed to Ward 4.

The time Bev spent with Tracy's mother wasn't easy but it would reveal yet more about Bev's fractured and dangerous mind. Eileen's health wasn't as good as it could be. She walked with a stick but she was still active and there was nothing she would not do for her daughter Tracy and 14-year-old son Jonathan. It was June when Bev moved in and at first all seemed to go well. However, before too long, Bev said that she sensed a ghostly presence in the house, some sort of poltergeist.

What followed was a bizarre catalogue of incidents. Jewellery would go missing, as well as money and ornaments, and they would crop up in odd places such as pot plants. Eileen had no time for the notion of ghosts but Jonathan was soon unsettled. Then the chip pan was switched on and left until it almost caught fire. The oven was set at maximum with food burning inside. A knife was embedded into Jonathan's pillow. Eileen suspected Bev but Tracy was furious at the suggestion. Bev was working hard to put a wedge between Eileen and her children and tensions in the house were rising.

At the same time, DS Clifton was receiving more results from the widening number of medical experts now involved with the case. The potassium found in Claire Peck's system had initially been dismissed as irrelevant as blood cells break down after death and release potassium naturally. But specialists in London and Birmingham reviewed the tissue samples and postmortems and concluded that Liam Taylor, Brad Gibson, Claire Peck and Tim Hardwick had been injected with potassium chloride. The potassium would explain why Brad had complained of pain from his IV drips.

A radiologist from Queen's Med examined X-rays and found that Katie's ribs had been fractured and saw the air bubble in Kayley Desmond's right armpit. It was evidence that she had either been injected with air – a potentially fatal act – or so quickly that air had entered her bloodsteam.

Meanwhile, the demon in Eileen's house would not rest.

Shelving was dislodged, more money stolen, bleach poured onto Jonathan's bed, Eileen's walking stick would be thrown across the room when her back was turned and both Jonathan and Bev were now complaining of feeling ill. Jonathan even went into a dead faint one day, as if his blood sugar had crashed. Bev gave him some fruit pastilles on the way to hospital and that seemed to help a lot. It was a difficult time. Eileen was struggling to cope but she began to notice something else. Something vital. Before the demon struck, she would hear Bev elsewhere in the house, whistling. It was no ordinary whistle. It was low, tuneless, almost trance-like. It heralded the demon.

Professor Hull completed his review. Based on revised analysis of samples and medical history, he believed that there had been four murders and eight attempted murders, all within the space of ten weeks. It was a staggering figure.

On 3 September 1991, Beverly Allitt was arrested for the murder of Becky Phillips. There would be a huge delay before the Department of Public Prosecutions were ready to bring the case and the trial would not commence until 15 February 1993, almost two years to the day since Beverly Allitt had begun work on Ward 4. By that point, she was facing 26 counts, ranging from grievous bodily harm to murder.

Life on Ward 4 appeared to return to normal. Allitt was an aberration and once removed, it could be seen that children were successfully nursed back to health without incident. But beneath the statistics, the truth was that Allitt's brief reign left no one unscathed. The medical teams were shattered by all that they'd encountered, their trust misplaced, their care abused by a girl who fed on their instincts to preserve life. As they'd flailed around blindly trying to save babies and children in their care, Bev was taking her fill. She had fed on the brutalised bodies of children, gorged on the misery she brought to families and sought to feed time and time again.

But with Big Bev removed from all she fed on, she transformed once more. On the day that the trial began, she was unrecognisable. She'd lost five stone over the months that she had been held on remand and, with no one in reach to damage, she had turned her rage back on herself. She'd spent a good deal of time being treated for a range of ailments, many of which were thought to be self-inflicted. The cause of one spate of vomiting was uncovered for example, when she was secretly observed eating her own faeces.

The trial was huge and Allitt would become notorious as an 'Angel of Death'. Tales of previous odd incidents started to emerge, such as that of the fire started in the nurses' home where she was a student. It would be all too easy to call her a monster but the task for the jury was to focus only on the evidence presented in court. By 17 May 1993, they were ready to give their verdict. Beverly Allitt was found guilty of the murder of Liam Taylor, Tim Hardwick, Becky Phillips and Claire Peck. She was found guilty of the attempted murder of Paul Crampton, Brad Gibson and of her own goddaughter, Katie Phillips. She was also found guilty of inflicting grievous bodily harm on six surviving children. She was sentenced to life and was taken to Rampton, the secure hospital.

Munchausen's syndrome was been given as one explanation of her behaviour. It was an addiction to medicine and to the attention it brings. Sufferers invent symptoms or even inflict harm on themselves to ensure that they receive an endless number of appointments and treatments. Munchausen's syndrome by proxy has greater risks, as sufferers inflict harm on others in an attempt to externalise their pain, so they can be at the beating heart of the drama as it unfolds.

Munchausen's goes some way to describing Beverly Allitt's behaviour but it does not address why this ordinary girl was capable of such appalling acts of murder and cruelty. What was it in her past that destroyed her capability to care for anyone outside her shattered mind? She has remained silent but answers may well lie in her past. Had she suffered a trauma perhaps at the hands of someone she trusted, someone who should have cared for her? With trust abused, did no one listen when she spoke out? A child will not understand everything about the adult world but the abused quickly learn that adults can present one face but, with the doors closed, reveal another.

Two ways of being in the world, one in the light, observed and protected, the other in the dark, unseen and feeding off dark desires. If a child speaks out against abuse and is not listened to, the impact can be devastating. The sense of worthlessness if ignored does not diminish pain and shame, it doubles it. Why doesn't anyone listen? It feels good when people do, when people show they care. You learn that concern can come to you in different ways, like when you tell people you are ill.

When Bev was 13, she had so many problems, stomachaches, backaches, headaches, bruises, cuts that needed bandages. People listened then. And if they stopped, they became interested once more when the injuries grew wilder, like stories of being hit by a car or falling off a horse. It felt good to be noticed but that warm feeling would melt away. It always did. What could fill her up next?

It was this fractured and damaged girl that would keep

seeking a way back to the light, to a place where she felt good once more, but in doing so, she would bring darkness to so many. Eileen Jobson did not believe in ghosts or demons and yet her home and her family were almost destroyed by one. Beverly herself had known what it was like to be without a place of safety, to be left in harm's way. Beverly doesn't believe in ghosts nor does she believe in fairy tales, because at some point in her young life she had to learn that there would be no Hansel to her Gretel. There would be no one to lead her out of the darkness.

7

AILEEN WUORNOS

HOW TO MAKE A MONSTER

'I pretty much had them selected that they were going to die.'

AILEEN WUORNOS INTERVIEWED IN PRISON

It took one year for Aileen Carol Wuornos to kill seven men, gripping the attention of America and the rest of the world. One year to create a media sensation that spawned money-spinning books, documentaries and films. But the question remains – how many years did it take to make a killer?

'We have evil in us,' Aileen said. 'All of us do. And my evil just happened to come out because of circumstances.'

The circumstances make for harrowing reading. Long before Aileen, or Lee as she was known to family and friends, ever got her hands on a .22 calibre pistol, the tool she used to execute seven men, her life had been destroyed through years of abuse and neglect. It is difficult to imagine that any child could emerge unscathed having endured the same upbringing as Lee. Boys who grew up with Lee testified at her trial that she would be regularly sexually abused. One described finding Lee in her fort, a den she'd built in the woods near her home, naked with Keith and Mark, two boys a year or so older than her. Keith was having sex with her. Keith was Lee's brother.

Hers was a case that cried out for social services to intervene from the start. Lee was born on 29 February 1956. Her mother, Diane, was just 16, yet had already given birth to her brother. Their father was 19-year-old Leo Dale Pittman but the couple's brief marriage was over before Lee was born. This would prove to be one of the few blessings in Lee's life as her father was soon convicted of kidnapping and sodomising an eight-year-old. Pittman would spend years in secure mental hospitals and committed suicide in prison.

The breakdown of the marriage and Pittman's arrest should have provided a narrow escape for Lee, saving her from being raised by a sexual pervert. Instead, it proved to be only the first step onto a path of a life marred by abuse. At the age of four, Diane took a trip with her two young children to visit her parents in Troy, Michigan. She asked her parents to babysit the children but later phoned to say that she would not return for them. Diane was exhausted by the struggle to raise two children and felt that the welfare she received was not enough to keep them as a family unit. She believed her parents were the best option for them all. Photographs of both children at this age give no hint to the brutal future in store for them. Both were good-looking children with white blond hair and wide smiles.

Diane's parents took the children in and officially adopted them both in March 1960. It was not until Lee was 11 that she found out that 'Aunt Diane' was her mother and the people she thought were her mother and father were in reality her grandparents. We can only guess at the emotional turmoil created when she realised that she had been abandoned. Sadly, by then, she would know all too well that even her grandparents didn't care for her properly.

Lauri Wuornos, Lee's grandfather, worked at Ford and her grandmother, Britta, stayed at home to raise their three children. Their home was unremarkable, a one level wood-clad house in an ordinary neighbourhood. Britta knew her daughter had made a poor choice when she decided to marry Pittman but she hoped to make the best of a bad situation and raise the two children alongside her youngest two, Barry and Lori. But it was not long before Lee began to display highly disturbed behaviour, trying to start fires in the home with lighter fluid. Lee suffered facial burns, the scars of which would remain throughout her life.

Grandfather Lauri did not hesitate to use severe physical punishment with his children. One of Lee's friends would later say at her trial that she witnessed Lauri force Lee over a chair and beat her savagely with a black leather belt.

'He was a bastard,' said Lee's friend.

By the time she was nine, all Lee's school friends knew she would exchange oral sex for cigarettes. Other children called her Cigarette Pig, yet teachers failed to raise the alarm. Alcohol was a factor in her life, perhaps an attempt to block out some of the pain that was being inflicted on her and drug abuse soon followed.

The kids continued to call her names. She was 'ugly' and a 'bitch' and one so-called 'boyfriend' threw rocks at her when she tried to join him with his other friends. Others recollect being at a party where 12-year-old Lee had passed out from drinking and lying in a foetal position. Two boys had sex with her and no one stopped it from happening.

Lee was just the vulnerable sort of character who was easy

prey for a local man named Chief. He was a suspected paedophile, always looking for ways to entice children into his house. Lee was a frequent visitor and when she found herself pregnant at age 14, many believed that the father of the child was either Chief or her own brother. The authorities intervened only to arrange for Lee's baby to be adopted. She came out of the maternity hospital and was returned to her home in Troy as if nothing had happened. Lauri thought differently and threw Lee out.

She had nowhere to turn and did not think about trying to contact her mother or the authorities. She slept rough in woodland at the bottom of her road, sometimes sleeping in the fort she had built or in abandoned cars. Lee was effectively homeless and yet was still a feature of life in Troy, someone to use for sexual favours, someone you could expect to turn up at houses where drugs were used and sold and someone who increasingly began to trade sex for money.

There is little doubt that Lee had been sexually abused since early childhood and psychiatrists record that young victims disregard and devalue their bodies. It is a paradoxical promiscuity. While it might be expected that the first instinct of the abused would be to withdraw from physical intimacy, the reverse can often be true. Studies have found that the long-term effect of early abuse can be devastating. Post-traumatic stress disorder, difficulty in forming and maintaining relationships, corrosive feelings of shame and anger and a higher likelihood of self-harming, suicide and delinquency are all factors that can ruin the adult life of child-abuse survivors.

There are other measures used to assess the likelihood of difficulties in later life: age, nature and the intensity of abuse all play a part. A very young victim of sustained abuse involving penetration will suffer most when they reach maturity. Furthermore, if a child comes to learn that sexual contact is conducted with coercion and that their bodies are an object used for the gratification of others, the impact it will have on sexual development can be disastrous. If the abuse has involved someone who should have been part of a caring and protecting relationship – as Keith should have been with Lee – the likelihood of the child trusting in the possibility of a loving sexual relationship can be reduced to nothing.

Even if she had entered therapy in her teens, it would have been hard for Lee to progress. Her primal need to protect herself was now almost entirely driven by anger. She had developed an explosive temper. When she was sent to the unmarried home to give birth, staff noted that she was hostile and could erupt into rage. That there was no professional intervention in Lee's childhood shows how easily a deeply traumatised and damaged child can be allowed to drift into a dangerous and unstable adulthood. It just needed a trigger.

On 7 July, Britta Wuornos died of liver failure, though Lee would later say that Lauri blamed her. Supposedly Britta was worn out with worry over her granddaughter's behaviour. Whatever the underlying reason for Britta's demise, Lauri saw this as another reason to cut all contact with Lee. It was really the end of the road for her life in Troy.

Lee embarked on a rootless existence that would dominate the next 20 years of her life and would end with a terrifying string of murders in central Florida. Yet the infamous images of her after her arrest would be very different from the fine-looking girl she was back in Troy. She had an enviable figure and she believed that she knew how to take care of herself. For good measure, she also began to carry a gun, a .22

calibre pistol, a weapon that first came to notice of the authorities in 1974 as she was arrested for drunk and disorderly conduct and firing off a few rounds. Lee gave a false name and skipped bail. The casual use of an alias and the ability to pack and leave town in a heartbeat would grow to be a permanent part of Lee's life. That she went on to abuse alcohol, prostitute herself and get into scrapes with the law would have surprised no one back in Troy. But Lee's next move certainly astonished everyone.

In 1976, a few of Lee's old acquaintances in Troy received some press clippings from the society pages of papers in Daytona, Florida. In them, they saw a smiling Mr and Mrs Lewis Fell. He was the 69-year-old president of a yacht club, a successful businessman who had made millions of dollars. Mrs Fell was a smiling 20-year-old Lee. It sounded like a fairytale ending. She had found a home and a man that could cater for her every financial need but the triumph over her early life was to be short lived. The seeds of destruction had already been planted.

Lewis had met Lee when she was hitchhiking, probably on her way to turning her next trick, as she used the highways as her place of work. Lewis Fell was blind to all this, seeing only a very young, slim, pretty and engaging woman. A proposal of marriage was soon made. That may seem extraordinary but Lee could charm. What was beyond her was the ability to form a lasting attachment.

Within weeks of the marriage, the new bride was back in bars, drinking to excess and raising hell. When her husband forbade her from continuing to behave in such a manner, she picked up his walking stick and beat him with it. The fairy tale was over. Their marriage officially ended on 19 July 1977, but Lee was out of the picture long before that, in trouble with the police yet again and pleading guilty to one count of assault.

If nothing else, she didn't have to worry about money. She had received a $10,000 payout from Keith's life insurance following his death the previous year from throat cancer. Within a few months however, all the money was gone and she went back to a life of hard drinking, fighting, fraud, robbery and prostitution. Lee was on her way to incarceration and her mental state was unravelling. She even held up convenience stores stripped down to a bikini worn as a disguise.

In 1981 she was arrested on charges of armed robbery, resulting in a year at the Florida Correctional Center. Whilst there she was held on six disciplinary charges for fighting. On release she amassed further felony charges, skipped bail and remained a volatile threat to others. The officer who ticketed her for speeding in 1986 probably did not realise how right his assessment was when he noted: 'Attitude poor. She thinks she is above the law.' She kept moving from motel to rented room and sometimes hooked up with an older man. This could have been the pattern of her life indefinitely but something did change. Lee walked into a gay bar in Daytona and met Tyria Jolene Moore.

From that moment, she embarked on the most significant love affair of her life. Lee fell for Tyria and fell hard and she would sell her body and what was left of her soul in the hope of keeping the two of them together. Tyria had occasional work cleaning motels but in the main she lived off Lee's earnings as a hooker. Lee was still only 30, but the years of alcohol abuse and bad living had taken its toll. Her street value was falling and it was harder to raise the money she needed to fuel the couple's lifestyle. She pulled little more than $30 a trick and would often have to start work at 6am just to keep a ready supply of money coming in.

They trailed from one temporary accommodation to the next, either having to pack up and leave over antisocial behaviour or simply through not making their rent payments. What friends they had were often ripped off, their money borrowed and never repaid, their ID documentation stolen.

If this was Lee's attempt to build a stable relationship, the first she would ever know, it was destined to fail. They were ordered off buses for foul and abusive behaviour: Lee even punched one bus driver for commenting on Tyria's looks. It was a mutually destructive partnership that was destined only to harvest more misery. But the price she would pay would not just be that of a broken heart.

Before Tyria walked out on her, Lee would orchestrate a campaign of robbery and murder in an attempt to keep Tyria at her side through money and gifts. As Lee was heard to say to Tyria in a conversation taped by the police: 'When I have somebody I love them all the way and I love them with all my heart and all my soul and all my mind. And I'll do anything. I go nuts.' She did go nuts, but it wasn't Tyria that tipped her over the edge.

Lee had traded sex for money for years without real incident. Once or twice she'd turn up after work and Tyria would see that she had a black eye. Lee would shrug it off. Most of her violence had been meted out during barroom arguments. She kept a lid on her temper in the main when picking up clients and if she was going to lose her cool, it was usually if she was turned down: her use of foul-mouthed expletives was well known and it would be a feature of her trial.

Lee was intelligent, she was able to talk fluently about politics, current events or religion if her clients wanted. But no matter how smart or how streetwise, none of her qualities were a match for the man she would meet on 1 December 1989. He would unleash a tidal fury in Lee that would not stop until her arrest a year later. His name was Richard Mallory.

The Mallory case still divides those who have looked deeper into Lee's crimes. This first killing was a turning point. Lee then showed no mercy and cold-bloodedly picked older men to rob and to kill. Her use of her .22 calibre pistol was brutal and her victims were often chosen merely because they in the wrong place at the wrong time. As Lee would later tell Nick Broomfield for his powerful documentary, *Aileen: Life and Death of a Serial Killer* : 'I pretty much had them selected that they were going to die.' But what happened on the night she killed Mallory was not so cut and dried.

Mallory ran an electronic repair shop in Clearwater, Florida. He had recently separated from his girlfriend and was 51 years old. Married several times before, Mallory was on his way to enjoy a long weekend in Daytona. When he failed to return on Monday to open up the shop, the staff weren't unduly worried. It was only when the police later found his abandoned Cadillac Coupe de Ville in a wooded drive in Ormond Beach that alarm bells began to ring.

Mallory's body was not found with the vehicle. In fact, it was not found until 13 December, when two men looking for scrap metal came along the dirt track off Interstate 95. It had only been two weeks but in that time most of his corpse, partially covered by old carpet, had putrefied beyond the point of recognition and the rest had been eaten away by insects and passing wild animals. Mallory's pockets were turned out and the first officers on the scene suspected that he had been robbed. The pathologist reported four bullets lodged in the torso. It was homicide.

There was a great deal more to learn about Richard Mallory, but they were facts that would later be kept from the jury. Mallory was a sex offender, a habitual user of prostitutes hired to act out his violent fantasies. At least one had brought a complaint against him for brutal sadistic ill-treatment after he'd tried to strangle her.

Years earlier, Mallory had been found guilty of housebreaking with intent to rape when he sexually molested a nurse. He was sent to a high security institution from which he escaped briefly, tried to abduct a young girl and was recaptured while driving a stolen vehicle. He spent a total of ten years in jail. This was no ordinary shopkeeper.

Mallory was released in 1968 and had kept out of trouble with the law. But he continued to feed his sadistic impulses through the use, and misuse, of call girls. His doomed trip to Daytona would no doubt have included stops at all his favourite strip clubs. He knew the regulars as well as the sex workers. They knew about his predilections and one or two had even traded sex for electronic goods from his store. That might have been one reason the shop wasn't doing so well and even when it was, Mallory needed all the cash he could get to fuel his leisure time. Perhaps he was putting all worries about mounting debt behind him as, on 1 December, he headed off for a weekend of partying. As it was, a motorway pile-up meant that Mallory got stuck in a huge tailback . Then he saw a woman in cut-off jeans and a baseball cap hitching a ride. He pulled over and a smiling Lee climbed inside.

Lee had been working the highway all day and the rain had kept falling. She was probably grateful to get into the warm of Mallory's car. At first, Mallory was easy going, happy to stop and buy liquor and even offered her a joint. It didn't take long to introduce the idea that Mallory could 'help her make a little money'. The negotiations opened: 'Head for $30, $35 for straight, $40 for 50/50 (half oral/half vaginal), $100 an hour.'

What happened after they left the Interstate and parked the car along a deserted track remains open to dispute. The prosecution at Lee's trial focused on the murder and that Mallory's possessions and cash had been stolen. They wanted to show the crime was a robbery-driven homicide while Lee said she acted in self-defence after Mallory turned violent, tied a cord around her neck, beat her and threatened to kill her. Lee gave her account at her trial. In it she talks of Visene, a US brand of eye-drops, and of rubbing alcohol, a chemical disinfectant.

Lee told the court what happened that night. Mallory said: 'You are going to do everything I tell you to do and if you don't I'll kill you right now and I'll fuck you after just like the other sluts I've done ... It doesn't matter to me, your body will still be warm for my huge cock.'

Lee added, 'He was choking me and I was holding [the cord] like this and he said, "Do you want to die slut?" and I (shook my head) "No."'

Lee said she was forced to lie down on the car seat. She said: 'He began having anal sex and he was doing this very violently... and I don't know if he came, or he climaxed, I talk street-talk so, he then violently took himself out and violently put himself in my vagina. I was crying, my brain was out.

'He takes Visene, he lifts up my legs and he puts what turns out to be rubbing alcohol from a Visene bottle and he sticks some up my rectum area and that really hurt pretty bad, because he'd torn me up royal, and then he put some in my vagina which really hurt bad. And then he walked around back to the driver's seat beside me and pulled my nose open like this... and he squirts rubbing alcohol down my nose and he says, "I'm saving your eyes for the grand finale," and he puts the Visene bottle back on the dash and I was really pissed, didn't care, I was yelling at him and everything else, he was laughing away...I thought to myself, I've got to fight or I'm going to die.'

Lee said she spat in Mallory's eyes and that gave her enough time to struggle across to her bag and fumble for her .22 pistol. Mallory lunged towards her and she fired two shots off into his body. She got out of the car but so did Mallory and she fired two further shots. It took up to 20 minutes for Mallory to die, during which his killer had dressed herself and sat down to watch and wait.

Tyria heard Lee arrive back early that morning in Mallory's Cadillac at the Ocean Shores Motel. Lee handed her a jacket and a scarf from the car. She told Tyria that she had shot and killed a guy and moved his body into scrubland and covered it with a red carpet. Tyria didn't call the police. Tyria later said that she was too fearful to call the police as she just didn't know what Lee was capable of. She was about to find out.

They used the car to move their stuff over to an apartment later that day. With the valuables that Lee found in Mallory's car pawned, Tyria and Lee had a little more cash in their pockets. They moved into a low-rent apartment and life got back to its usual rhythm of drinking and, for Lee, the search for work along Florida's highways. But there was no doubt that Lee had crashed through a psychological barrier that night with Mallory. With her explosive temper, Lee had long struggled to assess what was a real threat. Had she misread Mallory? He was clearly an unsavoury character but he would not have been the first that had Lee encountered.

Perhaps Mallory did not rape her, despite the detailed testimony she gave during her trial. But he'd done something. Was it an insult, a veiled threat, just something that reminded her a little too closely of Lauri or Keith or all the other boys and men who had brutalised her as a child? During the hours that they were together Mallory, knowingly or innocently, had dislodged the last remaining section of the mental dam that held back Lee's fury. Now she was going to make every other sucker pay.

In the years after her arrest, Lee's accounts of the reasons that she chose to kill the other men followed an eerily similar pattern: 'He tried to rape me'; 'and he said, "You fucking bitch"'; 'and I thought, you fucking bastard. I shot him'; 'I am going to kill you because you were trying to do whatever you could with me.' All her accounts led with accusations that a straightforward attempt to turn a trick was sabotaged by men: their violence and their need to humiliate Lee. In so talking, she wasn't so much recalling details of the nights in question but had found the voice to express the rage she'd harboured about her childhood abuse. What control Lee once had crumbled in the desire to execute any man who ever crossed her, be their crimes real or imagined. In her eyes, they'd beckoned her into their vehicles and were looking for ways to exploit her. She sat as judge, jury and executioner, waiting for them to make that first move.

Mallory was murdered in the early hours of 1 December

but Lee didn't kill again until the following May. Six murders then followed in as many months. Why was there a gap, why did she start to kill again and, when she did, why did she kill so regularly and so quickly?

It wasn't as if the police were hot on her trail. They suspected the perpetrator was an irate hooker but never came for Lee. She might well have got away with it. But in May of the following year, she got a new weapon, having dumped the .22 she had used for her first murder. She was picked up by 43-year-old David Spears, a man who didn't really fit the profile of a predatory man looking to exploit a highway hooker. By all accounts, even though he was a big and powerfully-built man, he was mild-mannered, courteous, hard-working and had a good relationship with his ex-wife, the woman he promised to call in on the following day. But, for him, that day never came.

Lee persuaded him to take a long detour to get her to Homosassa Springs. It wouldn't have been too long into the journey before she introduced the subject of 'earning a little money' and his fate was sealed. Nobody will every know exactly how the doomed transaction played out, but Lee ended up shooting six .22 calibre bullets into him. His body was not discovered for almost two weeks and when it was, off a dirt road and with a cap perched on its head, it was impossible to tell at first whether it was the remains of a man or a woman. Dental records were used to trace his identity.

Though the police didn't know why the construction worker had gone so far off his regular route, they thought his killing might have been the result of a robbery that had gone awry. He had been carrying around $600 to his ex-wife and daughter and his vehicle was later found stripped of valuables, the seat adjusted to suggest that whoever had driven it was much shorter than Mr Spears. A sexual motive was also considered, as a used condom was found among the beer cans by the corpse and a ripped packet in one of the foot wells. The pieces of the puzzle had only begun to be assembled when a call came through that another body had been found.

Charles Carskaddon left his mother's house to pick up his fiancée in Tampa. Things were looking good for Carskaddon, a 41-year-old former rodeo rider who had settled down to a new life of regular employment. Carskaddon also drove a Cadillac, a brown 1975 model which he had proudly restored himself. He picked up Lee somewhere out on the highway.

He was not a naïve man, carrying a .45 gun in the car in case of trouble, but its presence served only to infuriate Lee further. She shot him nine times – so many that she had to pause to reload. It later transpired that Carskaddon's gun was only for show: he had removed the firing pin.

The murders of the two men took place within five days. Money might have explained the first, but not the second. There was something new driving Lee. The first time she killed, the first time she watched another human being painfully gasp for air and reach the moment of death, Lee had experienced something wholly new. It was power, an absolute power through the knowledge that she was invulnerable at that moment and that the person who sought to cause her pain had ended up choking on his own blood.

She had probably replayed the scene of Mallory's murder in her mind as the days and weeks passed. Although she was agitated when she told Tyria what had happened, when no arrest took place, Lee would have returned time and time again to what she had done. She'd made him pay. Yet the thrill would not have stayed at the level of its original intensity. Why shouldn't she kill again? If 'they' messed with her, as Lee would later tell the police, 'it was pure hatred' and she was going to be the only one left standing. With the burst of adrenalin that hit in the moment of a kill, with the look of pure fear in the eyes of her victims, she had developed a taste for the rush.

'But like I say, it just happened that the last...this following year, that I kept meeting guys that were turning out to be ugly guys...to me,' she later told the police. 'That they were...fighting.' But the ugliness Lee had seen had been with her since childhood, the fighting she'd seen was her own flailing attempts to survive and now, psychologically, she had turned the tables.

Only two weeks from the day that she had dumped Carskaddon's naked body, covered with a green electric blanket, she was looking to kill again. And the killing of Peter Siems might never have been unearthed if it wasn't for the fact that Lee took a shine to his silver Pontiac Sunbird. Lee always used the vehicles of the men she murdered to transport their bodies before abandoning the car somewhere else, having disposed of the plates. But sometimes she'd hang on to the cars a little longer, to move to a new apartment or motel for example.

Peter Siems was a 65-year-old part-time preacher who would load his car with religious pamphlets to help him spread the word of the Lord. But at some point on 7 June 1990, he picked up an intoxicated Lee near the border with Georgia and it was the last time he was ever seen. Peter Siems' body has never been recovered and Lee claimed to be unable to recall where she dumped it. Tyria would later recall that immediately after killing Siems, and with a little extra cash in her pocket, Lee took her to Florida's Seaworld for a treat.

The Pontiac Sunbird was still with them a month later when it featured in another bizarre episode of the couple's life. Instead of lying low, Lee and Tyria decided to go on a drinking binge. Making their way home one afternoon, Tyria crashed the car off the road in full view of witnesses. The two women climbed out of the wreckage, had a blazing row about whose fault it was and, after rescuing their beer out of the back seat, started to make their way up the road. When a car came by, they ducked off the road and hid, all the while observed by another couple. Eventually they returned to the car and a bemused witness asked if they needed help. Their offer was turned down and after an aborted attempt to get the car started and with a plea that no one watching should call the police, they threw the registration plates of the car and its keys into the undergrowth.

Another driver stopped to ask the women if they needed help. Though both had superficial injuries, Lee met his request with a mouthful of abuse. The police later ran routine checks and realised that it was the car that belonged to the missing Peter Siems. Concern grew once bloodstains and smears were found on the fabric of the vehicle. Some attempt had been made by Lee to cover up what had happened three weeks earlier but alongside the junk found in the car were a number of receipts from gas stations along the highways that Lee used as her place of work. Police put together a composite picture of the two women and begin to piece together a rudimentary idea of their movements although they didn't take fingerprints. Lee was still not identified.

Eugene Burress was another man that perfectly suited Lee's emerging victim profile. He was 50 years old, a salesman who used the road routinely. Burgess was used to long trips: he would make deliveries for customers and could be on the road from dawn to dusk. When he failed to show up for his last scheduled stop one day, the customer called his head office. Alarm bells rang as it was out of character for him not to be in touch. If there had been a problem with his truck, his colleagues knew he would have called. His wife waited anxiously until 2am and then called the police, convinced that something serious had occurred.

The abandoned truck was quickly spotted because of the company logo on the side but it was another four days before a family looking for a picnic spot found its owner, about eight miles from the vehicle. Identification was hampered by decomposition and his wife had to confirm that she recognised his wedding band. The autopsy found two .22 bullets, one in the chest and a second in his back. Later Lee would again justify her actions on the grounds of sexual assault, or the threat of it. She did not deny that she shot him as he tried to flee the scene: she was beyond caring.

Christopher Berry-Dee is a criminologist and author who has spent many hours interviewing serious offenders. He interviewed Lee and wrote *Monster: My True Story* about her life and crimes. In it, he convincingly reconstructed what happened to Curtis Reid. He went missing on 6 September 1990, at the height of Lee's campaign of terror. His body has never been found and his car was discovered in a parking lot near one of the highways stalked by Lee. Much later, Reid's property would turn up in the possession of Tyria Moore. By that point, the police had all they needed to convict Lee, who denied ever coming across Mr Reid. It is likely that he was another victim and more were to follow.

It was on 9 September that Shirley Humphreys last saw her

husband alive. They had been married for 35 years, had raised three children and were hoping that Shirley's battle with cancer had been won. Charles Humphreys was a good husband who had always worked hard for his family, having served as a police chief in Alabama and then, at 56, using his experience to help protect at-risk and abused children. Shirley called the police at 8pm that evening. At 2.30am, she knew the knock at her door could only mean bad news yet she had no idea that she and her family were about to be catapulted into the heart of the one of the most notorious strings of murders in recent history.

Humphreys' Firenza car was found on 19 September some 70 miles from where he had been killed with seven bullets. Though the gun was confirmed to have been a .22, it was the car that provided officers with a link to Lee. Inside was a time-stamped receipt from a highway gas station where staff were able to provide a picture of Lee and Tyria. The pattern of homicides in which bodies were dumped away from their vehicles was established by law enforcement agents sharing intelligence across county lines. They realised they were looking for a sex-worker, possibly two, who were using highways to pick up men.

Lee approached Bobby Lee Copus at a truck stop to spin a plausible story about how she needed to get to Orlando to pick up her children from nursery. This may have been how she convinced other victims to give her a ride, not all were necessarily looking to pick up a hooker. Once inside, Lee soon switched from 'concerned mother' to openly propositioning Copus. Each time he turned her down, until she began to lose control. The truck driver managed to keep a cool head and gave her money to make a call about her children. As soon as she stepped outside, he locked the car and drove off. He watched a furious Lee gesticulating wildly as he drove away but probably would not have given the crazy hitchhiker much thought if the news hadn't broken all over the TV and press a few days later that another man, 60-year-old Walter Antonio, had been found shot dead. Copus reported his encounter to the police.

Antonio was found by an off-duty police officer, hidden in woodland, naked except for his socks. He'd been hit with four shots, the last to the head. Lee drove Antonio's car back to her motel and didn't dump it for a few days, by which time it had done almost a thousand miles. Police recognised the modus operandi – the plates kicked off the car, beer cans left inside, the body relocated and the vehicle and corpse stripped of valuables. But this was to be Lee's last murder. What remained of her life was about to fall apart and it was all down to Tyria.

Walter Antonio was killed on 17 November and Tyria went home to her family for Thanksgiving. The relationship rapidly disintegrated. Within a fortnight, Tyria had walked out and Lee began to unravel fast. She drank heavily, crashing out in a motel and was unable even to leave to raise the money she would need to avoid eviction. It was only a matter of time. The police were picking their way through Lee's life and her many aliases, tracking her career of petty crime over the years. It was while trawling through Lee's use of pawnshops that they hit pay dirt. Lee had left a thumbprint on a ticket used to pawn some of Richard Mallory's possessions. They found a match for a print on Peter Siem's car. They had a name: Aileen Carol Wuornos.

Christmas had come and gone and the police were closing in on Lee but needed to formulate a plan for her arrest. Early in the New Year of 1991, Lee was found in a bar in Daytona.

She had been drifting from motels to bars and sleeping rough, mostly drowning her sorrows over Tyria. Her favourite haunt was a biker bar, The Last Resort. Undercover officers Dick Martin and Mike Joyner spoke with Lee and even stood her a few drinks. While drinking, according to staff, she liked to listen to Randy Travis' 'Digging Up Bones'.

Lee was 34 but looked like a woman two decades older, washed up and ravaged by violent mood swings and alcohol abuse. Looking at the wasted, jittery, 5ft 4in woman, it was hard to believe that she had brought such fear and destruction to Florida. Keeping up their banter, Martin and Joyner persuaded Lee to leave the bar with them, where sheriff's investigator Larry Horzepa arrested Lee in connection with an outstanding warrant for illegal possession of a firearm. The murders weren't mentioned. The police were treading carefully, aware that any hasty moves could jeopardise the case.

The police caught up with Tyria the day after Lee's arrest on 9 January. She had moved in with her sister in Scranton, Pennsylvania, over a thousand miles away from Lee. Found with some items belonging to Lee's victims, Tyria was not in a great position but she improved it considerably when she agreed to co-operate with the police and testify against Lee. The police were right to guess that Tyria was Lee's Achilles heel and used her accordingly. They set up a series of calls – Lee even guessed that they were being taped and asked Tyria who she was with. But Tyria's rising hysteria that 'the cops were after her' proved too much for Lee and she assured Tyria that she would not let her lover down: 'I'm not going to let you get into trouble.'

Later, her assurance to Tyria was prescient: 'I would die for you…That's the truth. I'll gladly die for you.'

Believing that Tyria was going to be held for the murders, Lee chose to confess. Over the next few days, she gave the police a series of long and rambling monologues about Tyria's naïve nature and good character, continually stressing that her lover had no part to play in the murders. Lee was often vague on details, confused about sequence and even the number of men that died at her hands but she held on to her conviction that she acted in self-defence over the killing of Mallory.

On 28 January 1991, Aileen Carol Wuornos was indicted for the murder of Richard Mallory, her crimes igniting speculation across the US and much of the English-speaking world. By late February, she had also been charged with the murders of David Spears, Charles Humphreys and Eugene Burress, but it was the Mallory trial that would decide her fate.

On 27 January, the jury returned their verdict on the Mallory case after 91 minutes of deliberation. They found her guilty of premeditated felony murder in the first degree. Lee gave a violent outburst, telling the jury that she hoped they'd 'get raped'. The next day, Judge Uriel Blount sentenced her to death by electric chair and made the pronouncement: 'And may God have mercy on your corpse', an unfortunate departure from 'have mercy on your soul'. Perhaps Lee's verbal onslaught was still in his mind.

She repeated the performance when she was found guilty of three other murders. Lee changed from impassive listener to aggressive combatant, glaring at the court and spitting out: 'May your wife and kids get raped. Right in the ass.' There was now no control Lee could place on the anger that stemmed from her sense of victim-hood and desire that everyone else should taste what she had known. She was emotionally stunted, as one of her attorneys noted. Lee was 'a damaged, primitive child'. Psychiatrists who examined Lee assessed that she was legally sane at the time of the murders – she could appreciate the difference between right and wrong and understand the potential consequences of her actions. But all noted that hers was not a mind intact.

On death row, what was left of her capacity for thought deteriorated. Those involved in her case, including Tyria, sold the rights to their stories to movie producers. Lee herself claimed that she wanted to die and was infuriated when the State dragged its feet over her execution. David Damore, a prosecutor at her original trial, gave this insight: 'She's a ravaged soul who needs to be put out of her misery – wants to be put out of her misery.'

In an attempt to move things along, Lee changed her story and stated that she had never acted in self-defence but had selected men to rob and kill. Documentary film-maker Nick Broomfield asked Lee why she gave her original statements and she said: 'I was just doing the lying biz. It was just my lying gig, to try and beat the system.' Lee was playing a game she could never win. Now that Tyria had abandoned her, she wanted to die. She thought that by retracting her original statement that she had acted in self-defence, justice would speed up and she would be executed. The odds were always stacked against Lee. As the months and years dragged by, Lee would feel that the system that had failed her in life, had even failed in death.

There will always be people who believe that Aileen Wuornos was no more that a lying and cold-hearted serial killer. It is likely that they will also have sympathy with Volusia County Sheriff's Bob Kelley, one of the investigators, when he said: 'The pattern indicated she wasn't going to stop.' His assumption was probably correct. By the time of her arrest, Lee had lost all control over her impulses and could have easily killed again.

As it was, she was lost in delusion, believing her food was poisoned, that sonic rays were being beamed into her room to crush her head, that her room was rigged with devices to drive her crazy and that the police always wanted her to be a killer, to build up a story they could then sell. There were moments when Lee imagined how her life could have been if she had not grown up as she had. She said that when she was a child, she wanted to be an archaeologist, that she could have been 'an outstanding citizen for America'. Now all that was outstanding was the murders she was responsible for and the money that was being made as the Wuornos industry grew.

What sealed Lee's fate was beyond her control; Florida Governor Jeb Bush, campaigning for re-election on a strong law and order platform, signed her death warrant on 5 September 2002. At 5.30am on the morning of 9 October, Lee – having turned down her last meal – opted only for a cup of coffee. She was to face lethal injection. Strapped to a white gurney, Lee made no protest as she was wheeled into the death chamber, paramedics inserted needles and catheters into her arms and strapped a cardiac monitor to her chest. She made a statement that she'd be sailing to the Rock – Jesus – and that she'd return with him, 'Like *Independence Day* with Jesus, 6 June, like the movie, big mothership and all.'

The next injection would have made her feel light-headed. Then 15cc of saline was injected to ease the passage of 50cc of pancuronium bromide, which paralyses respiration. She gasped for air and coughed twice as her lungs collapsed.

Unable to move or breathe, she would have still been able to see and hear as the next dose of saline forged the way for the fatal dose of potassium chloride which burned through her until it reached her heart and stopped it dead. At 9.47am, the pronouncement of her death was greeted by silence from some and cheers from others who'd gathered at the walls of the Union Correctional Institution.

Lee arrived in the world an innocent but left knowing that she was hated and despised. Vitriol drove her to the end and she readily spoke about being filled with hate. No matter what a human being endures, they still have a moment when they choose whether or not to pull a trigger, when they choose to inflict misery and pain or not and Lee made her choice. She blamed everyone for her crimes but herself.

In the days before she died, she gave a hate-filled statement which it is impossible to read without thinking of a four-year old girl abandoned to a life of abuse. It is hard not to register that hers was a life destroyed before it began and that she had a mind which could not distinguish between those who had mistreated her and those who had not: 'You sabotaged my ass society...I've got a finger in all your faces, thanks a lot. You are inhuman. An inhumane bunch of fucking living bastards and bitches and you are going to get your asses nuked in the end and pretty soon it's coming.'

8

SARA ALDRETE
THE HIGH PRIESTESS

'I know what's going to happen to you. I can know everything
about you. It's all right here.'

ADOLFO CONSTANZO READING SARA'S TAROT CARDS

Two worlds are separated by a wide and lazy brown river,
the Rio Grande. On one side lies the Texan town of
Brownsville, on the other, Matamoros, a Mexican resort. But
law officials on both sides know that the border is an
illusion, the river is crossed legally and illegally every day
and the two worlds are one when it comes to drug-running,
smuggling and even murder. Work in law enforcement
agencies for long enough and nothing will surprise you. At
least, that is what Sheriff's Detective Ernesto Flores thought,
until a call came through one April morning.

It was 1989 and it had been a bad start to the year. US law
officials along border towns have regular dealings with their
Mexican counterparts, as both attempted to make an impact
in the 'war on drugs'. In reality, the war was floundering in
a complex net of corruption stretching for miles either side
of the border. There were any number of reports of *federales*

– the local name for the Mexican federal police – busting drug gangs only to sell the product themselves. Some officers were on drug-lord payrolls, providing drug runners with police badges to ease their way. There were always even a few who would quit in order to work full time with the gangs.

The temptations are hard to resist. Police officers work for a pittance and kickbacks keep their families together. It would take a good deal of courage and a high degree of risk for any officer to make a stand against colleagues he suspected of corruption. But it would be wrong to suggest that there aren't good officers working to make a difference – men such as Comandante Juan Benitez Ayala. He'd been brought in to Matamoros to arrest his predecessor, Comandate Perez, who'd made a fortune from the drugs trade and had recently absconded.

Although Perez had not been tracked down, Comandante Benitez had scored a number of other successes in the space of just a few months, more than his department had in over two years, and US officials were encouraged. But when Flores, a US law enforcer from across the border in Cameron County, was called by his superior and told to be at Benitez's office at seven the next morning, he sensed that there was more than a drugs bust underway. He was right.

All officers, on both sides of the divide, had been through a tough few weeks. A 21-year-old American premed student, Mark Kilroy, had gone missing and the US media was in uproar. The talented and good-looking student had been enjoying a holiday with friends and he'd disappeared one evening. His distraught parents and friends handed out flyers and gave interviews begging for information. Commercial leaders in Matamoros were agitating for the investigation to be resolved as the resort relied heavily on the flow of US tourist dollars. Talk of abduction and fears that Mark had been murdered was bad for business.

Scores of people go missing every year along border towns but Mark Kilroy had an uncle who was a customs supervisor in Los Angeles. That made him one of the police's own. The huge manhunt had pulled in hundreds of leads but they'd all led nowhere. It was frustrating but everything that could be done was in place. The case needed a lucky break and in the meantime, there were a great deal of other pressing matters competing for police time.

When Detective Flores reached Comandante Benitez's headquarters, he found two other Americans had arrived. They were customs officials, and together they watched preparations for the raid with a growing sense of concern. There was a Mexican SWAT team, in itself not unusual, but the atmosphere in the office certainly was. Tension was running high. Flores saw fear in the eyes of men who were ordinarily laid-back even if they expected armed resistance. Machismo and gun culture meant the Mexicans were usually relaxed around firearms but Flores found he could not even get the agents to reply to simple questions. They avoided making eye contact and filed out into the car park. Once outside, all eyes turned to watch Eluterio join them. He was a *curandero*, a healer. Eluterio climbed into the waiting police truck with a more specific task in mind: he was on his way to an exorcism.

The Americans regularly encountered superstition over the border. It was part of the landscape. They might be sceptical but they knew to keep their thoughts to themselves when they saw the good-luck charms and amulets worn by Mexican officers. They also accepted that in Mexico deeply-held beliefs

217

in Catholicism could go hand in hand with wariness surrounding darker, primeval religious forces. The drugs trade was savage and it was not unheard of for drug lords to buy the services of *brujos* – witches – to ensure good luck or to bring curses down onto their enemies. Some of those enemies would inevitably include police officers, and a *curandero* could be called in to perform a 'cleansing'. It is easy to laugh at a fear of the supernatural but by the end of that cold April day, Detective Flores would find it difficult to even raise a smile.

A handcuffed young man was pushed towards the waiting cars. As Flores watched the way he was smacked around the head, it was clear that the *federales* were in no mood for any show of resistance. He looked at the nondescript face of 'Little' Serafin – so-called to distinguish him from his father who was also named Serafin – with his classic Mexican moustache. He wondered what he'd done to inspire such loathing. It was a 20-minute drive out into the dusty and bleak countryside before the vehicles began to pull over and onto a track that would lead to Rancho Santa Elena, a run-down property with several shabby outbuildings.

The ranch was deserted, hidden from other farms that dotted the river, and it looked unremarkable. Standing with a machine gun, ready to fire, Flores was still at a loss as to what was going on until the chilly breeze changed direction. The smell that immediately hit him was unmistakable: it was the reek of rotting flesh. The handcuffs were taken off Little Serafin and he was pushed towards a small boarded-up shack. The door was pulled open and everyone fell back from the overpowering stench that rolled out.

Little Serafin was shoved in and when the eyes of the agents adjusted to the darkness, they saw the dank room was lit by two candles standing on the floor. The floor itself was caked with congealed blood, some of which came from black kettles filled with various animal remains. There was the head of a goat, a decomposing turtle and a headless rooster. Above them were two long wires with loops big enough for human wrists.

Little Serafin pointed to the restraints and said that was where human sacrifices were hung so their blood could be drained properly. But all eyes had moved to a large cauldron with sticks rising up from it. Little Serafin spoke again: 'That is Adolfo's *nganga* [a potion-filled cauldron]. This is where the spirits live. This is where Mark's brain is.'

Flores understood now why he was there and why the *federales* were happy to switch off the recording equipment they'd brought with them. They began to beat the nonchalant Little Serafin. The Mexican officials were very unnerved and clearly fearful of the evil spirits summoned to the isolated ranch, even though they were uncertain what the spirits were. They all looked not to Comandante Benitez but to Eluterio for guidance. The US officials didn't fear the supernatural but they were silenced by the sickening realisation that it was likely that Mark Kilroy had been murdered and dismembered in this bleak outhouse.

Eluterio ordered that the cauldron be dragged out in to the open. There was no thought given to the preservation of evidence. The desire to banish evil dominated all other concerns. The officials started to film again and Little Serafin was given the task of hauling the heavy cauldron out of the shack, retching as he did so, the black matter slopping against his shoes. Eluterio fired his gun into the sky as a warning that he was intent on expelling whatever evil possessed this place. The agents would not approach the *nganga* but even at a distance it was clear that a skull, with clumps of hair still attached, floated on the surface.

Eluterio ran into the shack and began to douse it with holy water. He smashed up whatever else remained and when he emerged to say that white magic rendered the space safe, the agents began to visibly relax. The Americans watched in silence. This was beyond anything they had experienced before and they sensed that this was only the beginning of what would turn up at Rancho Santa Elena. They wanted to know where the rest of Mark's remains could be found and Little Serafin began to walk. He assured them it would be easy enough to locate the remains. A wire had been threaded around Mark's spine. His body could be pulled up once it had decomposed sufficiently and the spine used for magical rituals.

Seeing the jagged wire sticking up from a mound of earth, the agents were right to expect the worst. Mark's body had been dismembered. His legs had been savagely severed at the knee and ankle, he'd been decapitated and his spinal column hacked out. It would later emerge that to feed the *nganga* of the man called Adolfo, the student was made to suffer horrifically. He was sodomised by Adolfo, who believed his power increased with his victim's torment. The agents would learn this and a good deal more about Adolfo and his followers over the next few weeks.

There were other mounds of earth near the makeshift grave of Mark Kilroy. More were buried. By the end of that day, Mark Kilroy would become one of 12 mutilated bodies unearthed by police officers.

The story was to become an international sensation. The Mexican press dubbed Adolfo's cult *narcosatánicos* – invoking as they did both Satan and drug-running. It emerged that Adolfo was a devotee of two strands of religious belief that originated in Africa but evolved as slaves were brought from that continent to the Americas. The first strand originated in Nigeria, where the Yoruba worshipped deities called Orishas. Each god possessed different powers and were asked to intervene in human affairs or appeased by offering sacrifices. Typically, this took the form of the blood of animals such as chickens or goats.

With the arrival of and imposition of Christianity, the Yoruba simply adapted their gods to the images they were now forced to worship. For example, Eleggua was an impish trickster god who became Christ as a child. There was a statue of Eleggua near the cauldron in the shack.

The religion grew to be known as Santería – 'the path of the saints' – as Catholic saints hid the true identity of these ancient gods. Santería is thought to have as many as one hundred million devotees throughout Latin America and, on the whole, is a benign faith, focusing on spells of protection and health.

The other strand of faith that Adolfo was immersed in has a more chequered reputation. Palo Mayombe has its roots in the Congo and that is where the *nganga* originates. Inside the *nganga* is the spirit of the dead that can be called on to act on behalf of the living. Palo simply means sticks and 28 sticks are required to be inserted into the *nganga*. Its followers are widespread but many are in Haiti where another faith system, Voodoo, shares many similarities.

Inevitably, these faiths travelled with the émigrés that arrived in the US, first and foremost to the closest port of arrival from Cuba, Haiti, the Dominican Republic and Miami. It was in Miami that Adolfo de Jesus Constanzo was born and grew up.

By the time Adolfo reached manhood, he shared the profile of many other dangerous serial killers. He was intent on creating a following. Fashioning himself as a father – el padrino – of his cult, he wanted a high priestess to share his vision and his spoils. Like that of fellow cult leaders Charles Manson, David Koresh or Jim Jones, Adolfo's was one of those messianic personalities which occasionally emerge and are skilful enough to manipulate and exert control over others. Few of their followers are aware that the path they are set on will not lead to spiritual enlightenment but to death and destruction.

From the outside, it seems implausible that any sane member of society could fall under the spell of these dangerous and deluded men, but many do. Maureen Griffo was a member of a cult , the Church of Bible Understanding, for ten years. She recognised that people find it difficult to imagine who would be gullible enough to be sucked in by a fanatical personality and has a stark warning: 'Who joins cults? They are anyone you could meet anywhere. I was a teen living in a small town when I was recruited... I was not a drug addict or a prostitute, but rather I had been a good student in school who worked two jobs.' It could almost be a pen portrait of Sara Aldrete.

Sara was born in 1964 to an ordinary and hard-working family in Matamoros, a couple of years before the arrival of her sister Teresa. Her father was an electrician and he held great hopes for his two daughters. Sara was schooled across the bridge in Brownsville and after graduating from high school, studied at Texas Southmost College. Looking at Sara back in 1987, you'd first be struck by her height. She was unusually tall at 6ft 1in, but beyond that, she seemed like a typical American student. She was bright and also excelled at sport and was talking about transferring to another Brownsville campus to work towards a teaching degree.

Sara was sociable and well-liked and had held down jobs

in part-time admin at the College to help support her studies. If pushed, college friends might say that Sara had been upset that at such a young age she had a failed marriage behind her, not something to be proud of as her family were conservative Catholics. There was also something else about Sara. She had a need to make herself centre stage to every story and would tell casual lies if it suited her to do so. There was a narcissistic fault line that ran though her character yet, in the main, people felt that Sara's future was promising. And that she could go on to achieve whatever she set her mind to.

Whatever Sara felt about her brief marriage isn't known. She hinted that her husband had physically mistreated her but she soon began dating once they broke up and was enjoying student life. Her one irritation was how small the worlds of Matamoros and Brownsville seemed. They were small towns with little ambition and even though Brownsville is American, it wasn't immune from the poverty found over the border and one-in-four families lived below the poverty line. Education was one way to ensure a better future but carving out a living in the town hardly filled Sara with enthusiasm. There had to be more to life than that and, like a lot of young adults, Sara sought something more. But she would have had little idea that her future lay in the hands of a driver who pulled his big silver Lincoln up in front of her car one July afternoon in 1987.

He had been signalling for her to stop but Sara had ignored him, so the driver pulled a dangerous stunt, first overtaking her and then executing a U-turn. It created a potential head-on collision that Sara only avoided by slamming on her brakes. No wallflower, Sara jumped from her car and demanded to know what the hell he thought he was doing. Traffic was backing up behind her, the Lincoln having blocked the road, and over the next few minutes Sara's life would change forever.

Adolfo emerged from the car, a vision in expensive white linen. He always wore white. Not as tall as Sara, he still managed to be an imposing figure, well-groomed, good-looking and entirely self-contained. Sara yelled at him but she was quickly unsettled by the man's calm manner, steady gaze and the way he quietly told her: 'I just wanted to talk to you.' He was hypnotic, no matter what she said, no matter the increased blares from the backed-up traffic, the man was intent on one thing alone: talking to Sara. There was something compelling about him. She found that her anger vanished and agreed that if he'd move his car, she would talk to him.

They sat in his car and Adolfo took control of the conversation, telling her that he was a lawyer from Miami, his family, originally from Cuba, were wealthy and influential and that he was there on a two-week break. Sara had noted the car plates were from Florida and there was little doubt that he was successful. Everything from the top-of-the-range car to the designer clothes he wore spoke of effortless wealth. He then hinted that he had clients that were Columbian. Sara was no fool and knew what this meant. The key trade with Columbians was cocaine and there on the border, you'd be hard pushed not to know someone who had a peripheral role in the drugs trade. She had grown up with people who had scored occasional and easy money that way and that included her boyfriend Gilberto. It wasn't for her, but like a lot of young adults living on both sides of the divide, she felt ambivalent about drugs.

'Let's get something to eat,' Adolfo said and Sara agreed. Sara knew that Adolfo was different from the men she grew up around but she also learned of other telltale signs that should have made her feel uneasy about the smooth Miami lawyer. He introduced her to Martin, a handsome and muscular man who was his partner in 'the clothes business'. Sara queried this, saying she thought he was a lawyer. He dismissed her with an assurance that he was involved in many businesses.

She noticed a beaded necklace that Adolfo talked about cryptically as part of his 'religion', something he would tell her about 'another time'. When Sara spent a while talking to Martin about sport, she also noted that Adolfo became agitated. He clearly needed the focus of her attention to be on him. It wasn't an attractive characteristic but it appealed to Sara's vanity: the man clearly wanted her. He asked to see her the next day and the incentive he provided was that he would tell her more about his religion.

She agreed and in fact spent part of every day over the next two weeks with him. The student was captivated. Adolfo strung her along, hinting that they were meant for each other. She was sexually attracted to him yet he made no move on her. He also lured her by talking about his ability to see the future through his reading of Tarot cards and saying that she was not ready for all he could disclose. He pulled stunts, too. Clearly not impressed with the presence of Gilberto in Sara's life he staged an outburst, warning Sara that her boyfriend was not good for her.

He also told Sara that he was a cop working undercover and as he did so he held her hand, staring deeply into her eyes – it would seem that no one but Adolfo was meant for her. She was being reeled in. The final ploy was a reading of Sara's cards where Adolfo made three predictions: that she would get college funding, that an old friend would call and finally, that another friend would call with a problem that only she could help with. Within a couple of days, the first two came true and Sara felt sure that Adolfo's powers were real. The third would take a little longer.

This last prediction was key. It would unlock Sara's devotion and it would lead Elio Hernandez into Adolfo's trap too. Elio was an old boyfriend of Sara's and he'd never recovered from the fact that she ended their brief relationship. He was part of a mid-level drug dealing family in Matamoros that had hit on a disastrous run of bad luck. Comandante Benitez had orchestrated the destruction of their marijuana crops and one of Elio's uncles had been arrested in the US after a tip-off. The real blow to the Hernandez family however was the death of one of the older brothers, Saul. He was the smart one in the family and he had slowly accrued wealth and connections for his clan until he got in the way of a bullet meant for someone else who was involved in a drugs feud. The family was now floundering badly, lacking strategic direction. Instead of examining how best to protect their business, they believed that they were cursed.

Adolfo knew all about the troubles the Hernandez clan faced and he was waiting for the opportunity to step in and take control. Whatever his belief in his 'religion' his desire to make money equalled it. He told Sara he was a witch and that he made his money through the accuracy of his predictions. There was some truth in this. Adolfo had quickly built a reputation in Mexico City since he had relocated from Miami three years earlier. He built a following amongst singers, actors, businessmen and drug dealers, eventually charging thousands of dollars for consultations.

But the accuracy of his card readings had little to do with magic. Adolfo was an excellent cold reader. Like any expert salesman, he was skilled at picking up on the verbal and nonverbal signals people gave out and could thread them into readings. People who seek predictions have a certain level of suggestibility too: predictions can come true if they are designed to be sufficiently open-ended. Plus, Adolfo relied on more than guesswork. He simply used research. In Sara's case, he used Salvador, a corrupt cop on his payroll, to find out all he could about her background and college life. A few checks gave Adolfo all the information he needed to make his predictions, such as notification of college funding, come true. Sara was hooked, as would be Elio and the Hernandez clan – with horrific results.

Adolfo had begun to reveal the secrets of his religion, Santería. He was also lavishing praise and expensive gifts on Sara and told her that she could become a powerful spiritual leader alongside him. He performed ceremonies and announced that she would be *la madrina*, the mother and high priestess of his faith. He built her an altar and introduced her to animal sacrifices. He pointed out that she killed and ate chicken but his beasts were serving a higher spiritual purpose. He told her that a call would come and that it would be Elio and that she was to tell him: 'I know a witch with great powers you should meet.'

As it was, Elio did not call. He met Sara on the street and they talked for a while, the depressed Elio hinting that all was not well in his world. Sara said he knew just the man he should meet.

With her altar and her brand new car, Sara was exhilarated by her new life. She still appeared at college and her admin job but had become an expert liar when asked about Adolfo, her expensive goods and a number of bizarre injuries, the results of ecstatic Santería ceremonies in which Sara would be possessed and fall into violent rapture. The only cloud on her horizon was Adolfo's waning sexual interest in her. Later, Sara would deny they were lovers but other members of the cult dismissed this, knowing that part of Adolfo's induction was sexual.

The truth of Adolfo's sexuality emerged when Sara turned up unexpectedly at his apartment. She found Martin and Adolfo together, they were lovers, and the charismatic leader also kept another man he'd recruited in Mexico City, Omar. Adolfo liked to aggressively dominate other men and the police would eventually find a hoard of violent gay pornography in one of Adolfo's abandoned apartments. Sara still maintained that Adolfo was obsessed by her but the infatuation seemed to be hers alone. A note from her read: 'I long to have your arms around me and feel your body against mine. I know you don't feel like I do, which is why I don't have the courage to sign this. But I just love you more than words can say.' Sara would later deny writing it, but by then, Sara had much to deny.

By late 1987, Sara was devoted to Adolfo and Santería and was happy for Adolfo to introduce her to his business contacts as his wife. They took trips to Houston and San Antonio and she regularly enjoyed the thousands of dollars she could spend on shopping sprees. When he wasn't with her, they would speak constantly on the telephone and she was happy to do his bidding, grooming Elio with tales of Adolfo's powers.

There was no doubt that Adolfo did have power – but it was of a very physical kind. Adolfo's hands were already bathed in human blood following a failed attempt to take centre stage with a drugs family called the Calzadas. He had used his magic to ensure good luck for Guillermo Calzada's drug deals but made the mistake of trying to muscle in on 50 per cent of their takings. Calzada was a hardened criminal and, flanked by his own bodyguard, he mocked and humiliated Adolfo. It seemed his charisma counted for nothing and it was a slight Adolfo could not shake off.

On 30 April 1987, Adolfo offered a free cleansing ceremony to patch up their differences and he lured Calzada and six other members of his family and staff, including his wife and mother, into their living room. But instead of a blessing, Adolfo drew a knife and two of his followers crashed through the door emptying bullets into the Calzadas. The bodies were not found until 7 May, when they washed up onto a river bank. All had been shot, mutilated and tortured, ears and fingers sliced off, the men castrated, their chests hacked open and hearts removed. One had a $20 bill rolled up and inserted into one of his finger cavities. The Mexican police knew that black magic had a part to play and blamed the spiralling carnage of the drugs trade.

Adolfo's plans to take an equal role in a drug family had not worked out with the Calzadas and now he wanted more. He wanted to control, he wanted a following. Within two months, Adolfo had engineered his meeting with Sara to put into action his plan to take command of the Hernandez family. They would prove much easier to manipulate. But the killing of the Calzadas had uncovered more than a lust for power. He had enjoyed the slaughter. It fed a desire in him and he knew that his followers would need to bring him more victims to feed his *nganga*. This was just the start.

On 23 March 1988, Sara left Matamoros and headed to Mexico City to be with Adolfo. She was leaving her old life behind. She'd known Adolfo for only eight months but it was all that was needed to persuade her that she would take centre stage in his religious following. She would be *la madrina* and caretaker of the *nganga*. Installed into Adolfo's luxury apartment, Adolfo instructed her to forsake her Catholic faith and to accept that her soul would die. For Adolfo it was simple: having no soul meant total freedom to act as he desired. Sara accepted.

She removed her clothes and stepped into a pair of white linen trousers and a white linen blouse so the ritual could begin. Omar led her by the hand to a door and she was blindfolded. She was led into a darkened room that was thick with cigar smoke and the stench of *aguardiente*, a particularly potent rum that can even cause brain damage in hardened drinkers. She was forced to drink, gagging on the liquid as it was held to her lips. Adolfo was chanting in Bantu, summoning the dead. His voice was distorted, possessed even.

She felt the feathers of a struggling bird brush up and down her body. It was decapitated and she felt the spurt of hot blood in her face. Then a goat was held behind her and slaughtered so her body was bathed in the animal's pumping blood. She enjoyed its warmth and the heady sense of power flowing into her. She felt her blouse torn from her and the feel of cold steel as Adolfo cut her shoulders to create ritualistic symbols.

'You are one of us now,' Adolfo said. 'Now you have the power.'

'I know,' Sara calmly replied.

She would not disappoint him. Her first task was to return to Matamoros and guide Elio, who had to report to her, his *madrina*. Elio had been initiated too and it was not long before other recruits were found. Like Elio, in the main these men were highly superstitious and easily swayed by Adolfo's predictions of good fortune. Working behind the scenes with

Salvador, the gang soon started to score major drug deals and the money started rolling in.

Adolfo was greedy and thought nothing of ritually killing rival drug dealers, opting to kill rather than pay for drug consignments. There can be little doubt that Sara knew of the bloodthirsty nature of Adolfo's business deals. Other cult members gave sworn statements of the central role she played in the group's psyche. She was their High Priestess.

She certainly profited from the group's criminal dealings and continued to orchestrate ceremonies and rituals to maintain their good fortune. It would have been likely that the gang would have continued with its dealings for years had it not been for Adolfo's insatiable need to feed his *nganga*. Traditionally, the skull needed to drive the power of the *nganga* had been secured by digging up a grave but Adolfo had gone far beyond traditional Palo Mayombe. He was a serial killer, intent on creating suffering in others to feed his own need for power. And the fate of La Claudia proved that.

La Claudia was the stage name of a drag artist called Ramon Paz Esquivel. He was a former lover and now a tenant of one of Adolfo's earliest recruits, an aging fortune-teller called Jorge Montes. Although Montes did not have a direct role in the drug dealing of the Hernandez clan, he did a lot to secure Adolfo's early reputation as a witch of great power and secured him his early celebrity contacts in Mexico City. Montes and La Claudia fell out badly but the transvestite refused to move out. In a fit of pique, Montes turned to Adolfo. What followed staggered even Mexico City's hardened police officers.

La Claudia was forced into the bathtub of the apartment that belonged to Montes. He was castrated, his fingers and toes were chopped off, his throat was cut and his skin peeled away from his face. His blood was drained and his brain and a shinbone taken away. His savaged remains were put into three bin bags, that a group of children found later the next day, dumped in a parking lot. Although sickened by what they found, police officers had no idea that this would be just one of several victims linked to Adolfo and his cult.

Most of the slaughter happened at the ranch outside Matamoros. Adolfo convinced his following that the sacrifices were made to ensure good luck for their drug deals and to aid their growing power, and with each death the cult members were also pulled tighter into Adolfo's world. They were all guilty and they were all growing accustomed to the process.

Sara maintains that she was not present at any of the human sacrifices but it would be difficult to believe that she was unaware of what was happening around her. After one savage rape, mutilation and murder of an unnamed hitchhiker, the gang retired to Sara's house for a cleansing ceremony. The High Priestess looked on and then joined them in a night of celebration. At other times, Adolfo would hold ceremonies at Sara's altar and demand sacrifices. But the most damning of evidence came with the death of Victor Sauceda, a former cop turned drug-lord enforcer.

Victor's background provides an insight into the muddied world of Mexican law enforcement. Victor had become known to US detective Flores over an investigation into a paedophile who drove over the border to prey on Mexican street children. Flores needed to trace a witness, a young street boy, but had got nowhere after months of extensive enquires. Victor's drug boss heard of the search and sent Victor to help Flores. Using his police skills and street knowledge, he found the boy in no time and brought him to Flores. The detective was impressed by the man's professionalism.

Early in April 1989 however, Victor was on a different mission. In his role as drug-lord enforcer he was looking for El Duby, one of Adolfo's key henchmen and El Duby begged his boss for help. Victor was brought to the Rancho Santa Elena. Little Serafin later told police that Sara was present and even stroked the cheek of the bound and gagged Victor through the car window once they pulled up at the ranch. Little Serafin also stated that Adolfo insisted that she stayed whilst the ritual killing took place. Victor's was one of the bodies later recovered at the ranch.

Adolfo's bloody reign suffered its first setback with the murder of a Mexican drug dealer who had tried to muscle into selling drugs in a tourist bar. He was dragged to the ranch but something exceptional happened. He didn't scream. No matter how brutal Adolfo's treatment, even with his ear sliced away from his skull, the drug dealer would not give Adolfo the satisfaction of seeing him submit and scream out. The cult members later said that after the man's death, Adolfo hit a crisis. He needed to see the agony and pleading in the eyes of his victims, he needed to hear their muffled screams of animal pain. But he heard nothing and, as he stood over the corpse, he made the fatal demand that the gang bring him someone soft, someone who would scream – 'a young American'. And so Mark Kilroy's fate was sealed.

With the disappearance of a US citizen, law officers were on high alert but after running down all leads, they knew they needed a stroke of luck. When it came, months later, it was as a result of Little Serafin's gullibility. As the number of sacrifices to Adolfo's *nganga* grew, Sara had assured him that their individual powers had grown too. It seemed to be true.

The police did not interfere with the Hernandez gang and Little Serafin was foolish enough to believe that he was actually invisible under the gaze of the *federales*. What was meant as a metaphor, Little Serafin took to heart and on 1 April 1989, he drove straight through a police checkpoint. The officers were stunned but two quietly followed him in an unmarked car. He drove to Rancho Santa Elena.

After Little Serafin left, they entered the grounds pretending to be lost and met the caretaker, a man called Domingo. They made a few enquiries of him and it was clear that he was not at ease. A preliminary search was organised and it was obvious from the guns found and traces of narcotics that the ranch was part of a drugs setup. It was this operation that also uncovered various black magic icons. They arrested Little Serafin, Elio and two other cult members, plus Domingo, but it was only during the following hours of interrogation that Comandante Benitez realised that it was no ordinary drug gang.

The cult members laughed at the officers: they were still convinced that they had special powers. It was Domingo, who was not an initiate, who revealed that he had felt sorry for the young man he saw there and had even fed him breakfast the morning before his death. The young man had spoken quietly and imploringly to Domingo but the caretaker didn't have a word of English. Benitez wanted to know what the young man looked like. Domingo confirmed he was blond and he nodded again when the police chief showed him a graduation picture of Mark Kilroy. It was then that Detective Flores received his call to attend the raid of 11 April.

The extent of Sara's involvement became clear as the interrogation proceeded. Little Serafin told police that he called *la madrina* after the abduction to tell her that they had done as they were asked. *La madrina* said that was fine and that they should all be at the ranch the next day for the ceremony. As details of the other cult members emerged, it was Sara who puzzled the officers the most. Ignorant drug runners they could understand but why would a young educated woman ever be involved in something so horrific?

Adolfo got wind of the arrests through one of the worried Hernandez family members. He immediately called Sara and arranged to meet her on the US side of the bridge. It was El Duby who picked her up and drove her to Adolfo and Martin at a Holiday Inn. Sara then made plane reservations for her and three others for the next day, 10 April. They planned to fly to Mexico City and then Miami. It was only en route to the airport that it dawned on Sara she did not have the visa and passport she needed to travel beyond the border area. They had to leave her at the bridge and she promised to follow them to Mexico City. If ever there was a time for Sara to turn herself in, it was then. The story had broken and it was huge on both sides of the border. There was no chance they would be able to get through the airport undetected, much less leave the country. But Sara joined them as she said she would. Later she would claim that she was forced to go but that seems unlikely as she travelled there independently. She also suggested that she only headed there for a holiday but the police pointed out that as she didn't even travel with a suitcase, it was just another attempt to talk her way out of her guilt.

On 13 April, yet another body was unearthed at the ranch. What distressed officers even more was the discovery of children's clothes and a small pair of shoes. But the investigation was hampered by a lack of cooperation between the various agencies and by a number of mistakes. One cult member known as El Gato was allowed to walk out of the grounds of one of Adolfo's apartment buildings saying he was just a student calling on a friend. In fact, it was El Gato who drove Mark Kilroy to the ranch. The media was running on overdrive, camera crews had shown up from around the globe speculating on what else would emerge.

The police arrived at the home of Sara's parents. They were devastated to realise that their daughter was part of a cult. The officers broke into the annexe and found one of Sara's altars, caked in blood.

By then the cult was on the run and reduced to its core members: Adolfo, Omar, Martin, El Duby and Sara. They all made attempts to alter their appearance. They stayed with a former cult member known as Karla and pressured her into finding a plastic surgeon. Adolfo watched TV and saw his ranch in flames and his *nganga* destroyed and he became increasingly hysterical. The gang drifted from chalet to chalet in resorts peppered around Mexico City, waiting for the police presence to die down enough to let them flee to the airport or for a surgeon to begin their transformation. Neither would happen.

Sara left the last apartment they stayed in, Rio Sena, to talk to a surgeon who turned her away. Once again, it was an opportunity to leave the gang, the others were trapped in their apartment and living from hour to hour, but Sara returned to Adolfo. She may have been infatuated but she wasn't stupid and knew that it was only a matter of time before they would be caught. Her 'religious' convictions didn't stand in the way of her self-interest. Sara wrote a note claiming she was held hostage and dropped it out of the apartment window. She felt this would be what she needed once the inevitable arrests came, proof that she was an innocent captive of Adolfo's gang.

The end when it came was as dramatic as any film script. With the net closing in, an officer was looking at an abandoned car outside the gang's fourth-floor apartment when Adolfo screamed: 'Mother, this is it!' and opened fire with the machine gun he had been nursing for the last two weeks. The officer was hit but managed to crawl behind the vehicle and fellow officers radioed for armed support.

The scene was one of utter chaos, Adolfo and El Duby fired from the apartment windows and Omar hid under the bed, Sara crouched in a corner. The gang were running out of bullets and after a failed attempt to explode a propane tank, Adolfo ordered El Duby to kill him and his followers and then turn the gun on himself. Omar decided not to die as did Sara. El Duby shot Martin and Adolfo but chose not to kill himself. Omar remained under the bed and Sara took her chance to run out to the police asking them not to shoot. 'Thank God. I'm saved,' she shouted, throwing herself into the arms of one of the officials.

At first the police were confused. Could Sara have been held captive and was this the notorious gang they'd been tracking down? During the questioning that followed, they were astonished by how much detail a 'captive' was able to furnish about the drug deals and the murders. The more she talked, the less she could avoid her natural instinct to place herself centre stage. She described the ritual killings with chilling clarity, even that of the man that was once her boyfriend – Gilberto. Throughout, she maintained that Adolfo was obsessed with her. When quizzed as to how she knew so much about the killings, Sara back-pedalled and said it was only because Adolfo told her everything.

One of the men present was Prosecutor Frederico Ponce. He dismissed Sara's efforts to claim that she was a captive by saying: 'If she wanted to escape she could have – because she was never a prisoner, except of her own crimes.'

Sara may not have been honest about her role in the many crimes that took place while she was *la madrina* but she did reveal a good deal more about Adolfo Constanzo's life. Holed up in various hideouts, the delusional Adolfo talked about his background as he never had before.

His introduction to Palo Mayombe and Santería came from his mother, Dina, in Miami. She was notorious in the many neighbourhoods for practising witchcraft and fouling everywhere they lived with animal corpses. Landlords would fight for her eviction and the scene of utter squalor she would leave was staggering. She would smear the walls with faeces and smash up every working item in the home. A deeply disturbed woman, she kept Adolfo isolated from other children and when he was bullied, taught him to create curses. She would scrawl the name of the child on a piece of paper and stuff it into the neck cavity of a decapitated chicken. Dina had a number of lovers and at least one beat Adolfo severely. She also introduced the boy to a Haitian witch, a man she believed would initiate her son into Palo Mayombe. The elderly Haitian did tutor Adolfo but he also repeatedly sexually abused him.

It was not surprising that Adolfo grew into a profoundly damaged man, determined to seize power and demonstrate it thorough the control and abuse of others. At Mark Kilroy's funeral service, his mother Helen gave a moving speech in which she asked for the congregation to pray not only for all the young men found with Mark but also those responsible: 'Pray that they will know that there is love.'

A loving and nurturing home was one thing that Adolfo had never known and as with almost every serial killer, that absence incubated a murderous rage and a need to prey on others. As part of the ritual killings, Adolfo sodomised his victims, the ultimate humiliation he once experienced himself. As Sara told police, he did so because, 'It satisfied him'. It satisfied a sickness in Adolfo's soul, the soul he claimed was dead but was in fact a corrupted soul that only brought death to others.

Sara was found guilty of aiding and abetting the gang and sentenced to six years, the maximum terms under Mexican law. In a second trial, she was found to be complicit in several of the cult's murders and sentenced to an additional 62 years. She has since protested that she is innocent, that she was coerced and abused by Mexican police into making false statements and has asked to be considered for parole. She will be eligible for consideration after a term of 25 years. In 2004, she told Dane Schiller of the *San Antonio Express-News*: 'I am at peace in my soul. I am clean.'

Her reference to being clean is probably significant. Cleansing was a key part of Santería's ceremonies. It held that it was possible to shrug off the evil around you. But what if the evil comes from within? When Adolfo chose cult members he chose carefully and he chose well. In the Hernandez gang he saw their misfortune, their lack of direction, their natural superstitious natures and their below-average intelligence. What did he see in Sara? He saw a link to the Hernandez clan but he also found a compliant and willing character who hungered for importance and a sense of power.

She was quick to adopt any means and methods necessary to acquire greater power and wealth. She was someone who lied easily, someone who relished a hidden life, where dark and vicious acts of abuse took centre stage. It was a life hidden from all who knew her and cared for her, her parents, her sister and her boyfriends and she took pleasure in deceit. She wore her mask well but someone saw it slip: her ex-boyfriend Gilberto and he paid with his life.

Mexican officers believe she enjoyed her role at the centre of the killing cult, a role she has never confessed to fully. We will never know if she stroked the cheeks of her victims, if she watched and if she orchestrated the slaughter. But we do know that she was the high priestess and as *la madrina*, she sustained and guided the evil that consumed her. And nothing can cleanse that.

9

KARLA HOMOLKA
THE PERFECT BRIDE

'Roses are red, violets are blue
There's nothing more fun than a pervert like you.'

KARLA HOMOLKA, IN A CARD TO PAUL BERNARDO

It had been the dream wedding and now it was the perfect honeymoon. Pretty Karla Homolka, newly-wedded Mrs Bernardo, gazed into the video camera recording in their Hawaiian hotel bedroom and said: 'The beauty of this ocean, this beach and everything here does not come close to equalling the love I feel for you, sweetheart.' The handsome groom, Paul Bernardo, looked on. Paul liked to watch.

Back in their home country of Canada, the waters of the man-made Lake Gibson, Ontario, were uncharacteristically low that summer. Police were fishing concrete blocks out of the water. They were uniform in size, approximately 2ft by 1ft and they had lids that could be prised open. A canoeist had found one beached in the muddy and debris-filled shallows. The lid had been dislodged and inside was something that looked like a human thigh. The canoeist called out to a nearby angler before staring again at the

241

remains. He was hoping his first instinct had been wrong. Perhaps it was the remains of some sort of fish. Then the two of them found another concrete block and when they looked inside, they saw something unmistakably human. It was a girl's calf and a foot.

It was 29 June, 1991 and the towns surrounding Lake Gibson had been unsettled by a string of vicious sexual assaults stretching back to 1987. A young man, presentable and well-spoken, was targeting women as they walked home. He waited until they were within sight of safety before overpowering them and subjecting them to horrific rape, both vaginally and anally. The press began using the name the Scarborough Rapist, as that was the town that was the focus of the attacks.

Paul Bernardo read the reports about the rising level of panic amongst young women and their families with great satisfaction. Only he knew that the assaults had begun a year earlier. Even before that, he had incorporated violent elements of his fantasy life to the lives of one or two of his more vulnerable girlfriends. He was a violent rapist but his crimes changed once he met his female accomplice, Karla. She nurtured new and sickening acts of savagery until her crimes equalled, if not outstripped, his. Their stories are intertwined and it is only by investigating Paul's life and how he came to meet Karla Homolka that it is possible to assess how willing a part she played in his schemes.

Paul got his thrills watching the humiliating powerlessness of very young women as they endured degrading acts. Preying on women so close to home was a part of that. Home was significant. Waiting until girls felt close to safety before snatching it away satisfied him most.

Paul Bernardo's upbringing was a case study in dysfunction. All the telltale signs were apparent long before he took his frustration out on innocent victims. His home life was chaotic and destructive. In time, his father would face a prison sentence for sexual assault on his own daughter, Paul's sister. Paul's mother was referred to by Paul as 'it' and she spent many years suffering with depression. Yet at other times, she would subject the family to violent rages. Later, with Paul entering his teens, she took delight in telling him that he was 'a bastard from hell' and that he wasn't the son of the man he thought of as his father.

All of the few friends that Paul allowed to see his home were shocked. He warned them that the house was filthy and that there wasn't any food and the claims proved to be no exaggeration. Despite an outward facade of middle-class respectability, the Bernardo home was disintegrating. Paul reacted to this by always being immaculately turned out. He quickly learned that good looks and a confident manner could get you anything you wanted. He was a diligent student, gaining a place at university in Toronto and he was taken on as a trainee at the prestigious accountancy firm of Price Waterhouse. No one would guess that his home-life was a mess.

Paul holed up in his room at home and surrounded himself with self help manuals and quotes from Gordon Gekko, the character in the film *Wall Street* who captured the 'greed is good' aspirations of the late 1980s. It seemed as if Paul had protected himself from his poisonous home environment and that he would go on to make something of his life. But he was already dangerously damaged and soon felt compelled to begin to inflict his rage on others.

It started when he found a girlfriend he could manipulate

and torment, but that wasn't enough. He took to carrying a knife and would grab women from behind at night, holding the weapon to their throats, groping them and then fleeing. At first it felt good, watching their terror. But soon he needed more. The rapes began.

The police were at a complete loss, though they recovered evidence from the scenes of the attacks. DNA evidence was in its infancy and it would take years for forensics to point to Paul Bernardo. The authorities knew they were looking for a man responsible for some 14 brutal assaults, but not that he had met someone who would help him go much further.

Karla Homolka, like Paul, understood the importance of appearance. The oldest of three girls born to Karel and Dorothy Homolka, she was a good student who had a passion for animals. Born in 1970, Karla grew up to be a young woman who looked like a poster girl for the *Baywatch* aesthetic. She was blonde, blue-eyed and slim, happy to sit all day sunning herself by the pool and chatting with her friends on the telephone. Karla would leave school with good grades and go on to become a veterinary nurse.

But her family, like Paul's, was very different under the surface. Karel Homolka was said to be something of a womaniser and one of his wife's work colleagues claimed that the couple had suggested a threesome to her. She turned them down. By her late teens Karla herself was sexually experienced, enjoyed role-playing and even owned a pair of handcuffs.

In 1987, when Karla was 17, she had a job in a pet store. Manager Kirsty Maan invited her to a sales conference that October with her friend Debbie to learn more about the business. They stayed in a hotel where Kirsty was shocked to be woken on the first evening by Karla bringing men back to her room. Kirsty told the men they had to leave but Karla immediately found another couple of men to invite back. And the one she was clearly interested in was 24-year-old Paul Bernardo. The two were soon inseparable.

Karla lived with her parents and sisters in St Catherines, almost a two-hour drive from Paul's home in Scarborough, but a journey he was happy to make. He spent a lot of money on his princess. One Christmas he bought hundreds of dollars worth of clothes, jewellery and a designer teddy bear that she called Bunky. They made a photogenic couple. Paul was a few years older than Karla but her parents approved. After all, he was a polite young man destined for success as a chartered accountant.

Paul thought he'd hit pay dirt. Here was a pretty girl who was sexually adventurous. Rather than resisting his suggestions, Karla was willing to let him do what he liked, be tied up or let Paul indulge in his obsession for anal sex. She would allow him to film her and to handcuff her hands behind her back as she knelt face-down.

When he was away, she would send him a barrage of notes and letters. Over the five-and-a-half years of their relationship, Karla penned more than a thousand messages. Some of them were written after the two had been fighting where she begged to be reconciled. Behind that outwardly respectable facade, Paul was often angry. She didn't give him what he really desired. She couldn't. She wasn't a virgin. And yet she seemed to understand his need. In a chilling note sent in January 1988, she wrote: 'I'm so sorry for what I've done. Hearing you say "I don't love you" was one of the worst moments of my life... If you find your virgin, there will be something wrong with her.'

On the one hand Paul demanded that Karla enact any depraved sexual fantasy of his choosing but he also wanted her to be sexually inexperienced. The inconsistency revealed an aspect of Paul's fractured and dangerous mind. He wanted the control he had felt stripped of as a child. He felt humiliated by his mother and may well have suffered other forms of abuse at the hands of his father. The ultimate expression of sexual control was to take virginity and it became an obsession. It would become his ultimate way of transferring the terror he once felt as an innocent.

Karla let him dominate her, let him lead her around with a dog collar around her neck, let him dress her as a schoolgirl, let him watch as she inserted a wine bottle into herself, but it wasn't her first sexual relationship and that frustrated him. But Karla understood. There wasn't anything that Paul could do which disturbed her. When he asked her what she would think if he told her that he was a rapist, Karla said, 'Cool'. The Scarborough rapes continued.

Police learned that the rapist would demand that the girls speak during their ordeals. They would have to say, 'I love you' as they were sodomised. But they were still no nearer catching him, despite forming a special force, or figuring out when he was likely to attack. In 1988, there were attacks in April, May, November and December, but then nothing for six months.

Karla however, thrived. She was deeply in love, and wrote in her last year book in high school that her dream was to marry Paul. The couple looked like they'd been cut out of a glossy magazine and so it seemed just right that when Paul proposed on 9 December 1989, it was as they walked hand-in-hand, with Niagara Falls as the dramatic backdrop, the snow softly falling and the scene lit by Christmas lights. Karla gave a gushing account of the proposal in her diary. A perfect prince for a perfect bride. Everyone around them was delighted at this romantic start to the festive season.

The police had less cause for celebration. They knew that the Scarborough rapist had struck over the Christmas period for the previous two years and, as they had feared, on 21 December, a call came through to say that another attack had been carried out. A young woman had been raped in an underground car park. The girl gave a clear account of all that her attacker had said and done but added a detail that the police had not heard before. She said that she felt someone else was with the attacker, someone filming. Asked to look through a photographic line-up, the girl picked out someone but it wasn't the attacker. The special force, Green Ribbon, logged what they found but knew that they were still chasing shadows.

With the New Year came Paul's resolution to leave Price Waterhouse. He was progressing well but at nothing like the rate he felt he deserved. He was snapped up by another accountancy firm and was to begin work that month for a bigger salary. It was how it should be, the couple were saving for what would prove to be a very expensive wedding in the summer. But Paul was no longer interested in accountancy and left the business.

He did so because he found that there was a good deal of cash to be made smuggling cigarettes over the border with the United States. Paul began to make huge sums while border and customs police never guessed that the clean-cut young man was engaging in illegal activity many times a week.

On 4 May 1990, Karla turned 20. She was enjoying her job and making big wedding plans. A few weeks later, another girl was raped in Scarborough after Paul had driven back from the Homolka household. The police recognised the attacker's pattern: threatening with a knife, tying and beating the victim, vaginal and anal rape and talking continually. But the ferocity of the attacks was increasing too. The girl had been slashed across her face with a knife and bitten on her breast. Police suspected that the rapist could become a murderer.

Again, the victim was able to give police a detailed account of what her attacker looked like. Alongside a reward, a picture was released and a bank teller contacted police to say that it looked like a customer called Paul Bernardo. But while the name would come up on a few occasions during the course of the investigation, the police were overwhelmed with calls. Paul was even interviewed by police in November 1990 but was able to present such a charming and pleasant facade, chatting happily about his wedding plans, that the officers found it hard to imagine he could be connected to anything as horrific as the Scarborough rapes. Paul's luck would hold for some time yet.

Meanwhile, Paul had turned his attention closer to home. He had developed an obsession with Karla's younger sister, Tammy Lyn. Paul openly told Karla that he felt Tammy was the prettiest of the Homolka girls. He flirted with her and took her out in his car too, knowing that it caused Karla distress. He demanded that Karla dress up as Tammy and have sex on the young teenager's bed when she was out. One night, Karla sprinkled Valium onto Tammy's food and stood guard as Paul masturbated next to the sleeping Tammy. Karla also knew Paul had filmed Tammy as she undressed. But they both knew that Tammy would wake up if she were touched.

Paul wanted more and Karla was happy to help. She had access to drugs at work, as she would administer them to pets before their operations. She brought a book home from the vet's called *The Compendium of Pharmaceuticals and Specialities* and decided on halothane, an anaesthetic used to keep pets under during operations. In a surgery, it is mixed with oxygen as even low doses could be dangerous. She'd need to take care.

Whilst everyone's thoughts were turning to Christmas once more, Karla and Paul refined their plans. Paul was staying with the Homolkas on 23 December and the couple prepared festive drinks for the family. They fixed Tammy a few cocktails and Paul filmed the family, the girls fooling around. It was the last night that the three pretty Homolka girls would spend together.

Tammy was persuaded to stay up and watch a movie with Paul and Karla. She soon passed out and Karla left to return with the halothane. She poured some on a cloth and held it to Tammy's face while Paul was filming. The shocking images would later be used in the court case when the couple were finally brought to justice.

Paul pulled down her tracksuit bottoms and Karla pulled up her top. He penetrated the unconscious girl first with his fingers then his penis and Karla started arguing with him. Not for him to stop but for him to hurry up and to put a condom on. As Paul held the camera, he instructed Karla to suck her sister's breasts and then perform cunnilingus, even though Tammy was menstruating.

Paul told Karla to insert her finger into Tammy and then to 'taste it'. Karla did as she was told but snapped, 'Fucking disgusting'. Placing the Halothane-soaked rag over Tammy's nose and mouth, Paul anally raped the helpless girl, who began to vomit. Karla panicked. Tammy had eaten earlier in the evening and Karla knew that animals were not allowed to eat before being anaesthetised. She hauled her sister upside down to try and clear her airway. The couple dragged Tammy into Karla's room, placed her on the bed and dressed her. Karla called 911 and, while waiting for the paramedics to arrive, hurriedly flushed away the halothane.

It was the commotion caused by the ambulance crew that woke Karel and Dorothy and Karla's other sister, Lori. Tammy was rushed to hospital with the chemical burn of halothane clearly visible on her cheek.

A police constable arrived to make initial enquiries as to what had caused the 15-year-old to stop breathing. He was concerned that Karla was cleaning the blankets on which Tammy had thrown up and asked her to stop the washing machine cycle. It was the same young policeman who took the call from the hospital to say that Tammy had been formally pronounced dead.

The family were taken to the police station but Karla and Paul had spent over an hour alone and so the statements they gave were exact and tightly-scripted. Tammy was buried on 27 December and the cause of death was given as accidental. It would be another three years before the truth would emerge.

Paul was in a terrible state as a result of the death which had deprived him of his fun. He would bang his fists into his head and accused Karla of incompetence. She wanted him to be happy again.

That January, Paul abducted a young woman and brought her to the Homolka house while the rest of the family were away and Karla watched him carry out a vicious assault. The name of this girl never became known to the police, she never came forward. Later Karla would refer to her as 'the January girl'. After her ordeal, she was driven to Lake Gibson and left at the side of the road. Paul wasn't satisfied. As the January girl was unresponsive and had not struggled or expressed her pain, Paul found her frustrating. To compensate, Karla dressed as 15-year-old Tammy once more and performed for him.

It was all captured on tape. Karla praised her 'King', Paul, for what he did to Tammy, telling him: 'I loved it when you took her virginity.' That wasn't all she had to say. He asked her what she learned from her experience with Tammy.

'Well,' replied Karla, 'we like little girls. We like to fuck them. If you're gonna fuck them, I'm gonna lick them.' She ended the session telling Paul that as she could not give him her own virginity, she gave him Tammy's. She produced a pair of Tammy's knickers and masturbated him.

There were other videos. There was footage of Karla in Tammy's room, wearing her clothes and placing a photo of the dead girl over her face as Paul acted out his fantasies. As they had sex, Tammy's stuffed cuddly toys were in the shot around them.

After the death of Tammy the Homolka family presented a united front. There was some discussion in the neighbourhood, as not everyone was convinced that Tammy's death was innocent. Karel and Dorothy asked Paul to leave the family's home in mid-January to allow them to grieve in private. Karla was furious and immediately began to look for somewhere for her and Paul to live together. She was also angered by her parents' suggestion that they economise over the size of the wedding plans and wrote angrily to a friend calling her parents 'assholes' and said their claims to be cash strapped after the funeral were 'bullshit'. The couple found an upmarket home to rent in Port Dalhousie, 57 Bayview, overlooking a pretty harbour.

Karla loved the house, and she worked hard to make it the perfect home, filling it with tasteful and neutral tones and decorative touches. Everyone who saw it was impressed, Karla was quite the homemaker. It would be where the couple would remain until Paul's arrest in 1993 and it would be where so much more horror would unfold.

In March 1991, Paul went on a break with friends, men far younger than himself who idolised Paul and all he stood for, and began a relationship with a nurse called Alison. He did not try and hide the sexual nature of the relationship from Karla, but he did lie to Alison, telling her that Karla was his sister. Again, Karla felt humiliated but a hint about how she might take centre stage in his affections once more came with a prescription for a sedative called Halcion. They had a bond that she did not want Paul to forget. But Paul continued to act independently of Karla.

In early April, a 14-year-old girl, out jogging early one morning, was seized from behind and pulled into woodland. She was stripped and raped and was convinced that her attacker would kill her. Again, the pattern of the rape followed the others and police noted that her attacker took some of the girl's clothing as trophies.

Karla later recalled how excited Paul was on his return that morning. He showed her what he'd taken from the girl. Then they had breakfast and played with their new puppy, a Rottweiler that Karla named Buddy. Their home seemed almost complete with Buddy as Paul worked on a few modifications of his own, like finding a way to film Karla's friends as they used the toilet.

Karla was unsettled by Paul's continuing interest in Alison and in other women and a letter from that time shows that Paul was quick to verbally abuse her and he threatened to end the relationship. Karla needed to make sure that didn't happen. She had always told Paul that she would do anything to keep him happy, and now the time was right to show him, once again, just how far she would go to please her 'King'.

Jane Doe is a pseudonym. The Canadian authorities gave the 15-year-old this alias in an attempt to protect her from the facts of her abuse as they emerged during Paul's trial. Jane met Karla when she was only 12, an excited young girl thrilled by the older woman's attentions. Karla had let Jane visit her at the vet centre and they'd talk about their love of animals. Paul and Karla were living in their own place and Karla saw it as an ideal opportunity to invite her to stay. Jane looked up to Karla like the big sister she never had, as she the only child of divorced parents. Her mother raised objections, wondering why the couple wanted to spend time with a 15-year-old. It didn't deter Jane. And every time Jane's mother met Karla, she found her very charming and friendly and so shelved her concerns. Neither Jane nor her mother suspected that Karla had been putting crushed Halcion in the girl's drinks. Or that Jane was filmed, unconscious, while being abused by both Paul and Karla.

Karla would call Paul on his mobile and tell him to come home for a 'surprise', when he'd find the girl naked from the waist down. Further footage showed Karla again using a halothane-soaked cloth with all the mundane details of a regular apartment bedroom coming in and out of focus behind as he wiped blood off the thighs of the comatose girl.

It isn't known how 15-year-old Leslie Mahaffy came to 57 Bayview. The police were able to establish that a friend had walked her home after a night out but did not go into her house. Leslie may have realised that she had forgotten her key and wasn't keen on waking her mother. What is known from what Karla later said is that Paul woke her up and that the girl was waiting, tied up downstairs. The filming began.

Leslie had to look towards the camera and give her name. She was filmed using the toilet, then stripped naked and forced into having sex with Paul and Karla. While the young girl was repeatedly assaulted over the next 24 hours, Karla made sure she found time to walk the dog. When she returned, she filmed as Paul anally raped Leslie and even as the girl screamed in pain, Karla never flinched. When she did move, it was to adjust the blindfold that was slipping from around Leslie's head.

Father's Day fell on 17 June that year. While Leslie's parents were frantically searching for their missing daughter, Karla cooked a meal and waited for her mother and father to arrive. Karel and Dorothy stayed until around 9pm that night, while Leslie Mahaffy's lifeless body, wrapped in a blanket, lay in a cupboard in the basement.

Paul was thrilled by their adventures. Karla really was shaping up to be the perfect wife. The wedding was to take place on 29 June. Karla was thoroughly organised when it came to planning her wedding and kept huge files containing every detail of the day. When it came, it was a truly ambitious wedding, one of the grandest in recent memory. The venue was an exclusive lakeside hotel, where the guests, who were to number over a hundred, would sit to enjoy a meal that included pheasant and veal. The bride and groom would arrive at the venue in a white, horse-drawn carriage. The bride's dress was an elaborate affair constructed from taffeta, with puffed sleeves and a long veil that was to frame her face with a cascade of tiny, white silk buds. Paul and Karla wanted to ensure that no one would forget the day and truthfully, as the golden couple arrived, they looked every inch the model of good looks and prosperity. They looked as if they had the world at their feet.

Long after the event, some of those present would talk about their suspicions. After the arrests and the trial, the story became a sensation. One of the guests sold his wedding footage to the highest bidder. Others talked about how police sketches of the Scarborough rapist looked uncannily like Paul and that they had always had their doubts about him. One of Paul's friends even approached the police to say that Paul's aggression and hatred of women made him wonder just what he was capable of. Yet most guests just enjoyed the day and were taken in by the perfect spectacle that they were there to witness. The couple could do anything they wanted.

By the time the couple had left for their honeymoon, they had dismembered Leslie's corpse, placed the parts in concrete blocks and dropped them into Lake Gibson. It was some time before the girl was identified, eventually, by reconstructing her jaw. Her dentist was able to positively state that the girl was Leslie. It was a heartbreaking moment made worse as Leslie's mother had initially been reassured that the girl found could not be her missing daughter as the eye colour of the corpse was brown. It took forensics to inform the police that if a body is immersed in cement and a mud-filled lake, even blue eyes will turn dark.

When the newlywed Bernardos returned, they were refreshed and ready to start abusing again. On 10 August, a call was put through to 911. It was Karla, asking for help: 'Please hurry, my friend has stopped breathing.' The friend was Jane, who had made the mistake of calling by to welcome the couple home. Within a few minutes however, Karla dialled 911 again to say that it was a false alarm, her friend was fine. The ambulance never arrived and Jane went home the next day, unaware that she had been assaulted by her friends once more.

Later that year, another teenager disappeared, 14-year-old Teri Anderson from St Catherines. The police were not sure if the girl should be thought of as another potential victim. Teri's father was a suspected drug dealer and they had reports that Teri didn't quite live up to appearances. Her friends confessed that the smiling cheerleader had been intoxicated the night of her disappearance and had even taken acid. All the details available were noted and the teenager's name was added to the missing persons list.

The following month brought scandal to the Bernardo family. Paul learned that his sister had gone to the police with allegations that her father had sexually abused her during her childhood. When asked why the allegation took so long to surface, Debbie broke down as she was overcome with fear that her own four-year-old daughter had been abused by Paul senior. The police spoke with the family and formally brought charges against Bernardo.

His son meanwhile was annoyed that Jane had decided that she no longer wanted anything to do with the couple. When she was conscious, she was frequently pressured by Karla to have sex with Paul. Karla regularly withdrew her friendship, manipulating the fact that the young girl idolised her. Paul had made any number of sexual advances towards Jane and Karla told her to 'lighten up'. It had got too much for the girl and she resolved to end the friendship. It was Jane's adolescent realisation that Karla wasn't a true friend after all that probably saved her life.

That year the couple held a Christmas party. Paul raped a guest in the bathroom. The attack made her vomit and Paul stormed out in disgust. She did not report her attack to the police. She wanted to forget that it had ever happened and shook from the shame of what Bernardo had done to her.

Life went on. Karla bought a new dog collar for herself for Valentine's Day 1992. She had taken to signing her cards and notes to him Karly Curls. Most of the notes were innocently phrased, if a little saccharine, full of gushing devotion. Others were more explicit, she'd sign herself off: 'Your little cocksucker', 'your little cunt', 'your little slut'. No matter who caught Paul's eye, Karla wanted to make sure that her husband realised who was central to their fantasy life and their lives as predators.

By April that year, the forensic net was beginning to close around Paul Bernardo. DNA tests in the early 1990s were primitive but when the Centre for Forensic Sciences contacted the investigative team working on the Scarborough rapes, they were able to narrow the profile to five men the police had questioned. Paul Kenneth Bernardo was one of those men. He remained confident that they were unable to detect him and his main concerns were working on ways to increase his cigarette-smuggling profits and penning lyrics for a rap album he thought would make him as famous as Vanilla Ice. Easter was approaching and Karla was due to have some time off. Their thoughts turned to the best way they could spend it.

At first glance, 15-year-old Kristen French was very different from Leslie Mahaffy. Kristen was dark rather than fair and their differences went beyond appearances. Whilst Leslie was known to have a troubled home life and had run away for short stints, Kristen was from a stable home and was a hard-working honours student at school. So when Kristen went missing on the afternoon of 16 April, the police switched quickly into a major hunt for the girl. She had disappeared during the 15-minute walk from her home and her parents had started to ring around to find out where she could be. It was completely unlike Kristen to go missing. Her parents' account of driving around trying to find a trace of their daughter is heartbreaking. Both were seized with a terrible sense that something was very, very wrong.

It was Karla who stopped the girl, calling her over and holding up a map while asking for directions. Kristen was a bright and helpful girl who would not have hesitated when Karla made her request. When she saw the map, there was probably a split second of confusion. The map Karla held up wasn't of St Catherines, but of neighbouring town Scarborough but, by then, it was too late. Kristen was bundled into the car and held at knifepoint as Karla restrained her by pulling her hair hard. It took very little time for Paul and Karla to drive up to their Bayview home and into the garage. There, they blindfolded Kristen and led her inside. The filming began.

Kristen asked for their help, she asked to go home. She knew her parents would be worried. She was filmed using the bathroom, crying as she was forced to undress and sitting in a Jacuzzi when told to bathe. Karla cooked dinner.

After they'd eaten, Paul decided it was time for them to act out a film of schoolgirls together. Karla's preparations were meticulous. She'd laid out make-up and perfumes and the outfits they should wear. They were to sit together chatting about make-up as a set-up shot. Paul filmed as Karla sexually abused Kristen. 'I like little girls,' Karla said for the benefit of the camera.

Paul began to lose his temper with Kristen. She was sexually inexperienced and could not follow his instructions. She was finding it difficult to masturbate him as he wished. To punish her, he pushed her to the floor and anally raped her, but the violence of his actions forced her to defecate. Paul was furious. He stood up and urinated on her, threatening to kill her. Karla watched through the video lens.

The abuse continued throughout the next day. Sometimes Karla would film, calmly issuing instructions to Kristen on what she should do to Paul. 'I want to see a mouth full of come, Kristen' she said whilst the whines of their dog Buddy could be heard in the background.

Frantic efforts were being made by the police, the community in St Catherines and Kristen's family. One of Kristen's shoes had been found at the spot where she was abducted and an eyewitness had come forward to say that she thought she'd seen the car involved – a Chevrolet Camaro. It was an unfortunate mistake as the police spent a huge number of man hours tracing Camaros, when the car Karla and Paul drove was, in fact, a Nissan 240SX.

The last segment of tape showing Kristen was the most harrowing. Paul and Karla sexually assaulted her with a wine bottle as she was handcuffed. Paul raped her vaginally and anally, angry that Kristen had called him a bastard. Kristen would not have known what a key word this was to Paul, triggering his anger towards his parents. Kristen was made to pay the price. Afterwards, he dressed and left the house to get a takeaway. When he returned, Kristen was dead.

Her body was discovered on 30 April, only a few hundred yards from where Leslie Mahaffy's body had been dumped. But the police did not make a connection between the two cases. They were both 15-year-old girls but Kristen's body was intact, even though her hair had been hacked off. Kristen French was buried on 4 May, 1992, the day of Karla's 22nd birthday. Reported sightings of Camaros were still flooding police information lines.

Two constables interviewed an old friend of Paul who called as he wanted to alert them to concerns he had about Paul's true character. The officers took notes as the man told them that Paul Bernardo harboured violent fantasies towards women and that in all likelihood, he'd already acted on them. He'd been violent towards other girlfriends and there was no telling what else he might do if given the opportunity. The report was filed and turned over to the task force.

Karla's and Paul's time was taken up with the more mundane matters of plans for the future. They had reached a decision on three things. They would change their last name to Teale, they would not have a baby until Paul had received a recording contract and they'd get a pet iguana and call it Spike.

Ten days after the report was processed by the investigative team, two officers were sent out to talk to Paul. Karla was out at work at the animal clinic and Paul gave a competent performance in front of the policemen, just as he had done two years earlier. He sat beneath one of his wedding pictures and explained that he'd given fluid samples back in 1990 just to help police with their enquiries. He was polite and the house was clean and neat and as he truthfully explained that he didn't drive a Camaro, he once again waltzed through questioning. By the time that Teri Anderson's body was fished out of Port Dalhousie on 23 May, Paul had once again been eliminated as a suspect.

The couple celebrated their anniversary and shortly afterwards sat through a current affair documentary about the abduction of Kristen French. Their confidence soared. Very few of the details the police gave were correct. The couple took a holiday in August, picked up a hooker and brought her back to their hotel room where Paul filmed the two women having sex. By autumn, they were increasingly busy stocking up cigarette runs in anticipation of high demand at Christmas.

Christmas was always a difficult time for Paul. The holidays represented something about an impossible family ideal that mocked his childhood and seemed to feed his rage. Unable to process his stress, he had repeatedly committed hideous crimes against women at that time of year.

Tammy Lyn had been killed at Christmas time. Paul had never forgiven Karla for allowing her to die and he still kept pictures of the teenager all over their home. He would fly into self-pitying rages that Karla had been so incompetent with the girl he had always wanted for himself. Karla knew the anniversary would be rough on Paul. The couple had been grooming another teenager, a girl called Norma. Karla thought it best to try and distract Paul by inviting Norma over. They drank heavily and Norma had to repel Paul's advances. He came into her room as she slept and despite being fully clothed, forced back her underwear and entered her. Norma fought and Paul left. He complained to Karla that he was getting nowhere with Norma. Karla suggested 'putting her under' with halothane and to her shock, he punched her hard twice, furious that he'd been reminded of Tammy Lyn. It was two years since Karla's sister had died and it was her death that would cause the couple's carefully-built world of serial murder, assault and deception to implode.

Paul was behaving in an increasingly deranged way, crying over Tammy and verbally attacking Karla. In contrast, his wife had grown in confidence. Paul left Karla over New Year, taking a break with some friends and drinking ever more. Karla probably hoped for the best on his return but this was the trigger point of their collapse as a couple. They argued and Paul attacked Karla, hitting her several times with a heavy-duty torch. Karla was a mess. Her face ballooned and both eyes were blackened.

Dorothy heard from a neighbour that Karla had been seen in a terrible state and she and Karel talked Karla into leaving Paul. She agreed but first went to the house while Paul was on another cigarette run and searching it frantically and would not tell her parents what it was she was looking for. Despite his splintering mind, Paul had still had the foresight to hide their video tapes.

The Homolkas took Karla to hospital where the doctor on duty noted that it was the worst case of spousal abuse he'd seen. Paul found the police waiting for him on his return to Bayview and he was arrested for the attack on Karla. Sitting in the same interview room that he'd been spoken to on the night of Tammy's death, he realised that the police were still utterly clueless about him. But everything was about to change.

Karla started a diary. In it, she retrospectively wrote down a catalogue of all the times that Paul had brutalised her. The pages were filled with more and more claims as Karla took time to recuperate at the home of her aunt and uncle. She read up on cycles of abuse in relationships and told all her old friends that she and Paul were over.

However, if she hoped to be free of Paul it wasn't to be, as on 1 February 1993 the Centre of Forensic Sciences finally completed their analysis of the DNA samples from the Scarborough rapes and there was only one name left standing – Paul Bernardo. The police immediately began a surveillance operation on Paul and checked if he had any criminal convictions. They quickly found that Paul had recently seriously assaulted his wife and detectives wanted to talk to her. They arrived at the Homolka house on 3 February but Karla said she was too busy to talk to the officers. It was decision time.

She had an idea of what her next move would be, but first she went out drinking on 5 February and picked up a man in a bar. It was the start of a new affair for Karla and she began staying overnight at his apartment. No doubt she was happy to put the whole of her marriage behind her but it wasn't to be. Karla learned that Paul had been running up all her credit cards and she was livid. She also knew that she was going to have to talk to the police at some point and so it was time to seize back the initiative. It was time to get a lawyer.

She knew one named George Walker who had his pet cared for at his local veterinary clinic where she worked. He imagined that he could give the young girl some quick legal advice on whatever was troubling her and wrap up before the rush hour began. The neatly-groomed Karla sat before the avuncular Mr Walker and told him that she had been with Paul when her sister was raped and accidentally killed, that she had also been there when Leslie and Kristen were attacked but that she had nothing to do with their deaths. Karla said there were video tapes but Paul must have hidden them. She wanted immunity. If it was offered, she would cooperate with the police and the prosecutors. Did he think that was possible?

In 30 years of practice, nothing came close to the story Karla told George Walker that winter afternoon. The brutality and degradation it revealed was on a level that no one had imagined. Walker struggled to maintain his professionalism but knew he had a duty to his client and said he would see if there was a deal on offer if Karla would testify. What followed created a storm of controversy that persists in Canada to this day. Whilst prosecutors were adamant that Karla could not remain immune from any prison sentence, it could be greatly reduced through a plea bargain.

Karla's lawyer made it clear that he would be adopting a 'battered woman's defence' as his client had been admitted to hospital earlier that year because of Paul Bernardo's violence and she had originally been coerced into acting on his behalf. At this point, the police did not have the video tape evidence and were persuaded that Karla's cooperation was key. Karla got her deal.

Paul was arrested on February 17 1993. In the hours that followed, he remained calm and detached, mostly fielding police questions with, 'No comment'. He was waiting for a lawyer. In a strange twist, when Paul went to court the next day to be charged, his father was also due to appear for sentencing. Police officers wondered just what kind of family the Bernardos were yet it was Paul's wife who still held the key for the prosecution.

It was a case that convulsed Canada. There were so many moments of high drama in the 18 months that followed that it was difficult to keep track. Paul had told his lawyer about the tapes and where to find them. They were hidden above a light fitting in the bathroom. Instead of handing them over to the police, the lawyer kept them in his possession for 16 months.

Karla's trial began at the end of June 1993. She had been free on bail and her parents and surviving sister accepted that she had been a victim, that Paul had tortured and manipulated her and that there simply was nothing that she could have done to save the girls Paul preyed on.

She pleaded guilty to two counts of manslaughter and received a 12-year jail sentence. At the time, again adding to the public outcry over the case, her pleas and statements went unreleased, covered by a publication ban, ordered by the judge, in an attempt to ensure that Paul would receive a fair trial. His trial was not scheduled until September. Despite attempts to create a news blackout, Karla's plea resolution was widely spoken of as 'a deal with the devil'. And still the video tapes had not been seen.

It was in September that Paul's lawyer hit crisis point. He fully believed that Karla was not a victim but an accomplice. He realised that he was in an impossible position as he had not made the tapes available to the police. He resigned from Paul's legal team, contacted another lawyer, John Rosen, and asked him to act on Paul's behalf. It was Rosen who handed the tapes to the police.

Paul's trial had to be rescheduled to allow John Rosen to build a case and it did not begin until May 1995. Karla testified at the end of June, by which time she had begun serving her prison sentence, her family still standing by her. Paul had entered a plea of not guilty to the nine charges against him, including two counts of first-degree murder. John Rosen knew that Karla was not on trial but took his time to pick apart the statements that she had given to the police about the part she had played in the abduction and assaults carried out on the girls. Despite maintaining that she was brutalised until she acted, reluctantly, at Paul's command, Rosen was effective at dismantling her stance.

It is worth noting that women who suffer at the hands of abusive partners often share similar backgrounds or experiences. The abuser first isolates the woman from family and friends, demolishes the woman's sense of self-worth and a cycle of verbal and physical abuse begins. It may be interspersed with periods of calm but the beatings are ongoing. Karla was savagely beaten at the *end* of their marriage. Despite what she had written in her 'diary' retrospectively, records show that she had regularly appeared at work, spent time with friends and attended many routine medical appointments with no sign of physical injuries.

Neither was she isolated, maintaining friendships and relations with her family throughout her time with Paul. It is significant that when Tammy died, Karla was living at home, and evidently not held captive by Paul. When battered women do snap after years of abuse, the object of their rage is the abuser, not an innocent third party. The woman will have spent years depressed, passive and confused. Karla displayed none of these characteristics.

Perhaps the most damning line that Rosen pursued was that there was no concrete evidence linking Paul to the deaths of Leslie and Kristen. Paul left both girls with Karla for periods of time, for example, when he left to buy takeaway food. He claimed that it was Karla, not he, who killed the girls.

Though he had taken the stand and sworn to tell the whole truth, Paul Bernardo would think nothing of lying. But it is plausible that he was not the killer. Karla said that Paul had used an electrical cord to kill Kristen but the pathology report showed that she had been beaten with an object and had aspirated blood in her lungs, which meant that blood had been breathed in through her nose or mouth before she died. The ligature marks were insufficient to have killed her as Karla described. But much earlier, Karla had admitted that in Paul's absence, she guarded Kristen with a rubber mallet, lest the girl try and escape. It was this scenario that Rosen presented. Kristen had made a bid to escape and Karla killed her, the dead girl had subdural haemorrhages on her head, consistent with hammer blows. After the blows, during her last breaths, she would have inhaled tiny blood particles. Leslie also had deep bruising on her back, consistent with pressure brought by knees holding her down whilst being asphyxiated in a pillow. Again, Rosen demonstrated that the marks were simply too small to have been made by Paul Bernardo.

Karla denied everything. It was all she had to do.

On 1 September, Paul Bernardo was found guilty on every charge and two weeks later he was sentenced to life. In November of 1995, he was declared a dangerous offender which made it unlikely that he would ever be released. It was a very different story for Karla.

On 4 July 2005, the following statement was made by the prison authorities: 'As of today, Karla Teale/Homolka is no longer under the jurisdiction of the Correctional Service of Canada. In collaboration with our partners in the criminal justice system, the Correctional Service of Canada has released Karla Teale/Homolka.' Teale was the name she and Paul had picked out, a homage to the rapist and serial killer played by Kevin Bacon in their favourite film *Criminal Law*. In the film, the character is called Martin Thiel, but it is pronounced Teale.

Karla had spent 12 years in correctional facilities. For the families of Kristen French and Leslie Mahaffy, there would be no release. That she has now gone on to remarry and start a family must be difficult to accept. Kristen and Leslie would never find happiness, marry and have children. Their futures were destroyed and their abuser walks free.

Using her fluent French, Karla lives in Quebec and has started her life again. She has apologised and said that she is haunted by her crimes but questions remain as to whether a character that took part in such acts of degradation and violence can be fully rehabilitated. Before her trial, she underwent psychological evaluation and traits surfaced that can be seen as compatible with a textbook psychopath. She fostered shallow and exploitative relationships, was narcissistic and egocentric and had a hostile and rigid personality that gave little thought to others.

Many within the prison system strive to make inroads into the minds of dangerous offenders. They set out to unpick their previous behavioural and psychological wiring, find what was at the root of the corruption and, in doing so, engender change. Central to changing behaviour is the ability to sympathise with others, to recognise the damage we can cause and to feel shame. Remorse and empathy shapes our humanity and allows us to develop as cooperative and caring human beings. But what if a mind can't learn these early and vital lessons?

Studying female serial killers, Dr Deborah Schurman-Kauflin has this assessment: 'Though it may sound dismal, no amount of therapy will stop a multiple murderer who has killed from killing again.'

She explains that the minds of serial killers are like houses built without a support structure. The inability to form early and vital human bonds leaves these minds damaged beyond repair. 'The house might look all right from the outside,' Dr Schurman-Kauflin warns, 'but at any moment, it could crumble.'

Karla has said sorry and that she was only a follower. She wants to be left in peace and doesn't expect people to forgive her for all she has done. In the interviews she has given since release, Karla has appeared well-groomed and well-rehearsed and she has said all the right things.

No one will ever learn the full truth of what happened to Leslie Mahaffy and Kristen French, no one knows if Karla has confronted her guilt and has found a way to change. But we do know that Karla has always been skilled at making a house look good from the outside.

10

JUANA BARRAZA

THE LADY OF SILENCE

'I got angry.'

JUANA'S RESPONSE WHEN ASKED FOR A MOTIVE FOR KILLING OLD WOMEN

It was a warm Wednesday afternoon in January 2006, a little after midday, when Juana Barraza saw 82-year-old Ana Maria de los Reyes Alfaro walking home from the market. Juana approached Ana Maria and asked if she might step inside for a glass of water. The older woman agreed. It took a second to decide to let the 48-year-old woman in the house but it would take Ana Maria many painful minutes to die.

Ana Maria's lodger thought he heard a noise. Approaching the room, he saw someone, thick-set and with cropped dyed hair, stumble as they stepped over Ana Maria's body. The old woman was lying on the floor. She was not breathing and the vivid markings on her neck and facial discolouring made it clear that she had been strangled. It was fortunate that a neighbour kept track of Juana over the next few minutes and that he was able to flag down a passing patrol car. Juana began to run but the two police officers caught her, handcuffed her and then walked her back to the street where Ana Maria lived.

Juana was searched and found to be carrying pension forms, false ID and a stethoscope. But far beyond that, the officer realised that this woman fitted the description of the bulky figure that had been bringing terror to the elderly in Mexico City for many years. The Mataviejitas, or Little Old Lady Killer, had finally been caught. Police believed that elderly women in Mexico City had been targeted since 2003. It was rumoured the killings had begun years before and that there might have been as many as 50 victims since the late 1990s. Working on assailant descriptions from previous assaults, many officers wondered if the old women were being attacked by a transvestite or a man using women's clothing to disguise himself. It was an obvious line of enquiry as the one consistent factor was the attacker's powerful and masculine size and build.

One victim's life had been saved when her son, recuperating at the house with a broken leg, disturbed the would-be attacker. He told the police that he had chased off a man. The raid on Mexico City's prostitute and transvestite community that followed produced nothing except a barrage of criticism from the press for the heavy-handed tactics the police employed.

By 2005 it seemed as if the investigation had failed. Despite an accurate description of a burly figure seen dressed in a large red blouse leaving one murder scene, the police had been led down too many dead ends. Valuable man-hours were lost trying to establish whether it was relevant that three of the victims had the same painting hanging on their walls. The original, *Boy in Red Waistcoat*, was painted in the

18th century by Jean-Baptise Greuze and prints of the image were popular. Its appearance at the crime scene proved to be no more than a coincidence. The media were convinced that a serial killer was on the loose and the police hit back with claims of press sensationalism. As the investigation floundered, the killer struck again and María de los Angeles Repper, 92, was strangled in her bedroom on 18 October.

There was panic in the air as the period of time between murders seemed to be narrowing. No women over 60 felt safe at home. Then, early in 2006, rumours spread that the police were checking the city's morgues because the Mataviejitas had committed suicide. Fingerprints had been taken and the painstaking process of matching them to the unsolved cases was underway when Juana Barraza was caught.

As if the arrest was not sensational enough, Barraza was also revealed to be an amateur masked wrestler who used the name The Lady of Silence. Wrestling, or lucha libre as it is called in Mexico, is hugely popular. Opponents use masks, evoking the country's Aztec past, and draw on images of animals, gods or demons. The contests are like a pantomime: the crowd roars its approval as the *técnicos* (good guys that fight within the rules) ultimately win out against the *rudos* (the bad guys that fight dirty). no one was surprised to learn that The Lady of Silence was one of the *rudos*, or as she said during one interview: 'Rudos to the core.'

Juana was a big fan who both organised amateur matches and sold popcorn at professional wrestling venues – not long before her arrest she was asked on TV for her opinion at a professional match. She was soon back on the small screen for a very different reason, paraded before the nation, and it was immediately clear from her size how easily she could overpower the elderly and the vulnerable.

The Mexican police held a press conference with Barraza standing behind a 3D cast of a head they had previously made based on witness descriptions. There was an uncanny resemblance and as the camera lights flashed, both faces remained similarly immobile. The police felt confident that they could secure a prosecution and announced that they had fingerprint evidence implicating Barraza in ten murders.

That was the case pretty much wrapped up. Mexican justice is very different from that in the UK. Here, the press are limited to reporting name, age and charges. In that way, a jury should not be at risk of being influenced by press coverage in advance of any trial. The Crown Prosecution Service then compiles the case against the accused and it is heard with the defendant fully represented by a counsel for the defence. In Mexico, there is no jury.

The courtroom is in the jail and the judges do not have to attend as they are free to give their verdicts in advance of the hearing after taking written submissions. Perhaps the biggest difference, however, is that in Mexico, the defendant is guilty unless proved to be innocent. And as the police present their findings to the press before any trial, that is often the forum for establishing innocence, or a lack of it.

Amnesty International has called Mexican justice 'gravely flawed' and once Barraza confessed to Ana Maria's murder after her arrest in 2006, it was clear that she would never see the outside world again. A thorough legal system, with full psychiatric evaluations, would have revealed a great deal more about the unnatural life of Juana Barraza. Through her, we can see how the mind of a serial killer is cast.

The only insight Barraza gave was that she was angry, very angry at the way her mother treated her and there was good reason to believe her. The facts were few. Juana was believed to have been born in 1957 in a poor district of Hidalgo, just north of Mexico City. Her life would have been a difficult one as she was not only hindered by poverty but had to contend with an abusive and alcoholic mother. She was rarely allowed to attend school. By the time she was 12, her relationship with her mother had disintegrated to the point that she was given away, traded for a few beers. Moved along like an unwanted object, Juana then suffered years of rape and abuse at the hands of her carer and others, resulting in pregnancy and she gave birth to a daughter. It was not clear what became of the little girl.

Yet Juana's anger did not ferment over the men who raped her. Her rage spilled out from the experience of her earlier years, the life she endured at home with her mother. Juana Barraza cannot talk to the outside world now and it is doubtful that she ever will. On 31 March 2008, more than two years after her arrest, she was found guilty on 16 charges, including 11 separate counts of murder. The prosecution linked her to a total of 40 murders and she has been sentenced to 759 years in prison.

Juana had a longer killing career than many male serial killers. Women like Juana are adept at exploiting the idea that women are ill-equipped to murder. With this advantage, the female serial killer can expect to last on average eight years compared to the four years that men usually manage. In addition, women do not want to be caught, they have no desire to become 'a story' and end up in jail. They plan meticulously.

The chief prosecutor, Bernando Batiz, described Juana as having a 'brilliant mind'. It seemed an odd way to describe someone who was barely literate and yet it did describe the careful and methodical manner of her slayings. Her career outstripped the average to last ten years: four elderly women a year savagely murdered in their own homes. Juana had a ruinous and violent desire to inflict pain and suffering on older women, a need that was unquenchable and without her arrest the murders would not have ended with Ana Maria's death.

In common with many other serial killers, Juana knew how to select victims, knew how to talk her way into homes and gain trust. Her false ID showed that she was equipped to pose as a government employee, working for social security. She told some of her victims that she was making sure that they had their full pension entitlement. That she was there to help.

Her potential victims were plentiful. There were many people desperate enough to accept assistance in whatever form it took in Mexico City. Despite its glass and steel skyscrapers, ambitious architecture and the broad boulevards presenting the trappings of successful modern living, poverty was rife in the city. Knock on one of the city's many less impressive doors to say that the occupant might be entitled to a greater pension payout and you would be welcomed by one of the many lone widows scraping by, especially if you were a woman yourself. Juana knew that and it was one way to ensure she would get a foot in the door.

Robbery was raised as a possible motive as Juana would take a few items, but over time, a far more disturbing pattern emerged. While some of the elderly victims were strangled and others were bludgeoned to death in a frenzied attack, some also showed evidence of sexual abuse.

Juana is The Silent Lady once more: she is lost in prison life and with no prospect of parole until she reaches 100, she will remain behind her mask of silence. But research carried out on other incarcerated female serial killers has uncovered an astonishing pattern, almost a template, that Juana will recognise.

It is possible to shape a breeding ground, to incubate a young mind in such extreme circumstances that they grow to exact a terrible price on the innocent and the unsuspecting. Juana's story is a textbook example. She was born to a family that was neither loving or stable. There is a good deal of research to back the requirement for a child to form early bonds with their carers. It is a very simple formula: if a baby is loved, it responds with warmth. If it is dealt with sensitively when it suffers, it will go on to become a resilient and caring human being. Place a baby in a chaotic home, a home were adults randomly terrorise infants, where physical punishment is indiscriminate, where pain is inflicted and the child is repeatedly told they are worthless, then the child will struggle to ever trust another human being.

Although Juana has only given a few sketchy details about her life growing up, a thread can be picked up from her final crime and traced back to a severely damaged childhood. Forensic psychologists are piecing together the pattern, not as an apology for the actions of serial killers, but in an effort to predict and prevent future predators taking to the streets to stage terrible acts of vengeance.

Dr Deborah Schurman-Kauflin interviewed seven female serial killers at length. They agreed to tell their stories if they remained anonymous. She found that the degree of abuse these women suffered was extreme. While drug and alcohol abuse was present in five out of the seven households, all of them reported sexual abuse. The assaults included vaginal rape, anal rape, forced oral sex and penetration with objects including pipes and bottles. Yet all also stated that it was the psychological and emotional abuse that proved hardest to bear. As one woman said: 'It is the emotional shit that drives you crazy.'

All found that abuse was hardest to endure when it came from the mother figure in their lives. They would be hit, cut and taunted but there was no clear trigger point for the mother's rage and the child learnt to become introverted and to watch continuously for the sea change around them. It is heartbreaking that when pushed for a 'happy memory' before the age of six, all struggled to recall anything of comfort. As most knew savage abuse by the age of five, it is hardly surprising.

A traumatised child will retreat and the majority will become introverted. Girls in particular are at risk of self-harming to create an outlet for the continuous pain they feel. No one seems willing to hear or help them. They are adrift and powerless to stop the abuse. Many will turn to alcohol and drug abuse, and drift into promiscuity and abusive relationships as adults. They harbour suicidal thoughts. But some are different. They number very, very few but they grow to have a disproportionate effect on all around them. These are female serial killers as children.

It starts with a dream. In this fantasy world, everything is different. Some retreat there when they are being repeatedly sexually abused, others retreat there afterwards, seeking comfort in the dark. It starts with fantasies of a perfect life, a loving home, of being reclaimed by a real mother, a rescue. You are taken away and no one hurts you anymore. Then the abuse begins again. The knife, the burning, the laughter as you beg for it to stop. What is the use of your dream life now? It takes shape differently this time. In your dream, you strike back, you see them recoil in pain and you feel soothed and feel calm for the first time. You watch, see someone other than you in pain and it eases you, knowing that this other world is always ready for you.

Your time is filled with these dreams; you look around the school yard and part of you knows, as you watch the boys chasing a football and the girls standing together laughing, that no one else has these dreams. But these children are nothing like you, they always seem full of light and you realise that it doesn't matter any more.

The violence in your mind increases in response to the violence around you. You use it to feed inside. You dream whenever you can now and it is more detailed, more elaborate, more real. What would you do before you hurt them, how would you prepare and what would happen afterwards, how would you get away? The planning excites you, it means so much more that way. But soon, even that fades. What sustains you now? It is funny how it happens.

One serial killer, we'll call her Lisa, attacked her mother's dog when she was young and as she did so, the thought came: 'I can make him die.'

Lisa recalled: 'I hated that dog, shit. I wanted him dead and I knew she [the girl's mother] loved him. She'd make all over him like this... But she couldn't love him no more because after I got a hold of him, he was as good as dead... No one could see what I was doing. I always made sure there was no one to see what I was doing. And I took the clothes line and I tied his back legs together so there was nowhere he could go. I picked up a stick and whacked him upside his head, and finally that little shit stopped yipping and I kept hitting him with sticks and rocks until he cried... the more he cried, the more I liked it. It was like, hey, finally, something else feels like I do. Let something else suffer for a change.'

It was a release and then there was calm, particularly when she saw her mother's frantic attempts to find her beloved pet. The girl grew up to murder five children in her care. All of the women studied said they tortured animals when they were children, and all confessed that it felt good to see something else suffer. There was also a curiosity, a wonder in the way they created death. It was real, it was a way to show yourself that you had taken back power. But even this was only a stage.

Adolescence is critical in the lives of female serial killers. At this stage, Juana was still being sexually abused and gave birth to a daughter. All the women Dr Schuman-Kauflin spoke to wanted to be mothers and, like Juana, they fell pregnant young. But caring for children was something quite apart from a desire to have them. Finding a way to provide a loving, consistent and stable home was too much. Parenting taxes every mother's emotional resources and these profoundly damaged young women had little they could draw on. Juana never developed a way to cope with stress when she was young, let alone cope with the frustrations of caring for a helpless baby every day.

Stress boils within and demands a release. Petty theft can be one release: stealing inconsequential items can be distracting for a while. Setting fires or drinking and drug abuse can be other outlets but underpinning it all will always be the burgeoning desire to see your pain live in others. Diversions only last so long.

Juana tried to build a life. But she was unskilled, barely able to read and write and found it impossible to sustain relationships with men. By the time of her arrest, she had four children by three different men and was living in a small ground-floor flat on the eastern edge of Mexico City.

Her eldest daughter had married early and had left to set up her own home and now Juana lived with her two youngest children, a boy of 13 and a girl of 11. She tried to support them with a number of street-vending jobs and domestic work and supplemented her meagre earnings by stealing occasionally.

But tragedy was never far from Juana's life. Her first-born son was mugged and beaten with baseball bats and later died from his injuries. Did she put it down to the realities of life on the city's poorest streets? Or did it trigger something far deeper?

Mexico City weighed heavily on Juana. Behind the gleaming spires and away from the tourists' lenses, the violence, the squalor, the corruption and the thick blanket of pollution never leaves you. It is hard to breathe. The still air above takes on a thick brown haze and the pavements wrecked by the great earthquake of 1985 remain broken. Only the litter fills the cracks. Walking through the maze of streets, you search for solace.

The dingy bars are operated by drugs gangs and gun fights are common but are largely ignored by an overstretched police force. The electricity supply is unreliable and the streets and houses soon retreat back to the dark they once came from. The old faiths are always with you, condemned by the Catholic church but always bubbling below the surface of belief: brujos (witches) sell spells to ward off the evil and it is easy to believe that you need all the protection you can get just to survive. Juana built a small altar in her room, an offering to Santa Muerte, the Goddess of Death, who is represented as a skull head draped in a woman's gown. Juana made offerings of rose petals, tequila, a dead snake and mumbled prayers. She petitions death, it is always with her, let it be on her side.

The conditions were ripe. She took the step from victim to conqueror. Juana has not talked about her first killing. The moment the old woman was selected, the preparations needed, the moment of truth and how it felt. Again, the women Dr Schurman-Kaufman spoke to can be our guide. The violent fantasies they'd harboured for years had never retreated. Then they killed. They talked of time slowing down and the peace of mind that followed. Juana selected a victim that resembled her mother. She would have dreamt of the moment many times, in many scenarios and then she would summon her anger. She would be her own Goddess of Death.

One serial killer who had been abused by her stepmother confessed that before she killed, she immersed herself in all she felt after she'd been abused and locked in a closet: 'It all started with me in the closet, but it'd end up as me being the one putting my hands on her throat. I did that so much of the time it was easy when I put my hands on [the first victim's throat].'

Juana used asphyxiation with the first and with many of her victims. She would often use what was at hand in the house: a curtain cord, a pair of tights or an electric cable.

To strangle another human being, even a frail one, takes a good deal of strength and control. Every one of the old women fought fiercely for their lives. After the struggle, she prodded the bodies, curious to see if they were alive or dead. Once satisfied, she slipped away. Sometimes she took mementos, perhaps an ornament or a religious figurine, then she returned home and slept soundly, her equilibrium restored.

Not every death was induced by strangulation. Sometimes she bludgeoned her victims, watching them writhe and waiting for the still point where there was no more resistance, the point where she could stand in the bedroom and be untouchable.

It is wrong to imagine that serial killers have one mode of killing. They adapt to environment and to their own mood. Sometimes Juana wanted to strike out, not squeeze the life from these old women. But these were the dangerous times, as blood loss was unavoidable. It was a messy process and easy to slip on the volume of blood generated from such an attack. Juana knew that there was little point in cleaning the scene. All she had to do was shrug off her nurse's uniform, if that was what she wore that day: she had a range of disguises. Sometimes she was a social worker, sometimes just a kind face there to help carry a heavy shopping bag back from the bus station. At other times she'd call with a clipboard in hand.

To the citizens of Mexico City, the attacks seemed random and undefined. Anyone was at risk, anywhere. It was easy to whip up an atmosphere of fear and police began to urge the over 60s to move in with relatives – particularly around November, as the killer always struck in November.

But the victims were not selected randomly. Juana took her time to pick out someone who reminded her of her mother. It didn't have to be a physical resemblance, perhaps just the way the older woman turned her head was enough to feed a new violent fantasy. After her arrest, Juana said she selected them because: 'They looked at me.'
John Douglas, an agent with the FBI who has tracked serial killers, has this insight: 'What they tell you is this, the thing that was really appealing to them was the hunt, the hunt and trying to look for the vulnerable victim.'

It seems extraordinary that at the same time as laying the groundwork for her next murder, Juana planned her appearances at wrestling festivals. There is a huge element of role-playing in lucha libre, and as a rudos, Juana had consciously selected the role of bad-guy. Something in the performance appealed to Juana. Even if the bouts were scripted and the outcome always the same, wrestlers still have to be self-reliant, quick and strong. These were elements that attracted Juana. It would have been how she saw herself at her best.

Juana was bulky and Dr Schurman-Kaufman could not help but note that all the female killers she interviewed shared the same physical build. All admitted that they battled with obesity as children and that it alienated them further from their peer group. They did not join in when other children ran around outside, they found it impossible to follow the subtle social interaction and instead retreated indoors and into their fantasy worlds. As girls, they were mocked as much for their size as their loner status. It seems that Juana learnt to use her bulk, turning a perceived weakness into a strength. She was rudos to the core with one vital difference. Outside the ring, the bad guy always won.

Once the crossing had been made, once murder was committed, there was no turning back. But one would never be enough. Like alcohol or drugs, the tolerance point got higher with use, more and more was needed to re-create the original rush. After a killing, the calm receded and feelings of stress and powerlessness began to gather once more. The state of mind of a female serial killer has been likened to a tornado. Powerlessness builds to rage, to violent thought, and spirals upwards until a murder is staged.

If it is true that Juana sexually abused some of her victims, it is a horrifying insight into the need to sadistically assert control over the mother figure. Sadists like to see others suffer and the greater the suffering and fear they observe, the more heightened their arousal. One of the killers interviewed, we'll call her Diane, revealed that after enduring repeated acts of sexual abuse as a young child, she grew to become attracted to inflicting suffering on others. Like Juana, Diane was caught up in a tornado effect and ended up taking the lives of six men and women. Her account of an attack that took a sadistic turn is terrifying:

'It was a pipe (I used). See what happens is I get a little carried away. I don't know why I do this. It seems like the more it hurts the other person, the better I like it. She had had a hysterectomy and I made her bleed real bad. She should've never been bleeding.'

It seemed that everyone's prayers had been answered when Juana Barraza was arrested. When her confession came, it was only to the murder of Ana Maria de los Reyes Alfaro. Later, three other confessions followed but Juana was belligerent: 'It isn't right to pin the others on me.' The time spent in the lead up to the trial would not have been easy. Mexican police apply what they refer to as *presion moral*, or moral pressure, to try and ensure that they gain a confession.

One method is to pin the suspect back in a chair and spray Tabasco mixed with soda water up into their nostrils. The foam overwhelms breathing temporarily and is then followed by a fierce burning sensation inside the soft nasal membrane. Confessions are usually secured.

Any ill-treatment will not have surprised Juana. She had known nothing but brutality throughout her life. Now she faces a life in prison and in fantasy once more. She will still harbour her rage and her dreams of retribution. She may come to realise that all her violence did nothing to repair the anger she felt about her childhood and that any release from inflicting abuse on others was momentary, an illusion. She was powerless as a child, but no amount of power she held in the bedrooms of terrified old women would ever fill the void.

There were two final statements Juana made before she fell silent again. When asked about her mother, about her feelings over her abandonment, she said: 'I felt rage, anger, rancour.' And when she heard her sentence read out, she added: 'Let God forgive me and not abandon me.'

Juana exists somewhere between rage and repentance. She may now understand that no matter the crimes committed against her as a child, her actions as an adult tie her to them forever. It is a prison of her own making and from that, she will never be free.

BIBLIOGRAPHY

Aileen: Life and Death of a Serial Killer, Nick Broomfield, Optimum Home Entertainment

BBC news archives

Buried Secrets: A True Story of Serial Murder, Edward Humes, New American Library

Beyond Belief: A Chronicle of Murder and its Detection, Emlyn Williams, Pan Books

CBC news archive

Daytona Beach News archive

The East Finchley Archer

Florida Department of Corrections archive

Florida Supreme Court archive

Fred and Rose, Howard Sounes, Time Warner Paperbacks

From Cradle to Grave, Joyce Egginton, Jove Books

Gloucestershire Constabulary archive

The Guardian archive

Happy Like Murderers - The Story Of Fred and Rose West, Gordon Burn, Faber and Faber

The Hendon and Finchley Times
International Cultic Studies Association archive
Invisible Darkness, Stephen Williams, Bantam Books
Will Johnson, Professional Genealogist:
  www.countyhistorian.com
Lonely Heart Lady, Joseph Geringer, Crimelibrary.com
Monster: My True Story, Christopher Berry-Dee, John Blake
  Publishing
Murder on Ward Four, Nick Davies, Chatto and Windus
My Life among the Serial Killers, Helen Morrison and
  Harold Goldberg, William
  Morrow and company
Myra Hindley: Inside the Mind of a Murderess, Jean Ritchie,
  Paladin
National Archive at Kew
The New Predator: Women Who Kill, Deborah Schurman-
  Kauflin, Algora Publishing
The New York Times archives
Salvaging the Sacred, Marian Partington, Quaker Books
The Selling of a Serial Killer, Nick Broomfield, DEJ Productions
A Shining Silence, Marian Partington, Western Chan
  Fellowship
The Tulsa Daily World
A Woman's Place, Elizabeth Roberts, Blackwell Publishing